FURIES

FURIES

War in Europe, 1450–1700

LAURO MARTINES

BLOOMSBURY PRESS

New York   London   New Delhi   Sydney

Published by Bloomsbury Press, New York

All papers used by Bloomsbury Press are natural, recyclable products
made from wood grown in well-managed forests. The manufacturing processes
conform to the environmental regulations of the country of origin.

LIBRARY OF CONGRESS CATALOGING-IN-PUBLICATION DATA

Martines, Lauro.
Furies : war in Europe, 1450–1700 / Lauro Martines.—1st U.S. ed.
p. cm.
Includes bibliographical references and index.
ISBN: 978-1-60819-609-8 (alk. paper)
1. Europe—History, Military—1492–1648. 2. Europe—History, Military—
1648–1789. 3. War and society—Europe—History—16th century. 4. War and
society—Europe—History—17th century. 5. Military art and science—
Europe—History—16th century. 6. Military art and science—
Europe—History—17th century. 7. Armies—Europe—History—16th
century. 8. Armies—Europe—History—17th century. 9. Mercenary
troops—Europe—History—16th century. 10. Mercenary
troops—Europe—History—17th century. I. Title.
D214.M37 2013
355.02094'0903—dc23
2012016390

First U.S. edition 2013

3 5 7 9 10 8 6 4 2

Typeset by Westchester Book Group

CONTENTS

Prelude

A WORLD AT WAR

In 1570, at the end of the third of France's Wars of Religion (1562–1598), the king's troops were at one point crossing the Loire River at the Pont-de-Cé, near Angers. As they went over the bridge, their progress was being cramped by more than eight hundred women, all camp followers. Sometime previously, Piero Strozzi, one of the premier generals of the age, had ordered that the women be dispersed. Now, in an outburst of angry impatience, he passed on the command that they be pushed off the bridge into the waters below.

We can only imagine the ensuing scene of panic, screaming, struggles, and violence. Strozzi was obeyed and the women drowned.

The reporter of this incident, Pierre de Bourdeille, refers to the women as "sluts and whores" ("*garces et putains*"). Many of them were perhaps prostitutes, but some—in keeping with the age and its customs—must have been companions or even concubines of some of the soldiers. However, it was a moment of crisis, and although Strozzi's solution came close to touching off a mutiny, his officers managed to control the exploding commotion. His luck held. He might have had to face a small army run amuck.

Female camp followers in the train of armies were a common feature of wartime, early modern Europe. But with their emphasis on factions at court and on the leading role of noblemen in the ranks of the Protestant rebels, standard accounts of the civil wars rarely even mention this fact.

Famine, too, could produce stupefying incidents, and the following event, like the preceding one, may be adduced to throw light on the way we write the history of war.

In the winter of 1630, a group of Italian villagers, subjects of the Duke of Mantua, caught a few disbanded soldiers out in the Mantuan countryside. The expert on the subject tells us that they proceeded to skin the captured men alive, to roast them, and then to eat what they had cooked.

An event like this, belonging to the moral setting of the Thirty Years War (1618–1648), is bound to trail an immediate, grievous history. And so it did. Floods and bad weather had stymied farming in Lombardy for nearly two years. The Po Valley lay steeped in famine. In September 1629, a few months before the grisly incident, thirty-six thousand Imperial soldiers had trekked down into Italy from Germany, intent on capturing Mantua. Two attacks on the city were bloodily repelled. The siege was lifted in late December. In the meantime, however, the soldiers laid waste to fields, plundered meager food supplies, set fire to houses, and treated peasants like pack animals by tying them to carts, using whips, and forcing them to pull loads.

When the villagers got their hands on the demobbed soldiers, their choking rage and hunger dictated the ensuing savagery. Skinning, roasting, and eating them became a ritual of revenge and nutrition.

A conclusion may be reeled out here. If we choose to write the history of war from the standpoint of diplomacy and high politics, the incidents at the bridge and in the Mantuan countryside need never be mentioned. For rulers and their ministers, affairs of state in early modern Europe were never about "little people": camp followers, peasants, commoners in cities, or the rank-and-file soldier.

When the historical analysis of war is masterminded by the ideas of "reason" and praxis in diplomacy and foreign affairs, war is negotiated into a rational and perfectly normal activity. Historians who see war in this light would seem to be taking a stance that puts them too close to the princes and ruling elites of past time. There were other voices, other testimonials, and so there must be other ways to take hold of the history of war.

"A War Mosaic"—my opening chapter—shows that from 1450 to 1700, Europe tended to be one world when it came to war. Professional armies of mercenaries were recruited all over the Continent. In the fifteenth century, Poland hired German, Spanish, Bohemian, Hungarian, and Scottish soldiers. Later, Sweden fought in Muscovy with Irish, English, Scottish, French, and German troops. Units of Croats, Germans, Walloons, Albanians, and especially Swiss served in French armies. In the Netherlands, Italians and Spaniards fought beside Irishmen, Germans, Dalmatians, and Walloons. Regiments of Swiss pikemen fought for Spain, France, and Venice, as well as for German and Italian princes. Companies of Poles, Hungarians, and Croatians fought in German regiments. And when it came to leadership in wartime, Italian generals—Piccolomini, Montecuccoli, Colloredo—distinguished themselves at the head of German Imperial armies. The famous Sack of Rome (1527) was the plundering work of Germans, Spaniards, and Italians.

In November 1494, as ten thousand mercenaries marched into Florence, Florentines looked into a polyglot of faces. They wanted to think of them as "barbarians," even though there were Italians among the Swiss, Dalmatians, Scots, and others, all marching under the banners of the king of France.

But it was more than the multiethnic stripe of soldiers that made Europe a single world in wartime. It was also the spin-off from the ascetic tradition of medieval Christianity: a tradition and a culture that promoted the punishment of the flesh as a beneficial action, not only in self-scourging (penitential) brotherhoods and in extremes of fasting, but also in the message-bearing images and icons of its bleeding, martyred saints. The sinister obverse of these images of heroic pain was the spreading use of torture: *official* violence against the person. As a way of ascertaining guilt, local authorities turned to it increasingly, and it came to be used everywhere in Europe by the middle of the thirteenth century, along with penalties that included branding, the lopping off of limbs, mutilation of the face, burning, and the spectacle of public execution. If pain was good for those who scourged themselves (good men), it was better for bad men, and might even serve to straighten them out.

When regarded in the light of confession to a priest once yearly, a requirement laid down by the Fourth Lateran Council of 1215, extorted confession in cases of capital crime looked very much like part of the same ritual of conscience.

It followed that war could easily be seen as punishment for sin. Preachers in wartime were only too ready to point this out. It was grist to their mill. And the great Martin Luther would give his authority to this claim. In the meantime, as heir to the proceedings of torture, Renaissance Europe would be no stranger to gore and carnage. By the testimony of their actions, princes and statesmen gave a voice to the assumption that war was the most natural ground in the world for barbarous activity.

Launched in the early 1520s, the Protestant Reformation would split Christianity and unleash new reasons for war. In fact, late-medieval heresy had already been met with pitiless military campaigns, notably against the Cathars in the early thirteenth century and the Czech Hussites of the 1420s and 1430s.

From the 1520s to the middle of the seventeenth century, as Protestants and Catholics clashed over questions of doctrine, many of them found that they could kill with a better conscience, because they were killing for God. When a town was stormed in religious strife, soldiers often shattered the bells of its churches, or took them down to sell as booty, or even awarded them to their master gunners. One of the messages behind such action held that it was wrong for bells to summon parishioners to ungodly church services.

Yet the persisting cause of atrocity in warfare was neither religious fervor nor the distorted, punish-the-body message of asceticism. It was the physical and mental condition of the common soldier. He often went unpaid and hungry, because those who had put him into the field and promised to pay him enough to feed himself were failing to do so. Nor did they then necessarily provide food as payment in kind. The result was that the wartime armies of princes could turn into a rabble of angry men, and this ugly mood was likely to be shared by their officers—noblemen, for the most part. Any ensuing consolation came from taking their rage out on the surrounding populace.

Fused to the question of paying soldiers was the problem of getting supplies to the needed military points: logistics. Above all, this meant the availability of bread or biscuit, rations of meat or fish, of beer or wine, and one other crucial need—forage for the horses and pack animals. Was it the case, however, that all this could be got for money? An army of twenty thousand men, even without camp followers, exceeded the population of most European cities; and when that winding horde of soldiers, with ten to fifteen thousand horses, set out on campaign, it could easily eat up, in a few days, all the food and fodder in the adjacent villages and countryside for many miles around. Such an army could not stay put; it had to move; it had to go on seeking new pastures and more stocks of food.

Stocks of food? Chapter 6 will show the awesome scale of the logistical problems embedded in any idea of supply depots, or of preparing armies to carry their own food and fodder. Columns of fifteen to twenty thousand men, foot soldiers and cavalry, generated such transport and food-supply problems that rulers came to be hounded by the need to change their ways. The outcome would alter the anatomy of the emerging state.

Either rulers turned to more realistic policies and stopped trying to assemble gigantic armies, or storms of unprecedented violence and brutality would reshape the nature of the state, leaving a trail marked by terror and blood.

★ ★ ★

NOT ALL OF EUROPE WOULD suffer the impact of armies. Even as the Thirty Years War (1618–1648) ravaged Germany, large parts of the country escaped the killing sprees of soldiers. All the same, the Continent's most populated areas—the river valleys, as well as its urban and more fertile regions—were always the primary ground of war. Here armies more easily found food, supplies, warmth, and the spoils of war.

We come to the question of "total war." This mode of warfare was certainly not an innovation of the twentieth century. Campaigns against civilian populations were already the ordinary business of wartime armies in the late middle ages. But after 1500, the new gunpowder weapons took destruction out to everything on the horizons: towns, villages, countryside, churches, livestock, and—with showers of explosive missiles—into the very middle of fortified cities. The ways of erecting a protective curtain of walls around cities had to be revolutionized. War was never a clean or simple matter of battles between armies. The besieging of towns and cities put the life of all people, over a radius of twenty to thirty miles in all directions, into grave danger.

Early modern Europe was the theater for "total war" in another sense as well. When engaged in armed conflict on a major scale, all the fiscal resources of the leading states, as we shall see, were pitched into armies and weapons.

THE ARGUMENT

Before proceeding to "A War Mosaic," I want to set forth the principal claims and themes that run through this book and guide its narrative.

War was by far the dearest of all government expenses in early modern Europe, and the ready income to pay for it never sufficed. The array of taxes could be complex, but it was also strikingly inefficient and easily corrupted. As a result, the big war-making states, tilting chronically into debt, verged not seldom on bankruptcy. But even when they were more or less solvent, the necessary life-giving funds (or credit) failed at times to reach the needy soldiers in the thick of war. Now, in hungry desperation, troops were likely to pounce on civilians for bread and other foods.

The massive bleeding of money that went with the movement of armies gradually altered the anatomy of Europe's emerging states: Spain and France first, then the Dutch Republic, Sweden, Austria under the Habsburgs, Russia, and Brandenburg-Prussia. In wartime, these states saw their cargo of debt all but driven out of control even as they levied new taxes, hired more contractors and administrators, created new departments, and gave rise to a civil service. But war and princely ambitions remained the impelling forces in the state, and they were seldom restrained for long by the scantiness of money or the complaints of their desperate armies.

After 1500, as rivalries and conflicting claims among princes were ramped up and war was intensified, armies swelled or were held in the field for longer periods. They became a common sight on the roads and rivers of Europe's most populous regions. In the course of the sixteenth century, a mix of mercenary, conscripted, and forcibly impressed soldiers began to appear on the scene. The traditional reserves of volunteer mercenaries no longer sufficed to meet the demand. War was depleting them. The conscripted and impressed men could not begin to match the battle skills of the professionals, but they were not nearly so expensive. The hard men were the backbone of the mixed armies and commanded higher rates of pay.

By their surprising capacity to go on fielding large numbers of troops, the developing "power" states acquired a thickening carapace of authority. They used it to extend their power over the institutional churches, over regional assemblies of citizens, over private income, over commoners, and over the lesser nobility. The great nobility long retained special privileges, but by the end of the seventeenth century these too were being sharply whittled away. Soldiers were sometimes deployed to impose compliance.

Most of the foregoing observations are scattered throughout the better war studies of the period 1450 to 1700. But they are seldom, if ever, drawn together into an overall view. I take them from a rich body of scholarship that is often cited in my endnotes, and I owe a debt of gratitude to the authors. Over the past generation, the new social history of war has shifted the direction of study away from narrow military concerns and out to a quest for richer contexts, for the condition of the common soldier, and for the voices of civilians caught up in the tangles of war. But an immense amount of research remains to be done, above all with regard to the magnitudes of violence, the outbreak of diseases, the practice of quartering soldiers on civilians, the place of women in the society of the wagon trains, relations between officers and their men, and essential logistical questions. These major gaps in the scholarship justify the assertion that in the ongoing work on war and armies, there is still too much devotion—at least for me—to the fine details of the great battles, as well as to the lofty designs of foreign policies. Not one of the major battles of the Thirty Years War was politically decisive, and much the same may certainly be said about the Italian Wars (1494–1559), the French Wars of Religion (1562–1598), and the wars of the Spanish crown in the Low Countries (1567–1648).

What, then, to say about what is new or different in this book?

In the supply and transport conditions of the day, raising an army of twenty thousand men was always an undertaking of awesome difficulty. The task depended first of all upon hundreds of captains and colonels and contact men, fanning out to find recruits. Next came the need to move and supply the enlisted men, and this called for careful organization, along with ready access to massive amounts of labor and capital. Only a great prince or a wealthy republic (Venice, the United Provinces) could aspire to such a venture.

These considerations are seldom far from the unfolding picture in *Furies*. They take cognizance of the fact that in the final analysis, the large armies of early modern Europe were frail monsters subject to diseases, desertion, lack of pay, mutinies, and wild episodes of violence.

I have also given considerable attention to a strange paradox: the spectacle of states that are able to raise exterminating armies, while also nursing financial black holes at the center of their being. The contradiction was resolved, as we shall see, by the use of ingenious expedients and credit mechanisms. Now bankers come forward as key figures in the business of war.

If we define the ground of war as being in those places where military violence is taking place, then the history of war in the sixteenth and seventeenth centuries should concentrate on relations between soldiers and civilians, and particularly on their ugly encounters. For European warfare in that period was directed overwhelmingly against civilians in town and country. Which is why *Furies* is focused on the siege and sacking of cities, on the incidence of plunder and killing in the countryside, on the wretched condition of the ordinary soldier, the terror of forced recruitment, and the rampant incidence of disease. In a sense, the point of such a wide-angled view is to transform the abstractions of social and political analysis into their flesh-and-blood results on the plains of war.

It only remains to add that weaving horror into a true narrative is a matter of measure, pace, and shifting stresses. I found this the most difficult part of the composition of *Furies*. War stretches the resources of writers to their limits.

A War Mosaic

The incidents and mini-tales that follow will at first seem disjointed, because they break up the arrow of time by moving sharply back and forth over countries and over more than two centuries. But taken together, they glide into a pattern: the undreamed-of pattern of war in Europe between about 1450 and 1700. Suffering civilians, cruel hunger, penniless soldiers, dying armies, and merciless conduct push forward to dominate the view. Wonder will play its part, if not pity. War has many faces, yet one face everywhere: anguish for the victims in the middle of it.

If it can be told at all in a single book, a history of diverse wars must be a mosaic, or, in a different key, an X-ray of war, of what the major wars of the age had in common. This is all the more true of a time when gunpowder, swollen armies, blundering princes, and flaring costs transformed the nature of warfare.

A PEASANT BOY (1634)

At the height of the Thirty Years War in Germany, the Imperial city of Augsburg suffered a punishing siege of more than seven months. One of the richest "free" cities in southern Germany, it was home to the Fuggers, Hochstetters, and Welsers, international bankers to kings and emperors. Two armies, Catholic mainly, surrounded the city in September 1634. Made up of Bavarian and other German units, they also included companies of Croatians, Spaniards, Poles, Italians, and soldiers from other parts of Europe. The siege began with work that aimed to cut off all incoming food supplies and to block the River Lech, whose waters flowed toward the city.

Sometime in late October, on the outskirts of Augsburg, a peasant boy was caught carrying three larks, with a view, it was claimed, to smuggling them into the city. He was forthwith hanged, almost certainly within sight of the city walls, and the larks were tied ostentatiously to his belt. The exhibit carried a warning to travelers and onlookers of the hazards of trying to sneak foodstuffs into the beleaguered city.

The officer who ordered the boy executed may have been more severe with him than with others who had tried to run the blockade. Life-sparing but bloodier, a lesser penalty involved cutting off the noses and ears of people who were caught breaching the ban.

Jakob Wagner, the Augsburger who noted the incident in his chronicle, does not comment on it. Nor does he record the name of the youth, despite the fact that he is a stickler for names. In this case, understandably, he was unable to provide the identity of a simple peasant. But his recording of the incident fell into line with his chronicling of other cruelties. Of these, indeed, he was to see and hear about many more in the course of the Thirty Years War.

DESERTERS

On the twenty-first of April, 1705, somewhere in the heart of France, Pierre La Sire, an illiterate countryman, was condemned by a court-martial for having deserted his infantry company. He was sentenced to have his nose and ears cut off, and to be branded on one cheek with the royal fleur-de-lis. The rest of the sentence was worse, arguably, than the penalty of death: commitment to the galleys as a slave and oarsman for the rest of his life.

The case could be regarded as typical, even if La Sire's judges seemed to shatter the bonds of reason. Desertion from the French army was rife in those years, and the punishments directed against it varied, because the laws governing desertion were changed several times. Royal authority dithered. But capital punishment, mutilating the face, and slavery at the oars were the principal penalties. Sentences might also be less extreme, such as when branded deserters were pressed back into military service.

La Sire's fate points to the omnivorous manpower needs of the French army around 1700. In some cases, men were even allowed to enter the army in order to evade trial for murder. France had long provided ample pools of volunteers for its armies, but the foreign policies of Cardinal Richelieu first, and then of King Louis XIV, demanded bigger armies. The result was that by the early 1690s, France's standing land forces had risen to a total of 320,000 men from about ten or twelve thousand in the 1620s. The only way to reach the new figure was to dispatch recruiters and press-gangs out into the rural districts, where they frequently used deceit and violence to ensnare the recalcitrant. And Pierre La Sire had almost surely been one of the young men spirited forcibly away from his village.

In the seventeenth century, Sweden's peasantry would face harrowing recruitment calls. England, Spain, and Germany also experienced the like. Two fleeting vignettes from other parts of Europe illustrate the savage extremes of the need for soldiers.

In 1712, straining to halt desertion from his armies, Peter the Great of Russia brought in "the practice of branding recruits in much the same way as common criminals . . . the mark of a cross was burned into their left arm and the wound rubbed with gunpowder."

In northern Italy, just a few years earlier (1707), Prince Eugene of Savoy, commander of Imperial forces, laid it down "that any soldier found more than a hundred paces away from the army on the march . . . should be hanged."

FLORENCE AGAINST PISA (1406)

Early in 1406, an army of mercenaries closed in on the old seaport of Pisa, using boats and carting in supplies for a stubborn siege. The paymaster of the professionals, located forty-five miles east of Pisa, was Europe's most literate city, the Republic of Florence.

Pisa had once ranked as a near rival to the two seafaring republics, Genoa and Venice. In the twelfth and thirteenth centuries, Pisan boats, laden with goods and merchants, had sailed regularly across the Mediterranean to Acre, Constantinople, Alexandria, Tunis, and then, closer to home, to Sardinia and Sicily. Now, however, an ancient hostility, pitting two close neighbors against each other, was at fever pitch. Pisa, a dwarf republic, had in effect been sold by its temporary overlords; and Florence, seeking possession of it in the late summer of 1405, had paid out part of the 206,000 gold florins demanded by the bosses of the unhappy city.

But the buyers had ignored the pluck of the Pisans. Having occupied the fortress on the fringes of the city, Florence suddenly saw itself robbed of this prize by a surprise attack, and thus far had not been able to make good its claim. The people of Florence already saw themselves as the rightful owners of Pisa, although no one had consulted the Pisans.

Between November 1405 and June 1406, the steely resistance of the *Pisani* repeatedly repelled the besiegers, preventing them from fording the great moat and storming a curtain of defensive walls. By the middle of May, a stranglehold had cut off the entry of food supplies into the embattled city. Neither by land nor sea could any provisions be got past the ring of soldiers on horse and foot. The seaport was in the grip of starvation. Cats, dogs, vermin, roots, and every scrap of greenery in the city ended by being devoured: "The grass in market places had been torn up, dried, and ground into a powdery dust for bread." Ships, loaded with Sicilian grain for the Pisans, were halted near the mouth of the Arno River and their cargoes resold, instead, to the Florentine enemy. The price of grain in Pisa jumped to such heights that smugglers from Lucca, clutching small loads of it, risked their lives by trying to steal into the city in the watches of the night.

Owing to the horrendous costs of the siege for the Florentines, there was always a chance that Florence would call it off. In late April, making a desperate new bid to hold out, Pisa's commanders began to expel "the destitute and useless people" (beggars and poor folk) from the city, in the effort to stretch the remaining stores of food for the defending soldiers and for the better-off. Charitable handouts to the starving had continued, hastening the depletion of food stocks.

Florence's "commissaries"—the civilian bosses in the field—reacted to the Pisan decision with an equal lack of pity. They ruled that any-one coming out of Pisa was to be hanged. Heralded by trumpet blasts, this ordinance was read out, or rather cried out, at Pisa's city gates. The besiegers were counting on starvation to force a swift surrender. Moments of dramatic cruelty had already been seen. Some weeks earlier, a captured Pisan soldier had been trussed up and turned "like a stone" into a projectile; he was catapulted over Pisa's ramparts, on to one of the streets, his shattered corpse bearing a sign that said something like, THIS IS THE KIND OF DEATH AWAITING ANYONE ELSE WHO COMES OUT OF PISA.

Digging in, each side was determined to have its way. When the first group of poor women, now expelled from Pisa, appeared outside the city walls, Florence's mercenaries refrained from killing them, in a show of mercy, but cut off the backs of their skirts and all the clothing over their backsides. They then proceeded to brand their buttocks with the fleur-de-lis, one of the devices on Florence's coat of arms, and pushed them back toward the walls. When branding failed to stop the exit of poor women, the soldiers took to cutting off their noses and then driving them back again. Pisan men—the few expelled from the city—were instead either hanged on the spot or at select points up high: a sight and a lesson for those looking on over the top of Pisa's ramparts.

To the pincer of hunger in Pisa the Florentine army added death and injury from an occasional shower of missiles. Europe had first seen the tandem of gunpowder and artillery in the 1340s; and Pisans heard "bombards" in 1406. But the new weapon had no true accuracy until after 1450. Just as lethal in 1400, however, were huge stone-casting catapults (perriers). And the besiegers used these to spread terror inside Pisa. The claws of war also moved over the Pisan countryside, over great stretches of farmland, villages, and little towns, where mercenaries burned and plundered at will. Much of the loot, including stores of grain, found its way to Florence.

According to the civilian supervisor in the field, the Florentine politician Gino Capponi, Florence's mercenaries were driven by golden prospects. Their successful capture of Pisa—they had been promised—would be rewarded with double their wages, a sacking of the city, and a bounty of 100,000 florins. But during the summer, as it became clear that Pisa would be starved into a surrender, thus exposing its mobile wealth to freebooting soldiers, Florence drew back from the violence of a sack, in a retreat oiled by self-interest. Why let all that wealth fall into the hands of predatory mercenaries? Much of it would be taxable, disposable, useful.

The commissaries now issued strict orders. When Pisa fell, there was to be no looting, on pain of death. The takeover had to be disciplined and seemingly magnanimous. Months earlier, the first captain-general of the assault on the seaport, Bertoldo degli Orsini, a Roman nobleman, had turned out to be so much greedier for plunder in the countryside than for seizing Pisa that the Florentines had dismissed him and his little army.

In the end, Pisa was turned over to the Florentines by the treachery of the city's jumped-up lord and citizen, Giovanni Gambacorti, who was rewarded with 20,000 florins and properties in Florence. Tax-free Florentine citizenship was also thrown into the deal. All the treacherous arrangements had been wrapped in secrecy. Just before dawn, on October 9, 1406, with Pisa's inhabitants still asleep, the city gates were thrown open and in marched the Florentine army, doubtless to the sound of drums and instantly waking the citizenry. Stunned at first, as they looked from their windows, how could they conceal the effects of starvation? One Florentine reported that the appearance of the Pisans "was repugnant and frightening, with all their faces hollowed out by hunger." Some of the soldiers went into the city carrying bread. They threw it at the starving inhabitants, at children in particular, and the reactions they got were shocking. They were seeing, they thought, "ravenous birds of prey," with siblings tearing at each other for chunks of bread, and children fighting with their parents.

Back in Florence, news of the surrender caused a burst of exaltation and mad glee. The city's many church bells resounded. Then came three days of celebration, with bonfires, processions, parties, jousts, and a solemn Mass in the Baptistry, the church of San Giovanni, where special thanks were offered up to God for the glorious, heaven-sent destiny of the Florentines. Now at last they had a great seaport of their own, one to match, as it were, their literary prowess. Florence, after all, by 1400 had already produced a literature that whole nations could be proud of, not to speak of a single city: Dante's *Divine Comedy*, Petrarch's *Canzoniere* (his great sonnet sequence), and Boccaccio's hundred tales, *The Decameron*. Machiavelli, Michelangelo, and other luminaries still lay in Florence's future.

Pisa's hatred of the Florentines would burn brightly for more than a century and would be vividly displayed in 1494, with the outbreak of the Italian Wars (1494–1559), in the city's spirited revolt against Florence.

IN THE PATH OF WAR: RUMEGIES (1693–1713)

At the end of the seventeenth century, one of the major lanes of warfare ran through the French-speaking village of Rumegies, near Lille, on the border between Flanders and France. Alexandre Dubois, a local man and the keeper of a journal, was the parish priest of

Rumegies, a community of eighty-four families. His journal captures the voice of a sharp, committed, ironic, wise, and likable cleric. He was also remarkably well-informed about European events.

The region was crisscrossed by armies, domestic and foreign, for about twenty years, in wars between the France of Louis XIV and the Dutch Netherlands allied with England, Spain, and a league of German princes. Dubois's pages provide a record of what happened in and around Rumegies.

The money pinch on the village began in 1691, with the royal creation of new local offices, solely with the intent of selling them to raise cash for the crown. The village itself was rather forced to buy the offices.

In 1693, the Duke of Württemberg arrived on the scene, at the head of twenty thousand men, and at once demanded "contributions." Rumegies was assigned a staggering levy of 30,000 florins. Hostages were rounded up, picked from the larger district, and dispatched to Ghent, to be held there until payment was made. But a French victory at Neerwinden, "the glory of France and the ruin of our village," diverted the contributions into French hands, and although these were now lowered to 18,000 florins, cries of bitterness rang out. Food prices had soared; the well-off saw their surpluses vanish in the contributions; and the poor agonized, with the price of bread itself beyond their reach. No grain had been harvested locally that year. Yet the Nine Years War (1688–1697) went on.

With people dying of hunger in the winter and spring of 1694, every day brought a stream of strangers to Rumegies, to the church, to beg Dubois for bread. In 1695, the crown levied a general head or poll tax to help pay for the war, despite the fact that all "contributions" also went for the upkeep of the king's armies. In June of that year, driven by hunger, seventeen Spanish soldiers—almost certainly deserters from the anti-French ranks—were caught in the Rumegies wheat fields, evidently stripping off stalks. The villagers killed one, but the other sixteen got away.

Grain prices in the Rumegies region remained too dear for most people, and Dubois lashes out at the "new rich" who had battened on the profits made from the hoarding and timely sale of grains. The year 1697 resulted in a terrible harvest for the village, owing to torrents of rain. Rye was the only cereal to be reaped. In his entries for 1698, Dubois calls attention to the three brothers of a difficult local family. One was hanged for stealing a horse; another was serving out his life as a galley slave; and the third—weaving with the fortunes of war—had soldiered in both French and Spanish armies but had deserted five times, on each occasion pocketing the join-up money.

The famine of 1699 would long be remembered. Every day the poor lined up "by the hundreds" to beg for bread. Yet not long after, in preparations for war (1701), the poll tax was again levied, now in perpetuity, and five local boys were taken into a militia, while three others were pressed into the king's army.

A few years later (1708), a Dutch army, with strong British support, lay siege to Lille, and the entire region was overrun by scouring French soldiers, horsemen foraging for hay from August to December. That difficult year was followed by the wet and freezing winter of 1709, lasting until April. Then, too soon, the relief promised by spring died in Rumegies. The French army had been forced to retreat. On May 27, a pillaging army of more than ten thousand of the Dutch Republic's mercenaries entered the diocese of Saint-Amand, which included the parish of Rumegies. In less than three months, 180 villagers would perish. Alexandre Dubois sees the invaders in the imagery of the Last Judgment. Speaking a language incomprehensible to the village, the Dutch "were armed with pistols, bayonets, swords, and great staffs . . . and they destroyed everything. They took fifty cows and thirty horses; and having stolen things at will . . . they violated some of the women and killed several villagers with staff blows." Breaking into the parish church, they "pillaged and profaned it" and gave a beating to our diarist, Dubois. Showing "faces that breathed nothing but carnage . . . they delivered Rumegies to their fury."

Dubois and the villagers fled. But when they returned two or three days later, they found their houses with "nothing but walls—no doors, no windows, no glass, not a scrap of metal, and worse still not a single bale of hay. In fact, there wasn't one in the entire Tournai region, and that led to the death of nearly all livestock by the following winter." Dubois noticed that malnutrition also killed villagers, for although many were dead by Christmas, not one, he observed, was from among those who had been well fed. "Most of the dead had neither money, nor underwear, nor even hay to sleep on." And people were eating the sort of bread "that dogs would not have eaten the year before."

Easter of 1710 came with an army that cut through Rumegies on its way to besiege Douai. The soldiers robbed whatever pleased them. A year later, for six weeks, the village had to offer food and lodging to soldiers from a Hanoverian infantry regiment. In March 1712, it was saddled for ten days with demanding French horsemen who took wood, carts, horses, and hay. "Had they stayed any longer, we would have been forced to abandon the village. These gentlemen take all the horses . . . keep them as long as they like, till they wear them out, giving them nothing to eat and nothing to the owners either. They are the despair of our poor peasants."

Between 1709 and 1713, the neighboring town of Saint-Amand changed hands several times, passing back and forth between Dutch and French armies, and each time Rumegies had to cough up hay, tools, money, and food in measures that kept the villagers destitute. In the end, to feed the poor folk of the parish, Rumegies, like all neighboring villages, had to sell off some of its common lands at prices fallen to less than half of their normal value.

The priest closes his chronicle of the 1709 fury by fixing on the efforts of Dutch soldiers to dismantle and cart away the three bells of the village church. Giving up in frustration, they tried to shatter them. Failing in this, too, they swung and half-threw one of the bells out of the belfry. But when it failed to break after striking the ground, they dropped another down on top of the first. Now the two bells ended with fine cracks, so that in time they had to be melted down and recast. This expensive work was done in Tournai, and the bells got their final blessing on Sunday, October 29, 1713.

The scene of violence over the bells had in it something of the religious fumes of the Thirty Years War (1618–1648), or even of the French Wars of Religion (1562–1598). Louis XIV's soldiers had seized the Protestant city of Strasbourg in 1681, forcibly restoring Catholicism there; and in 1685 his revocation of the Edict of Nantes (1598) put all French Protestants outside the law. When, therefore, confronting the "papist" church bells of Rumegies, the wild anger of the Dutch soldiers was a likely reaction to the suppression of the Protestant church in France. No doubt French Huguenots marched in their ranks.

ANIMAL SKINS

Let's go back to the late sixteenth century, to consider the face of famine.

Over an anxious stretch of nine months, ending in late August 1573, the hilltop town of Sancerre, near Bourges in central France, lay under the siege of a royal army. A religious civil war raged between Catholics and Protestants ("Huguenots"), and fortified Sancerre, teeming with Huguenot refugees, had been reduced to the most desperate measures because its food supplies were all but gone.

Jean de Léry, a Huguenot pastor, produced an account of the experience almost at once. He was in the town throughout the length of the siege. Chapter 10 of his story, dealing with the impact of famine on the little town, ranks as one of the most harrowing stretches of narrative in the chronicles of Europe. Here, for the moment, suffice it to say that he tells his readers how the *Sancerrois*, in their feverish search for food, cooked animal skins and leather, including harnesses, parchment, letters, books, and the membranes of drums.

Some of the people who perished in Sancerre also ate pulverized bones and the hooves of horses.

The skins, he tells us, including drumheads, were soaked for a day or two, and the water was often changed. They were then well scraped with a knife and boiled for the better part of a day, until they became tender and soft. This was determined "by scratching at the skins with your fingers and seeing if they were glutinous." Now, like tripe, they could be cut up into little pieces and mixed with herbs and spices.

In proceedings of this sort, the impact of war speaks for itself.

PIONEERS

In the sixteenth and early seventeenth centuries, "pioneers" accompanied armies as diggers, excavators, and miners. From the moment an army laid siege to a city, working in the most dangerous circumstances, hundreds or even thousands of pioneers would be called in to excavate trenches around the besieged city and, if the need arose, to dig mines under the great curtain of walls. At select points in the mines, they would deposit barrels of gunpowder and then explode the lot so as to shatter the walls above, opening the way for the besieging army to burst into the beleaguered city.

Astonishingly, we know almost nothing about pioneers, mainly because their lowliness and the presumed inferiority of their labors condemned them to a near silence in the historical record. Even foot soldiers looked down upon them as noncombatants who drew a more pitiable wage than the common soldier himself. Combing through the indexes of books by military historians and the social historians of war, we look in vain for entries on "pioneers."

In June 1573, when the royal siege of the great Protestant seaport of La Rochelle was lifted, following a five-month blockade, more than 50 percent of an army of eighteen thousand men lay dead, dying, or had fled in desertion. But of the two thousand lowly trench and mine diggers at the start of the siege, only two hundred were still alive.

A GERMAN SHOEMAKER (1630s)

Alexandre Dubois's chronicle of woe in the village of Rumegies had been prefigured by the diary of Hans Heberle, a shoemaker from the village of Neenstetten, about twelve miles north of Ulm, one of the largest cities in southern Germany.

As the Thirty Years War peaked, the wide territory of Ulm, with its rich sprinkle of villages, was crisscrossed repeatedly by Swedish and Imperial armies with their many units of foreign *Soldateska*: Finns, Scots, Irishmen, Spaniards, Poles, Czechs, Croats, Hungarians, Italians, and others. The shoemaker reveals that Neenstetten and the adjoining village of Weidenstetten were assaulted time and time again by plundering soldiers on horse and foot. Their raids frequently ended in the mass theft of livestock, fodder, grain, tools, carts, and horses. Villagers were beaten, killed, and held to ransom; and women were sometimes raped or occasionally abducted. Arson was frequent, employed most particularly against obstinate peasants.

Local folk could handle random freebooters, but the approach of regimented units often terrified them. They would then sweep up the best of their movable goods, foodstuffs included, pack their carts or wagons, and make for Ulm, to seek protection inside the city's defensive walls. Heberle, our shoemaker, counted no fewer than thirty such flights in the course of the 1630s and 1640s. Hunger, malnutrition, sickness, exposure to freezing winters, and living in crammed wagons—sometimes for many weeks on end—became a way of life. In those circumstances, relations between refugee peasants and Ulm's burghers were bound to be charged with acute strains, especially if the refugees showed signs of disease, or if their food supplies ran out and they became beggars.

But soldiers, too, were prey to fortune. They could be punished.

The Imperial armies had commanders who worked, when possible, to establish a climate of control, and these officers could impose harsh justice on their men. Hans Heberle, a Lutheran for whom priests were "ravenous animals," witnessed the doling out of justice by Catholic officers. He saw soldiers condemned to capital punishment—on one occasion a group of ten, some of them "distinguished and high-ranking officers. They were beheaded in the [Geislingen] marketplace."

As a victim, what Heberle could not possibly see was the fact that the horrific cruelty of soldiers in wartime had a story behind it, a story driven by the necessities of life itself. It will be told in a later chapter.

WIPING OUT A MALE POPULATION

The great Protestant hero of the Thirty Years War, King Gustavus Adolphus of Sweden (d. 1632), was the prime mover of policies that bled his country's farming communities of their able-bodied men. Like King Louis XIV, he needed soldiers, and he needed them desperately to pursue his grand policies. Six wars with Denmark alone in the seventeenth century, not to mention the country's major role in the Thirty Years War, turned Sweden into a "tax and power" state, as well as into a great recruiting ground. In 1648, "there were 127 Swedish garrisons, scattered all over Germany."

Yet Sweden, a country of farmers mainly, was sparsely populated. Peasants comprised more than 90 percent of the population. Their farms were small, suitable for the labor of individual households, and many of the plots were located on the estates of noblemen. From the 1620s onward, every parish in Sweden had to maintain and equip specified numbers of soldiers, as fixed by the crown on a year-by-year basis. The conscripts were selected by the parishes themselves.

A study of the community of Bygdea reveals that in the eighteen years from 1621 to 1639, the male population there, ranging in ages from fifteen to sixty, fell from 472 to 294 men—a drop of nearly 40 percent. The drop was caused by the great loss of life in Sweden's wars, mainly from diseases picked up in garrisons. Thus, of the men conscripted in 1638, numbering twenty-seven, "all but one died prematurely abroad." In Geoffrey Parker's words, "Enlistment . . . had become a sentence of death." To satisfy its conscription quota, the parish of Bygdea had to scoop into the teenage pool, with the result, in 1639, that half of the conscripts "were only fifteen years old and all but two were under eighteen."

In effect, war losses "led to an almost catastrophic shortage of adult males in the parish. By the end of the 1630s, there were 1.5 women per man in Bygdea." Indeed, if we omit children and old men from the count, the figures reveal that "there were about three women to each grown man." In other words, much of the arable land was without adult male labor, and "women were in charge of a growing number of farms."

The example of Bygdea had affinities in other parts of Europe: in the heart of Spain from the late sixteenth century onward, as its Habsburg kings struggled to hold on to the Netherlands; in Germany, during the Thirty Years War, as rampant disease and armed violence decimated populations, males especially; and in France, after about 1685, as Louis XIV's wars ate up more and more men.

But war could also eliminate the men unwanted by their communities: sturdy beggars, the idling poor, troublemakers, vagrants, and others on society's margins. The coercion of neighbors and local authority put the undesirables into the hands of the recruiters who came around to take men by force, in chains if need be. Between 1627 and 1631, about twenty-five thousand men were shipped from Scotland to Germany to serve in Danish and Swedish armies, and among these were many "masterless men" who had been kidnapped or otherwise forcibly seized. The rigors of Scottish Calvinism called for a disciplined life, and the men grabbed for war in Germany— unemployed and seen as shiftless—would no doubt have been numbered among the undisciplined.

VANISHING ARMIES

In late June 1406, as a Florentine army was attempting to scale the walls of Pisa, an outbreak of disease suddenly cut through its ranks. Swarms of flies seemed to come out of nowhere. That was the first sign. Then came an assault of fleas and lice, followed by a plague of mice and frogs, but of a sort that "even the filthiest peasant" could not have tolerated. A brutal heat had settled into Pisa's river valley. "The contagion in the air was such that even the healthiest bodies were afflicted by violent fevers. And the soldiers were overtaken by so disabling a weakness and such exhaustion, that all they could do was to lie about on the ground." Surprisingly, the symptoms, reminiscent of typhus, seem not to have been fatal. The commanding officers were able to separate the different units and to move them about. Overcoming the malady, the army returned to the siege.

But soldiers were not usually so fortunate in their encounters with disease. The unforgiving cause of dying armies was any infectious, fatal malady, likely to turn rampant in a few days.

In April 1528, in the middle of the Italian Wars, the distinguished French general, the *vicomte* de Lautrec, arrived outside of Naples with an army of twenty-eight thousand men. He laid siege to the city, proposing to take it from the occupying Spanish and Italian soldiers. In the heat of July, typhus—caused by the feces of body lice—suddenly began to wind through Lautrec's ranks. More than half of his army was dead within thirty days, and some accounts claim that "of 25,000 men, only 4,000 remained." Lautrec himself perished, along with most of the other commanders and an array of French noblemen. The retreat of the besiegers began on August 29, but they surrendered on the thirtieth, as they were being cut to pieces. Without horses or pack animals, the survivors, when not killed by local peasants, were forced to walk back to France, begging for alms and bread along the way.

Even more dramatic perhaps, nearly one hundred years later, was a campaign that miscarried for one of the great generals of the

Thirty Years War—Wallenstein. In August 1626, in a mere twenty-two days, he marched an army from Zerbst in Germany to Olmütz in Moravia, for a distance of 370 miles. "Twenty thousand men started from Zerbst. Five thousand . . . were left by the end of the campaign." Plague, dysentery, exhaustion, and desertion had eliminated the rest. Dying armies were vanishing armies.

BILLETS

In July 1649, to the east of Paris, near Chalons-sur-Saône, a French regiment demanded billets in a village that claimed to be exempt from the quartering of soldiers. When the regiment met resistance from the villagers, and the commander, a baron, was wounded by a musket shot, the soldiers threw themselves on the village, intent on sacking it. They stormed the church, where most of the villagers had taken refuge, killed one man, and then tried to hang the peasant suspected of shooting the officer. Next, grabbing thirty to forty of the villagers, they carted them off to Verdun to be held for ransom.

The unit was soon dissolved, and the soldiers were transferred to other companies. But no other punishment was meted out. The village had either bought the exemption from billeting or had contacts in high places, for the practice in seventeenth-century France was to quarter soldiers on civilians. But of course officers, too, might have lofty contacts. In the winter of 1640–1641, a regiment billeted in the town of Moulins went on the rampage while the commanding officer, Roger de Rabutin, Count of Bussy, was off having a love affair with the Countess Helénè de Busset. His penalty for failing to control his men was a prison term in the Bastille. But calling on his roundabout connections with the most powerful politician in France, Cardinal Richelieu, he was set free three months later.

A COMMANDING OFFICER: BLAISE DE MONLUC
(c. 1500–1577)

The eldest of eleven children, Blaise de Lasseran Massencome, *seigneur* de Monluc, was born into Gascony's nobility. The family had a château near Condom, eighty miles south of Bordeaux, and although down-at-heel, they had grand connections. Monluc's brother Jean rose to become the bishop of Valence.

When the family decided that Monluc's future lay in soldiering— their income from properties being too skimpy for a life to be lived in style—he was thirteen years old and straightway sent to Antoine, the Duke of Lorraine, who took him on first as a page, then as an archer (an aide to a heavy cavalryman) in one of his companies. By the age of twenty, Monluc was campaigning in the Italian Wars and taken prisoner at the battle of Bicocca (April 1522). From this point on, his life would be all arms, campaigns, horses, and deployments, except for intervals when string-pulling got him snubbed at the royal court, or when he was sidelined in disgrace for being too outspoken. But he always rebounded; he served in Italy with the well-known general Lautrec (Odet de Foix); and meanwhile he was forging a reputation.

Captured again at the battle of Pavia (February 1525), where the king of France was also taken prisoner, Monluc's captors demanded ransom money, in keeping with practice that lasted down to the eighteenth century. All noblemen generally, when captured in battle, had to buy their release, and ransoms were dear, often adding up to a year of the captive's annual income. On this occasion, however, exceptionally, Monluc seems to have got away without payment. Thereafter, he turned up as an officer or in combat at Naples, Marseille, in Artois, Perpignan, Cérisoles, Boulogne, Moncalieri, Siena, La Rochelle, Thionville, and many other places. His combat experience took him through five battles, nineteen assaults on fortresses, eleven sieges, and about two hundred skirmishes.

In time, Monluc's fame collected around his actions as commander of the besieged city of Siena in 1554–1555, but even more so around his feral activity in the 1560s and 1570s, in the clutch of the French Wars of Religion. A pitiless fighter for both the king and the Catholic Church, he peopled "trees with hangings" and put "the inhabitants of entire Huguenot towns to the sword," such as at Monségur, Targon, and Vergt in 1562.

His body ended as a map of war wounds. He came very close to losing an arm, owing to an act of foolish bravery; a shoulder and wrist took serious gunshot wounds; one hip was knocked out of line; and after 1570 he wore a leather mask, cut and sewn to conceal the oozing results and horror of an arquebus shot that tore away his nose and part of his face. Yet he did not therefore try to keep his family away from war. His ways suggest that he could imagine no other life. Widowed at the age of about sixty-four, he had four sons and three daughters by his first marriage. Three of the sons, soldiers, were killed in battle; the fourth entered a military order, the Knights of Malta, and later became bishop of Condom. But two of his daughters went into convents. King Henry III made him a field marshal (*Maréchal de France*) in 1574.

In the early 1570s, provoked by an inquiry into his financial doings as governor of Guyenne, Monluc dictated a long, self-justifying letter, which he then expanded and recast as *Commentaires*. The work is an absorbing memoir, while also profiling a life that was typical in many respects of the kind of noblemen who embraced the profession of arms with a lasting passion. He appears to have been unhappy and fidgety only when forced to be away from armed men, cavalcades, battles and battle dress, positions of command, and grand gestures.

As a young man and even later, King Henry IV (d. 1610) of France was rather like Monluc: He loved horses, companies of armed men, and the hurly-burly of war. So too did King Gustavus Adolphus of Sweden. They thrilled to the galloping plunge into battle, and were usually flanked by men from the ancient lineages.

Europe's armies, however, pulled in every kind of man, from the hardened criminal to the cavalier who proposed to fight for his religious faith, his king, his honor, money, or a sprint in status. Noble causes and "base" self-interest marched hand in hand. Motives were blurred, protean. And if acute necessity, such as hunger, pulled many a poor man from town and country into the ranks, this was not usually the case with well-born officers. The exceptional cases of this sort—such as in Sweden, Spain, or Germany—involved mercenaries who came from the gentry's social margins, wretched "gentlemen" without the income to outfit a horse or themselves. But even these men, like their comfortable brethren, went to war to improve their financial lot, dreaming of "higher" causes, in search of adventure, or even—more sociably—to be able in time to show off their scars. The Danish general Count Josias Rantzau boasted sixty wounds and "certainly lost an eye, foot, hand, and an ear over [the course of] his career." Prowess in battle had been a mark of the nobleman since time out of mind.

REVENGE

In 1633, not many miles from Munich, angry peasants murdered several soldiers—freebooters—in two separate incidents. In the first incident, finding two Swedish soldiers concealed in chests of grain in the village of Erling, they killed one and buried the other alive with his dead companion. Then one night, in December, about eight months later, "fifty armed peasants from Seefeld went to Aschering, where they surprised a band of mounted thieves [soldiers], who had made off in the early morning with five of their horses. They shot the leader dead, put the others to flight, and went back home with their horses." Germany was traversing the bloodiest decade of the Thirty Years War.

Fighting on the Protestant side in this war, the Scottish colonel Robert Monro (c. 1590–1680) served for seven years with Swedish forces in the 1620s and 1630s. He found that peasants "are ever enemies to Souldiers." In April 1632, he was with the army of King

Gustavus Adolphus near Freisingen and Memmingen, in Bavaria. Commanders had imposed "contributions" (war levies) on two walled towns, Hohnwart and Pfafenhowen. Responding violently, the neighboring peasantry "on the march cruelly used our Souldiers (that went aside to plunder) in cutting off their noses and eares, hands and feete, pulling out their eyes, with sundry other cruelties which they used, being justly repayed by the Souldiers, in the burning of many Dorpes [villages] on the march, leaving also the Boores [peasants] dead where they were found."

The peasants were doing little more than responding with the cruelties which the laws of princely authority had used on them in the past. A punishment widely and often used against rebellious peasants was that of mutilating the face by cutting off the nose and ears. Revenge brought some satisfaction. One report had it, in 1620, that armed villagers had killed four hundred of the Count Ernst of Mansfeld's soldiers—an entirely believable claim. And an experienced officer would not have left a wounded soldier in a village, expecting the villagers to look after him. He knew that they would probably murder the man.

Since bands of mounted outlaws had plagued many parts of early modern Europe long before the outbreak of the Thirty Years War, propertied peasants almost everywhere had learned how to use firearms, and many of them owned guns.

SOLDIERS IN TATTERS

In an entry of December 1633, at the height of the Thirty Years War, the diary of a Benedictine monk, Maurus Friesenegger, arrests us with a haunting image.

Witness to a formal mustering of Italian and Spanish regiments in a Bavarian village, he observed that the ordinary soldiers, with their "blackened and yellowed faces, were emaciated, only half dressed or in tatters, and in some cases even looked like masked figures in stolen women's garments. This," he says, "was the visage of hunger and suffering. But next to them were the officers, handsomely and splendidly dressed."

The armies of Louis XIV were often speckled with men in rags. In 1673, one of his war commissaries took notice of a company "which had 26 or 27 men as naked as a hand and the majority without shoes or socks." The like could easily have been encountered a century earlier. In 1573, when the king's commanders finally lifted the failed siege of the Protestant stronghold of La Rochelle, the diseased besiegers were "covered with rags." Three years later, a French army of ten thousand men, commanded by the Duke of Mayenne, moved around unpaid, unfed, and living off the countryside, "their clothing in rags."

Badly shod soldiers in ragged dress were a commonplace in early modern Europe's wartime armies.

LOOKING BACK

The scatter of images and pared-down details in this chapter range over a continent awash with pain and anxiety: suffering generated by war and by bigger, hungrier armies. The pivotal events lay in payment for war, in sieges, and in the snaking marches of large armies with their long columns of horses, pack animals, carts, wagons, artillery trains, camp followers, and roving bands of foraging horsemen. Here was the monster that forced taxes to climb relentlessly, testing the ways of princes and oligarchies, shattering the productive routines of farm life and urban labor, and creating avenues for wholesale corruption in the spending of public moneys.

But while prices, crop yields, and economic trends may be quantified and charted, human woe never can be. It has no mouths for a thermometer, no places for listening to heartbeats, and no numbers to be tabulated, except for the dead, though even these are too often a matter of informed guesswork. The maimed and the mutilated of wartime Europe were never counted.

Aside from treating us to descriptions—and these can defeat novelists—historians of early modern Europe do not know how to deal with the human suffering caused by armies in action. Their narratives rely on abstract and prosaic turns of phrase, such as the "untold misery" of towns that were "horribly sacked." They—historians—far prefer the technicalities of battles, weapons, logistics, prices, markets, or, even better, the close analysis of alliances, treaties, personalities, and foreign-policy discussions. Yet war is something more than a sequence of strategies, clever statesmen, or an event ("armed conflict") in economics and international politics. Its effects weave through the moral and psychological life of communities, stamping the ways people see, compare, and judge human action. In the study of war, historians should also be positioned where questions of right and wrong move into view.

SOLDIERS: PLEBEIANS AND NOBLES

THE SCUM OF THE EARTH

Europe's upper classes—whence officers came—tended to regard their soldiers as the scum of the earth. The evidence for this is conclusive in word and deed, resoundingly so in the way rulers and their ministers treated the rank and file of their armed men. King Louis XIV (d. 1715) wanted humble service in his armies to be regarded as honorable, as activity that a Frenchman could be proud of. But the force of tradition, the pressing needs of recruitment, and the conduct of officials made a mockery of his dream.

In a world of blood nobilities, of privileged castes and hallowed hierarchies, social identity was as if ordained. Elites and clergymen, Protestant and Catholic, argued that the stations of the high and mighty were anchored in the natural order of the cosmos. The blaspheming soldier—mostly illiterate, filthy, and easily insulted or kicked around by his superior officers—was bound to be seen as a lowly creature. Besides, was it not the case that he was also a thug, and likely to be a gambler, an idler, a drunk, or a former jailbird?

These claims and caricatures had their many exceptions, to be sure. Large armies often had a sprinkling of clerks, students, and the sons of sturdy farmers and small-time merchants. The ranks were even likely to conceal impoverished and illiterate noblemen, eager, by their contact with officers, to get their hands on booty and to better their status. Louis XIV would make it illegal for such men to serve alongside commoners. The ranks of every army also included skilled artisans—varieties of smiths, leather workers, and carpenters. But these were men who performed humble work with their hands. They could not elevate the name and face of the soldier, and nor could the fragile lacing of recruits who came from people of "the better sort." Only in religious warfare, when men appeared to be fighting for God, might lowly soldiering be perceived as honorable.

Late in 1552, at the disastrous siege of Metz, where his soldiers were dying by the thousands, the Emperor Charles V opined that since they were mostly poor commoners, no harm was being done because they were rather like caterpillars or grasshoppers, "which eat the buds and other good things of the earth . . . If they were men of worth, they would not be in his camp for [a pitiable] six *livres* a month." He was talking to one of the leading generals of the age, the Duke of Alba, who looked upon most foot soldiers as "labourers and lackeys." This was a commonplace view, shared by commanding officers almost everywhere.

At the end of the century, the eminent Spanish jurist Castillo de Bovadilla declared that "[war] is also useful because, with it, many men who are the feces and excrement of the Commonwealth are expelled and cast out as soldiers. If they were tolerated, they would corrupt, like the body's ill humors whose expulsion improves the good humors." Nearly two hundred years later, in the 1780s, France's minister of war, the Count of Saint-Germain, observed: "As things are, the army must inevitably consist of the scum of people and of all those for whom society has no use." And in the early nineteenth century, the Duke of Wellington considered that the army he led against Napoleon was composed of "the scum of the earth" and drunks—men best disciplined, he believed, by means of severe floggings.

It was a view—the soldier as scum—that refused to die.

At the beginning of our period, despite being feared and disliked, the small armies of fifteenth-century Italy were spared much of the later class venom. Commanded by private field officers (*condottieri*) who served rulers on a contractual basis, they were troops of volunteers, more cavalry than foot soldiers: better dressed, less brutalized, and seldom forbiddingly hungry, because they were seldom wholly cut off from food supplies. They, too, now and then, went unpaid, but their campaigns nearly always had them close to thriving cities. The stinging contempt for soldiers was more a product of the later sixteenth century and after. It was tied to the century's galloping inflation, which aggravated poverty and the desperation of soldiers; but it was more especially a by-product of the spreading practice of "impressment," the brutal pressing of men into armies. Which usually meant taking "the lowest of the low."

In the 1620s, Thomas Barnes argued that impressment was the way "to cleanse the city and rid the country of such as may be struggling vagrants and lewd livers . . . which do swarm amongst us." He felt that if they were pushed up close to death in wartime, men of this sort might be made to think about their souls. In Bristol, in 1635, the preacher Thomas Palmer also saw impressed men as "the scum of the seas" and "the excrement of the land." But he wanted a different kind of army in the fight for Protestantism in Ireland: "It is no Christian policy to choose such sinful instruments for such a serious action."

The cat was out of the bag. If the practice of forcing men to bear arms was not fairly and universally applied, it could easily turn into a policy of social cleansing.

How were men identified by recruiters? Among Protestants as well as Catholics, the church was the great institutional avenue of control. Their records of baptisms and deaths, kept in the different parishes, provided names and identities for governments, the names too for the rosters of those fit to bear arms.

As long as Europe produced enough volunteers and mercenaries to fill the regiments of professional armies, rulers and their field officers had no reason to complain of manpower shortages. Where payment of some sort added up to a living wage, men were ready to bear arms, a fact best thrown into relief by the sixteenth century's armies of Swiss pikemen and German pike infantry, the Landsknechts. Then and later, stark hunger also propelled men into Europe's swelling armies, where they hoped to find enough to eat, as in the ranks of the Dutch Republic's mercenaries in the early seventeenth century, or in Germany in the 1630s and 1640s.

On the whole, Europe's pool of volunteering men remained deep enough to satisfy demand until the mid-sixteenth century. Now the tide of princely ambitions and religious controversy began to turn and to require more soldiers, or to require them more often.

RECRUITMENT AND DESERTION

The need to force men into taking up arms was first sharply experienced in England, next in Spain in the late sixteenth century, then in Sweden in the 1620s, and thereafter in France and Germany in spite of the fact that states continued to hire armies of mercenaries. The Venetian and Dutch republics always depended on mercenary troops. They were reputed to be more generous with their disbursements, particularly in the seventeenth century, when they faced stiff competition for the hiring of troops on the international mercenary market. France, Spain, and the German princes were also casting about hungrily for men.

I propose to emphasize compulsory recruitment, because this policy, along with the capacity to go on raising the level of taxes and inventing new ones, marks the coercive trail of the emerging power state.

In the 1580s, when Queen Elizabeth I of England ramped up the campaign to impose her Protestant will on Catholic Ireland, her Privy Council began to ship more companies of pressed men across the Irish Sea. The war there had crossed over into something bitter beyond measure. Welsh and English soldiers saw Ireland as a graveyard, a place of hunger and fatal disease. Word of this had made the rounds, and men resisted the summons to go there. They had to be strong-armed into serving her majesty. There was even a saying in Chester: "Better be hanged at home than die like dogs in Ireland." And it was highlighted in 1600—to take one example—when a scant fifteen hundred men remained in the Derry garrisons out of the four thousand who had arrived at those outposts only the year before. The rest had been done away with by dysentery, typhus, and other causes. No wonder, then, that impressment for Ireland provoked mutinies "in the vicinity of Chester in 1574, 1578, 1580, 1581, 1594, and 1596." Mutiny was the first act of determined resistance. The second took the form of mass desertions. Although well guarded and frequently locked up, large numbers of gang-pressed men found ways of absconding even before they set sail.

Estimates indicate that thirty to forty thousand men from England and Wales were shipped to Ireland in the years between 1585 and 1602. The numbers included a smattering of the sons of small farmers: volunteers seeking social advancement and eyeing the possibility of becoming officers. But the large majority were pressed men, and their condition, physical and moral, could be the despair of officials. Describing recent arrivals, one report from Bristol said that "most of them [were] either lame, diseased, boys, or common rogues. Few of them have any clothes; small weak starved bodies taken up in fairs, markets and highways to supply the places of better men kept at home." Officers in charge of musters occasionally returned whole troops of men back to their dispatch points. One contemporary claimed that impressment was being used to purge parishes "of rogues, loyters, drunkards, and such as no other way can live." Another observed that he would have liked to paint a group of recruits, and thus depict "so many strange decrepid people" who looked as though "they had been kept in hospitals." In March 1595, about fifteen hundred men who had served in Brittany reached Waterford, Ireland. On looking them over in Dublin, the new lord deputy, William Russell, remarked, "What . . . are these the old soldiers we hear of? They look as if they came out of gaols in London."

The search for men could indeed be so urgent that criminals were sometimes released from prison to be pressed directly into military service for action abroad.

The English practice of impressment went back to the middle of the century, to the reign of Henry VIII, and passed into the nineteenth century. It would always smack of social cleansing, owing to its illegal methods and selection criteria. In the 1640s, during the English Civil War, Parliament itself accepted the use of impressment. The first targets were the "masterless men": the unemployed, vagrants, "idlers," and beggars, but also men grabbed from among the poor in town and country. All these were perpetual fair game, and London was always the main center for the violence of well-spoken recruitment bullies.

The poor lands and people of Scotland saw even more male disappearances than England and Wales. Estimates hold that twenty-five to fifty thousand Scots served in foreign armies during the Thirty Years War (1618–1648). In the Netherlands and Germany, they were so numerous that they were considered at times—in nasty hyperbole—"to be as ubiquitous on the battlefields of Europe as lice and rats." Many were volunteers, borne away from Scotland by their faith in the Calvinist fight against "popery," or by gnawing hunger and the hope of loot overseas. But many more were pressed men, some of whom, before departing, were made to swear that they would never return to Scotland on pain of death.

The British pressing of men into ragtag armies had its equivalent on the Continent, and first of all in Spain.

In their Eighty Years War (1567–1648), the Habsburg kings of Spain used armies of foreign mercenaries to press their dynastic claims on the Netherlands. Ordinarily, not more than 15 percent of their soldiers were likely to be Spaniards. But this percentage was drawn almost entirely from Castile, and by the late sixteenth century, the Castilian male population was being drained. Faced with a chronic shortage of soldiers, the crown now turned to a policy that would produce explosive emotional scenes—even when it drew on the local support of class-conscious communities as they helped to engineer episodes of social cleansing. In the effort to be fair, Spanish towns also held recruitment lotteries of the eligible men. But aside from leading to mass desertions, the use of lotteries elicited every device of the law, of trickery, fraud, and social connection, as the manipulators jockeyed to keep their men out of the army. The most common expedient had the well-off paying local men to go to war for them. Or, failing this, they called in and paid strangers or outsiders, so as to meet the local quotas. There were always categories of exempt men: nobles, town officials, tax collectors, university students, servants of noblemen and of the Inquisition, and even shepherds and particular classes of workers. But the policies of the kings kept up the relentless pressures, and by the 1630s, even the exempt *hidalgos* (gentry) fell subject to special levies, although many of them were so poor that they could barely afford to keep a horse.

The king's Council of War took for granted that 18 to 25 percent of the men picked for mustering would desert on their way to the points of embarkation: "a gross underestimate," according to I. A. A. Thompson. For "Companies might easily lose a half or two thirds of their men on the march." In September 1636, in a letter to King Philip IV, the archbishop of Burgos noted that in his diocese most of the men taken, whether by lottery or by force, "die of hunger before they reach the garrisons." In Zamora and Salamanca, pressed men were "carried off in ropes and handcuffs." It was also common practice to jail the new recruits until they were marched off. In the summer of 1641, the town of Béjar was holding seventeen men in jail for a garrison levy. Only three were locals; the others were "bought" outsiders.

In the early seventeenth century, the Iberian peninsula must have been crisscrossed daily by thousands of deserters on the run: dodging, begging, hiding, trying to get back home or somewhere else. Others sought to return to their commanding officers or sat in jails, awaiting trial. Some towns simply rebelled against forced recruitment, such as coastal Murcia, with people ready to kill royal recruiters. In Alburquerque, in August 1641, two hundred armed men freed a group of recruits, removed their handcuffs, and told them to flee, while at the same time threatening to kill their military escorts. In September, just inside Portugal, another group of handcuffed and chained recruits was freed by an armed band.

But Castilian resistance to forced soldiering paled by comparison to that in Catalonia, a province of the old kingdom of Aragon. Here, in 1636, as the historian Luis Corteguera has pointed out, royal agents were able to recruit only "criminals whose death sentences were commuted for military service." In June of the same year in Barcelona, when six reapers were tricked into enlisting and detained by force in the recruiter's house, a group of their fellow workers turned up to protest, only to be greeted by armed men who were there on orders from the regional governor. Soon five hundred reapers came back. They stormed and sacked the house.

Only the threat of war with France could rally the people of Catalonia to the defense of the larger realm, if with little enthusiasm. In August 1639, aiming to halt the advance of a French army in the province of Rosselló, the northeastern province of Spain, officials had managed to raise a force of ten thousand men. Almost immediately, however, two thousand defected, and by November more than nine thousand "Catalan soldiers were missing" from the Rosselló campaign, although many of the losses were the result of disease and casualties. Early in January 1640, when the French finally surrendered the fortress of Salses, the price was found to have been the death of "4,000 to 10,000 Catalans," including "a quarter of the nobility," victims all of "disease and wounds." A great and unprecedented Catalan revolt broke out before the end of the year, when it was discovered that the royal government proposed to keep and billet troops in Rosselló, in preparation for a springtime campaign against France. Repudiating their allegiance to the king of Spain in January 1641, the angry Catalans "elected France's Louis XIII as their new king." And therein, for a time, lay a different history, well told in J. H. Elliott's *The Revolt of the Catalans.*

In eastern Europe, starting at the Elbe River, where serfdom saw a resurgence and had deeper roots, hauling men away was also a labor of brutality. Tsarist Russia brought in a compulsory draft in the 1630s, taking one peasant from every ten or twenty households, including even boys of fourteen and fifteen. Noblemen, poor ones in particular, were also subject to enlistment, and they nearly always opted for the cavalry units. Under Peter I, around 1700, the men borne away numbered from one in fifty to one in 150 households, depending upon need.

Conditions in the Russian army were the very ones we have come to expect. Soldiers often went cold and hungry, and they were seldom if ever paid on time or in full. Aside from the fact that half of their pay was routinely deducted for clothing, they were sometimes also paid in kind. Captains beat their men, in a replay of lord beating serf. Desertion was rife, and in the early eighteenth century gangs of disciplined deserters occasionally terrorized rural communities. Peter I had recruits put in irons, in the clasp of which they might be marched hundreds of miles to their destination. Punishment for deserters was inevitably harsh, ranging from hanging and flogging to sentences of hard labor for life. "On the march back from Pruth in 1711," Hughes tells us, "gallows were erected in camp each night to remind deserters of the fate that awaited them." But the hunt for runaway men could also lead to stiff reprisals against their communities or families, with the former compelled to provide substitutes or guarantees, and family members "seized as hostages until they [the deserters] gave themselves up." John Keep observes that recruitment in Russia generated furious debate, "for everyone knew that . . . a recruit was unlikely ever to see his family again."

THE REASONS FOR THE PASSIONATE resistance to being pressed into a soldier's life were not hard to fathom. In Spain, as in England, it was clear that forced recruitment was crudely one-sided, or given to every degree of string-pulling and favoritism. Where choosing the needed men was the job of the local lord or community, as in Sweden,

Brandenburg, and Russia, parochial interests, and local likes or dis-
likes, came quickly into play. In the world of early modern Europe,
with its "natural" hierarchies of privilege, this had to be tolerated.
Such was life. What was *not* life in the rebellious popular imagination
was the life of the common soldier. Whether by lottery, selective conscription, or kidnapping, impressment was often seen as a kind of
sentence of death. Men knew—the knowledge circulated—that
armies were unhappy hosts to disease, hunger, and other forms of
wretchedness, such as the effects of freezing cold and dogs' abuse
from officers. What lesson was to be drawn from this? That it was
better to die at home, in one's own squalid poverty, than to die even
more wretchedly in a foreign land. The devil you knew was better
than the one you didn't know.

In Sweden, a needy nobility and the overriding ambitions of the
Vasa kings carried that agrarian country into a close series of wars in
the late sixteenth and seventeenth centuries. The call for fighting
men, hence for peasants, became acute during the Thirty Years War;
and at one point the ordinary peasantry had to offer up one son from
every eight households. Replacement pressures became pitiless. Between 1626 and 1630, the Swedes and Finns (then under Swedish
rule) supplied Gustavus Adolphus with 51,367 conscripts, of whom
35,000 to 40,000 had perished by 1630, mainly from disease. Too
dispersed to resist, peasant communities appear to have cooperated
with this cull, thereby keeping control over the question of the men
who would be picked for war in distant fields. Well-off farmers took
little poor boys into their houses, fed and clothed them, drew on their
labor, and then, when the summons came, turned them over to the
army as substitutes for their own sons. Now neither the farmers nor
their offspring would be drawn for the carnage in Germany.

Reflecting on the foregoing practice, the historian Robert I. Frost
has concluded that in view of "a growing landless proletariat" in
Sweden and Finland, from which "the military state drew its cannon fodder," the designated system of culling "was beneficial for all:
the government got its soldier, the farmer did not have to go to war,

and children from poor households received a more comfortable upbringing." Indeed, he opines, the poor families also "benefitted: they did not have to feed an extra mouth." Never mind that the chosen young man now went off to die of disease, starvation, or wounds.

THE EUROPEAN POPULATION EXPANDED IN the sixteenth century, passing from nearly 62 million souls in 1500 to about 78 million by 1600. But by the 1590s the rate of growth began to slow down, stunted by plague epidemics, ruinous weather, and harvest failures. Spain, Germany, and Italy saw declines in their populations. War, too, impeded growth by spreading disease and wrecking the productive cycles of rural life. With their demand for longer-serving or bigger armies, princely states scooped down more deeply into the pools of men fit to brandish pikes and guns. By the early 1630s, at the peak of the all-European Thirty Years War, field commanders had seen such a dramatic wastage of soldiers that it became impossible to find the needed volunteers—or even to find enough men to press quietly into the ranks of mercenaries. The result was that battles usually ended with the impressment of large numbers of the captured enemy soldiers, who now passed to the winning side. In the wake of their shattering victory at Breitenfeld (1631), Gustavus Adolphus's Protestant army took in the Italian regiments of the defeated Imperialist commander, Tilly. But happily enough for them, "they all deserted the next year, as soon as they came in sight of the Alps."

Although triggered by religious conflict, the Thirty Years War turned into an outright bloody contest for territory and loot, while always being passed off as a conflict over dynastic, religious, or security claims. Hence pressing the captured enemy into the ranks of the victorious did not always make for strange bedfellows.

Under the guidance of Cardinal Richelieu, France entered the Thirty Years War in 1635, in pursuit of a policy aimed at stopping the supposed expansionist march of the Spanish and German dynastic houses. From this point on, in their clamor for soldiers, the French began to turn to the practice of forcible recruitment. Thanks to the sway of aristocratic authority in the local communities, many officers (noblemen born) were able to drum up companies of volunteers: tenants and servants of theirs, as well as retainers and others. But these numbers no longer sufficed for the ambitious needs of the crown.

In the 1640s and 1650s, French recruiting parties used alcohol and trickery to catch their men. They would get them drunk, or have them enticed by prostitutes, or slip coins into their pockets and then swear that their victims had accepted the binding enlistment money. But quotas were more often reached by means of violence. Recruiters would seize travelers, grab men off the streets, break into houses, or even lay hands on their prey in church. Force was more easily used in the country than in towns, and peasants were likely to flee or hide when hearing about the approach of recruiters. In the 1670s, officials "reported that, owing to the threat of forced enrolments, markets were deserted and peasants feared leaving their homes." During the Nine Years War (1688–1697), writing from Orléans, an officer of the crown claimed that "the markets are full of people who carry men off by force." The War of the Spanish Succession (1702–1714) set off another flurry of impressments. Now and then, bands of peasants responded by assaulting recruiters and releasing the kidnapped men. In the 1690s, a leading minister frankly admitted "that enrolments are still almost all fraudulent," and he repeated this claim in 1706.

The activity of press-gangs was an embarrassment for the government, and edicts were issued against the practice. But the demands of war, widened by Louis XIV's aggressive foreign policy, imposed connivance on his ministers. And army officers, more than conniving, were the linchpin of the system. They "themselves forcibly enrolled and kidnapped men and even boys, including monks, notaries, geriatrics, and shopkeepers whose relative prosperity would have given them little incentive to take the king's silver." In one case, Paris's top policeman had to force a cavalry captain to abandon his

possessive claim on a boot maker. The claim was based on a signature fraudulently obtained, and the captain had threatened to kill
the cobbler if he refused to join his regiment.

Recruitment officers also worked with gangs of thuggish "en-
rollers" (*racoleurs*), who plied their trade in Paris, Lyon, and other
cities. Having caught their prey, they would lock them up and sell
them, as new enlistees, to officers eager for men. The king's recruitment money thus passed through different hands.

THE THIRTY YEARS WAR AFFLICTED Germany with such storms of
carnage that after it ended in 1648, regional elites began to give way,
by the approval of tax hikes, to the pressure of princes, who were
now determined to have permanent armies. These would serve—so
ran the argument—to guarantee security. But problems of recruitment quickly surfaced. As the German economy picked up after the
war, and men were able to make a living from daily work in town
and country, territorial princes found that they could not afford the
sums required to attract the needed numbers of men into their bud-
ding armies. Taxes would not allow it, and there were seldom enough
volunteers. In the crunch, one partial solution was—as in France,
England, and Spain—to let men out of prison to be pressed directly
into armies. In the duchy of Wolfenbüttel, even before the 1630s,
serious criminals were regularly "condemned to war," or were often
freed from prison to serve in the front lines. Their destinations might
be the Netherlands or the Hungarian-Turkish borderlands. Later, it
became common for Germany's princely governments to offer army
service as a substitute for prison and even, occasionally, for the penalty of death.

Generally speaking, however, snooping recruiters, such as for Brandenburg and Saxony, more often resorted to cunning and to brutal
grab-and-lock-up tactics. Having concealed his helpers, a recruiter
would turn up in "dives" or "low-life" inns and taverns, where the
case of a man whisked away would raise no great hue and cry. Wine
or brandy often worked when the sign-up money was not enticing

enough. "Malice and beatings also helped." And so it happened that in East Frisia, as poor Hilke Wessels complained in 1665, if her vanished husband had not been brutally assaulted, "he would never have dreamed of becoming a soldier!" In Prussia, right up to the 1730s, the army recruiter was "the most feared individual in the land." To escape what they saw as a life of abuse, young peasants maimed themselves or fled from home. Indeed, now and then entire villages fled, so that in the face of resistance to recruitment, "the killing of [Prussian] subjects . . . was not rare."

Recruiters sometimes had secret agreements with local tavern or innkeepers. But they could get their signals crossed, and fights occasionally broke out between preying parties of recruiters, with each claiming the same man. Recruiting was a business, and there was keen rivalry here and there among the predators. Agents for recruiting officers haggled over their prey. They spoke of "delivering," "owing," "lending," and "borrowing" men, such as when they "sold" new recruits to captains or colonels. Yet for all their cheating and lurking in the shadows near the scenes of their thuggery, army officers importuned their governments to take stern action against runaway men. They insisted on their rights over deserters, and in dogged pursuit of them might break into houses in the middle of the night to pull their victims out into the streets and drag them away.

In the sixteenth century, Germany's Landsknechts, professional pikemen, had a notorious reputation. With their gaudy dress and codpieces, they were seen as troublemakers, devils, gluttons, and braggarts who hated the routines of ordinary life. But the dominant adjectives for them did not necessarily turn them into "lower-class scum." Later, in the turmoil of the Thirty Years War, some contemporaries, looking back, would even regard them as patriots. After 1650, however, Germans began to see soldiers in a different light, owing to the recruitment of criminals and to the organized pressing of men from the unsavory reaches of society: vagrants, beggars, misfits, and the unwanted poor. No hardworking peasant or craftsman wanted a place in the ranks alongside such men, unless he was fleeing intolerable strains at home, or foolishly imagining a life of adventure and easy-come loot.

Yet impressment parties also got their hands on men of a more solid type, with the result that German armies, like the armies of Louis XIV, came to be plagued by the scurvy of desertion. Men had deserted massively in the moil and toil of the Thirty Years War—out of fear, hunger, lack of pay, and even religious conviction. But desertion after 1650, which went on in a rising tide through much of the eighteenth century, was the natural consequence of impressment and biased, selective conscription. To cut off escape routes for aspiring deserters, army officers in Prussia even sought to avoid night-time marches and camping in the vicinity of forests, or marching through them, unless they were flanked by Hussars—cavalry. Now, however, in that climate of repression, civilians were more willing to help runaway soldiers—despite the risk of dire penalties, the alarms raised against desertion in Sunday sermons, and the publication of long lists of deserters in the newspapers.

The conscripted permanent army had arrived, and recruitment was moving in a new direction, now chiefly by enforced enlistment under the rule of the state. It was the route most prominently taken by Sweden after 1620, in the reign of Gustavus Adolphus.

OFFICERS AND ENTERPRISERS

Jan Werth (1591–1652), one of the leading generals of the Thirty Years War, was born a peasant near Cologne. He joined the Spanish army in about 1610, turned into a fearless horseman, and became—riding over every social obstacle—the top general of cavalry in the Bavarian and Imperial armies. The convulsions of the Thirty Years War fostered the rise from "nothing" of several other generals, including Johann von Aldringen (1588–1634), Peter Melander (1589–1648), and Guillaume Gil de Haas (1597–1657). Aldringen was the son of a town clerk from Luxembourg. Melander, born into a Calvinist peasant family in the Low Countries, managed to get a university education before becoming one of the Empire's most important generals. And Gil de Haas, a stonemason from Ypres, ended his life, like Aldringen, as a Bavarian general.

But these men were wonders. With a few exceptions in Italy, including prominent *condottieri*, such as the humbly born Niccolò Piccinino and Gattamelata (Erasmo da Narni), the like had almost never been seen before, and would not be seen again until the end of the eighteenth century. Officers came overwhelmingly from the nobility, above all in the upper grades of command. Yet enormous disparities cut through Europe's noble ranks, with great lords at one extreme, possessing vast tracts of land, towns, and rights over people, while at the other were Prussian junkers with a little house on a tiny farm, or Spanish *hidalgos* who might have trouble finding the money for a decent pair of shoes. Still, all claimed (or aspired to have) a family coat of arms and clung to privileges that set them apart from the multitudes of commoners, especially with regard to taxation and army service. Taxes were customarily weighted in their favor, or, in many parts of Europe, they paid none at all, apart from indirect sales taxes.

It did not follow that poor noblemen, if so minded, were alone in turning to look to the profession of arms for income. Younger sons of the well-off nobility also directed their ambitions that way.

One of these was Caspar von Widmarckter (1566–1621), born in Leipzig to a line of army officers on his father's side. Unusually for an officer and military entrepreneur, he studied philosophy and law in Paris for six years (1580–1586), passed into the service of a German general in France, fighting for the Huguenots, and in the late 1580s was taken on both as a soldier and diplomat by King Henry IV. Caspar would be greatly engaged in recruiting German mercenaries for the Huguenot cause. Along the way, he was granted French noble status by King Henry and afterward, on embassies, he would be given precious golden chains by King James I of England and King

Louis XIII. In July 1597, he was hired by Moritz, the Landgrave of Hesse-Kassel, again as a diplomat and soldier; and by 1609 he was a leading member of Moritz's privy council.

Caspar married a young widow in 1598, amassed a large fortune, much of it from the business of war, and had a grand house built in Vacha. By 1614 he wanted to leave the Landgrave's service and retire, but he was promised promotions and pressed into staying on in his official roles. Three years later, the most remarkable campaign of his life—he kept a record of it—took him and his regiment into France, Savoy, Piedmont, and the vicinity of Milan. In a war between France and Spain, parts of northern Italy became contested ground, and Moritz had sided with the French against the Spanish. Caspar was the sort of man who could stand up to the Landgrave, and there was sometimes tension between them. Combing through his campaign diary, we get the picture of an officer who had no trouble doling out stern punishment, such as by having a would-be mutineer strangled and then shown off to convey a lesson to the other soldiers. Throughout the campaign of 1617, lasting from late March to November, regimental wages came in late, and his troops often went hungry, on at least one occasion seeing no bread at all for three days. Resentment swelled and there were mutinous rumbles. Soldiers fell seriously ill by the hundreds, with the result that during their trek into Italy, Caspar and the regimental commander, C. von Schomberg, were forced to leave behind five hundred sick soldiers. Many or most of these would perish, and some of them were killed by villagers, their supposed caretakers. After the regiment engaged in bloody skirmishes with Spanish troops, the gravely wounded were also abandoned.

It was a hard campaign, and the next year, ailing already, Caspar again sought to retire. But the Landgrave insisted, yet once more, on his continuing service, and had him mustering Hessian troops in 1619 and 1620, which must have helped to bring on a fierce attack of rheumatism. The attack would lead to his death in September 1621. In a time when so many colonels and lieutenant colonels perished in combat, Caspar was fortunate to die in his own bed.

But let's look next to a major figure, Bernhard of Saxe-Weimar (1604–1639), the youngest of eleven brothers, dukes of Weimar, and the most daring of them. Bred to arms, he soon became an outstanding commander, attracted the loyalty of soldiers, and proved able to raise large levies of armed men. Having no state of his own, he passed easily into the role of military enterpriser, intent on putting his troops—with himself as general—into the wartime service of others. His aims were to multiply his earnings, to raise still larger armies, and to acquire a large principality—that is, his own state.

In late October, 1635, he signed a contract with the king of France, Louis XIII, who had just barged into the Thirty Years War to pursue a policy against the Habsburgs of Austria and Spain. Bernhard "promised to raise an army of at least 6,000 horse and 12,000 German foot" in just under three months, in return for the sum of four million *livres* per year, to be paid quarterly. He had to field a full array of seasoned officers and produce an artillery train "composed of at least 600 horses." The money would go to pay for salaries, supplies, horses, and cannon. His foot soldiers had to be armed with "good muskets and bandoliers, or with pikes and corselets," while the horsemen were to carry two pistols and wear a cuirass. Bernhard was importuned to be as careful with the king's money as he would be with his own. Since fraud, however, was only too common, because "of the greed of the officers, who try to fill up their companies with *passe-volants* [walk-on impostors], on the day of the muster [or whenever required] . . . the army is to be formed up in battle order for a new review to be made . . . [and] a reduction shall be made, in his Majesty's favour, of 14 *livres* for every cavalryman who is lacking, and 12 *livres* for every infantryman."

Here, then, in the deal cut by king and nobleman, was a classic (early modern) arrangement between a mighty sovereign and a military enterpriser, a bond between power politics and the soldier as entrepreneur. There was also another bond in their tacit understanding that the four million *livres* (about 1.67 million talers) would be far from sufficient: Bernhard's troops would also have to

live off forced "contributions" from surrounding civilian populations.

In the world of that day, noblemen were meant to live from landed
income, office, or soldiering, and to have a head for honor, for "higher"
things—not for "trade" and the tang of profit. Yet it was altogether
honorable for them to have proprietary rights over a mercenary force,
to treat it as a business, and to want to turn a profit. The traditional
métier of the medieval noble, that of warrior, had thus passed into
early modern Europe in a new form and with enough élan to vindi-
cate all the moneymaking ploys of the nobleman as military entrepreneur.

How much wealth or "social capital" (honor, prestige, or public
standing) could be acquired in war may be gleaned from the fact
that in northern Italy, in the late sixteenth and early seventeenth
centuries, noble families of ancient lineage strained to have their
men taken on as officers in the Spanish army or in the armies of the
Venetian Republic. In fact, when a lineage had wealth enough, it
might be ready to disburse large sums for companies of mercenaries,
if this was the way to obtain an exalted officer's rank. In France, the
social-climbing "robe" nobility (risen through legal study) com-
peted fiercely for the purchase of captaincies and colonelships, hence
for the buying up of companies and regiments. And there was bitter
complaint about this from the "sword" nobility, who saw themselves, in many cases, priced out of that honorable market.

The greatest banking families—even they—produced men who
happily embraced war and arms. Ambrogio Spinola (1569–1630), a
Genoese billionaire, was the outstanding example. While serving as
commander of the Army of Flanders in the first decades of the seventeenth century, he was also for years a creditor of the Spanish
crown for a loan of five million florins, a sum—depending upon the
year's take—in excess of two years of royal income from the wealth
of the Indies. But more than the men around Spinola, the Catholic
Fuggers of Augsburg, celebrated bankers, were massively intent on
gaining glory and money for themselves in war and arms. Three of

Hans Jakob Fugger's sons went into the Army of Flanders as colonels in the second half of the sixteenth century. And during the Thirty Years War, seven Fuggers at least served in the armies of the Empire and of the Duke of Bavaria, where they ranged in rank from captain to field marshal and general. War and arms seduced them not only because of the attendant social capital, but also because they expected the commitment (and their investment of capital) to bring in handsome returns from booty, officers' pay, and "contributions."

Educated by Jesuits in the classics, Ott Heinrich Fugger (1592–1644) went on to study at the universities of Ingolstadt, Perugia, and Siena. He began his military career in 1617 as a self-financing colonel in the Spanish army, and by 1618–1619 he and his regiment of three thousand men were seeing action in Lombardy and then Bohemia. Thereafter, Ott would serve in Austria, Hungary, and the Low Countries, and next—for the Catholic League and the Duke of Bavaria—in northern Italy again, Franconia, Swabia, and other places. As military governor of Augsburg in 1635, and then as the city's commandant from 1636 to 1639, he held two of the most lucrative posts of his career. Meanwhile, as his earnings swelled, he was assembling a rich collection of pictures.

Ott's biographer, Stephanie Haberer, found that in the course of the 1620s and 1630s, he earned scores of thousands of florins (*gulden*) in salaries, "contributions," and other forms not itemized by his accountant. There were also rich gains from the Imperial confiscation of enemy properties, which were then cheaply bought up by well-placed insiders. In this fashion, Ott got the Hessian lordship of Speckfeld, as well as other lands later on. His earnings enabled him to live in grand palatial circumstances.

All told, then, this entrepreneur cannot be said to have done less well as a soldier than he might have done as a banker. In 1620, the emperor confirmed the Fuggers in their title as counts, and in 1627 Ott was made a Knight of the Golden Fleece by the king of Spain.

★   ★   ★

IN ITALY, THE COMPANIES OF the leading professional soldiers (*condot-tieri*) were among the first of the well-organized mercenary forces. Pulled together and captained by noblemen with distinguished family names, they were hired out by contract to princes and city-states. There was money in such activity, lots of it, and honor too, in spades. And by 1450, Italian warlords were employing more and newer types of gunpowder weapons.

But in the autumn of 1494, when the king of France, Charles VIII, marched some twenty-five thousand men into Italy, the *condottieri*—war captains from the Orsini, Vitelli, Baglioni, Dal Verme, and other such families—met more than their match in the king's guns and mercenary troops from Switzerland, Germany, Scotland, and France. From this time on, more than ever, serious war on a larger scale, heralded by the French invasion, would be dominated by hardened professionals: enterprisers who raised armies not only for money, or to acquire noble estates and princely titles, but also with a view to marching them across distant frontiers. They flourished on war. Peacetime garrisons were of no use to them. Without wartime salaries, or booty and so-called "contributions," the army of an enter-priser fell apart, and he went back home to Scotland, Gascony, Castile, Switzerland, Saxony, Bohemia, the Balkans, or the mountainous parts of Italy.

Europe was seeing dynasties of once stay-at-home noblemen pass into the profession of arms. Between 1500 and about 1680, as a new tax-and-power state came into being, the raising of armies was mainly in the hands of enterprisers. The most successful of these were themselves fighters. They had direct contacts with colonels and captains: men who could draw on their own networks of friends and acquaintances in town and country. And they used those contacts to raise regiments of mercenaries whenever the call came from princes or urban elites. At the peak of the Thirty Years War, at least fifteen hundred such enterprisers were supplying the needs of princes. Among these, for example, were the Scottish nobles Sir Donald MacKay, Colonel Robert Monro, and Alexander Leslie, who led volunteers and pressed men into Sweden's armies and even into Muscovite Russia.

Some enterprisers were themselves princes, such as the Duke of Saxe-Weimar, Christian of Brunswick-Wolfenbüttel (1599–1626), and Charles IV of Lorraine (1604–1674), who could raise armies of up to twenty thousand men, foot and horse, and then negotiate profitable hiring arrangements with a superior power. More remarkably, brilliant generals such as Pappenheim and Wallenstein, turning their armies into private enterprises, were even able to double their numbers while on the march, largely by having their men live off extortion and plunder. Their outstanding reputations—Pappenheim's on the battlefield—drew men into their ranks. In the late 1630s, the leading Swedish general, Johan Banér, came close to owning his own army of desperados.

At the lower end of the scale, small enterprisers might raise and captain units of anywhere from two hundred to two thousand men. In January 1525, a contract between the Emperor Charles V and Giovanni Maria da Varano, lord of the city of Camerino, called for the Italian to provide Charles with "1500 well-equipped infantry and a smaller cavalry contingent." In May 1484, another petty warlord from the da Varano family bound himself to serve Venice with a force of twelve hundred cavalry and fifty mounted archers. The contract was for two years and a sum of 50,000 gold ducats. Hired units, however, also came in even smaller numbers. In 1490, in a war between the city of Metz and the Duke of Lorraine (René II), the city brought in twenty-three hundred mercenaries: "'Burgundians, French, Lombards, Spaniards, Biscayans, Gascons, Hainaulters and Picards, as well as Germans, Sclavonians and Albanians,' and each 'nation' had its own captain." In other words, this patchwork was the product of ten or twelve enterprising captains, likely subcontractors, under the command of the chief enterpriser, a higher officer.

But there had to be volunteers in enough numbers to satisfy demand, or the ugly art of selective impressment would come into play. With its scale of wars, epidemics, and stunted populations, the seventeenth century posed grave problems for recruiters, and no enterpriser could get around this. One illustrative example tells much of the story.

Early in 1644, Cardinal Mazarin, France's chief minister, decided to raise troops for the embattled Amalia Elisabeth, the ruler (Landgravine) of Hesse-Cassel, a Protestant ally threatened by Imperial forces. He commissioned the Count of Marsin, a colonel, to raise four thousand mercenaries (half horse and half foot) in the neutral bishopric of Liège and in other parts of the Empire's Westphalian circle. Marsin's recruiting captains ran into trouble at once. They found that a Spanish general and a French field marshal were also recruiting in the region. As a result, recruitment bonuses were driven up sharply, bribes were offered to likely enlistees, and Marsin failed to accomplish his mission. The French would have recourse to impressment.

Captains were the key to the business of recruitment. They were meant to look after their men, handle wages, arrange for supplies, and in wartime were apt to dispose of the power of life and death over their charges. Ideally, they captained infantry companies that ranged in size from one hundred up to three hundred men, or cavalry companies of about one hundred horse when at full strength. But as war and disease took their toll, numbers plummeted, and in the seventeenth century, many infantry companies on campaign comprised no more than sixty to eighty men. A lieutenant and an ensign served as aides to the captain, these too usually drawn from the nobility, although commoners also turned up in these grades.

Armies were clusters of regiments, and these were made up of companies. From about the middle of the sixteenth century, infantry regiments were usually under the command of colonels. A regiment might number eight hundred to three thousand men at full strength; but it was in the companies that officers, especially the captains, truly knew their men, thus making them the pivotal recruitment figures in villages and urban neighborhoods. Working with their lieutenants, they conducted the face-to-face dealings and clinched arrangements.

But the men who most counted for princes and other big warlords were the regimental commanders, the colonels. These were the enterprisers of substance, the men who often had proprietary rights over a regiment or two, or simply owned them outright.

In the 1590s, ailing financially, the Spanish crown let more and more of its authority slip into the hands of its local elites and captains as it scraped about, desperate for more soldiers. Royal government now saw the passage of "the officer as crown-appointed functionary to the officer as crown-accepted entrepreneur." In the Netherlands, recruiting was wholly the job of entrepreneurs. There, in changing circumstances, 80 to 90 percent of the Spanish army was composed of mercenaries from Germany, France, Ireland, Italy, Switzerland, Austria, and the southern Netherlands. Already organized into companies and regiments, they were marched in from abroad by enterprising officers—men moved primarily by the business of profit and loss.

WAGES AND PROFITS

When soldiers were made to go hungry, regulations and promises concerning their expected food rations were turned into a jeering mockery. Everywhere in Europe these called for a daily diet of one and a half to two pounds of bread (or groats for gruel in eastern Europe); from eight ounces to a pound of meat, fish, or possibly cheese; measures of beer or wine; and specific amounts of salt, vinegar, and oil. Government ministers were well aware of what the stomachs of active men required. In Russia and parts of eastern Europe, owing to population scarcities, armies often aimed to carry enough food in their wagon trains to cover basic wartime needs. In the west, instead, in war zones, although efforts were made to carry some food, or even grain and portable ovens for the making of bread, it was frequently taken for granted that soldiers on campaign would be able to pick up food along the way. And wages were supposed to cover the costs of daily food rations, unless the army itself was providing all or part of the food. What really happened?

It is easy to come on itemized facts concerning the wages of soldiers. The German Landsknecht of the sixteenth century received a basic sum of four *gulden* per month. A frontline Spanish soldier in the 1590s got a wage of forty-five *maravedís* per day. In 1699, in the Russia of Peter the Great, soldiers were being paid five to eleven roubles per year. Around 1700, a peacetime musketeer in France got five *sous* per day. And Venice paid foot soldiers about three ducats per month during the sixteenth century, although this sum came to less, because it was paid out in petty cash, not in the valued gold coin, the ducat.

But all these figures ring through to us as meaningless until we put the soldier into the world of his social peers: the landless peasant, the poor artisan, the wage laborer. Now his earnings are converted into a standard of living, and in this light, pairing soldier with lowly civilian, historians have found that the two were in a match in which the civilian was usually better off. Famine could drive peasants and craftsmen into armies, such as in France in 1694 and 1709, or in parts of Germany during the Thirty Years War. In serious scarcity, a good 40 percent of populations were likely to depend on charity or on begging in the streets and village byways. In France, bread claimed one half the budget of the poor. Geoffrey Parker has held that in the Low Countries, possibly "half the income of the average poor family went on bread," their "staple diet [being] a bowl of salt soup with black rye bread." All told, indeed, 75 percent of their yearly income was apt to be spent on food. Here at once we begin to pick up a sense of the struggle for survival in the social milieux from which most soldiers came. No wonder then that food was so important for them. There had to be this, at least, or why volunteer for the army?

Along came a rational solution: payment in food, the basic stipend of Sweden's armies in Germany during the Thirty Years War. This policy was frankly laid down by Gustavus Adolphus in 1632. Running short of the needed cash, he saw no better way out of his fix.

But there was also another, if more devious, route. It was described by the Swedish chancellor Axel Oxenstierna in 1633. He estimated that if the army's seventy-eight thousand men were paid on a monthly basis, as was their due, the yearly wage bill would be in the region of 9.8 million Reichstalers. But if he paid them for a mere month, holding on to the rest, and dispensed one pound of bread per day to each soldier, plus occasional small sums of money, he would then be able to keep the yearly bill down to 5.4 million Reichstalers. And this is what he tried to do. Within two years, however, in 1635, though having already confronted a major mutiny, Oxenstierna was again faced with an army in a state of mass mutiny, and he had to rush into negotiations with the officers.

In the late sixteenth and seventeenth centuries, the mercenary armies of the Dutch were alleged to be the best paid in Europe. Yet "the pay was half that of a day labourer," and the Dutch were capable of callously dismissing, without pay, newly recruited mercenary companies on suddenly finding that they no longer needed them, as happened in 1658. The ruling elites of the United (Dutch) Provinces were not in the least generous with their armies; no European state ever was, because paying wartime soldiers was the dearest by far of all government expenses. Hence the Scottish, English, and German mercenaries of the Dutch occasionally bordered on mutiny, their cries a litany against arrears in pay. Still, by managing to pay more regularly than princes, thanks to a booming seventeenth-century economy, the Dutch were nearly always able to attract mercenaries. Even local journeymen, who often lived on the verge of unemployment, despite the boom, might join a home regiment for the simple reason that it "held the prospect of continuous income." But just as temporary hard times could bring this on, so better times were likely to result in mass desertions. Army life was a choice of last resort.

Military historians point out that when the opportunity arose, soldiers in garrisons were allowed to work at their trades, if they had one, with an eye to extra earnings. But only peace could impart substance to this rosy view, and even then the working soldier might have to share that extramural income with his commanding officer. War itself—the actual ground and times of warfare—offered few opportunities for workaday labor.

The Peace of Cateau-Cambrésis (1559), ending the Italian Wars, released thousands of French soldiers, including officers, back into civilian life, and many would soon be sucked into the French Wars of Religion (1562–1598). In this "higher" conflict, the will to provide soldiers with a living wage quickly floundered. Within weeks of the start of a campaign, Catholic and Protestant princes would find themselves unable to go on paying the sums due. Their armies now began to go hungry, or to strike out in search of edible plunder. The practical solution—and this occurred repeatedly, on the government side especially—was to call a truce and disband the troops. Crown and Huguenot opposition would then begin to cast about for ways to raise more funds for a new round of warfare.

But such proceedings could pave the way to horror. In October 1562, over three days, contrary to the pleas of the queen mother, Catherine de Médicis, an unpaid and resentful royal army sacked Rouen, the second-largest city in France. Some of the captains simply stole away with the silver for the wages of the soldiers.

If we turn to the late fifteenth century, to Renaissance Italy and the world of the Sforza dukes of Milan, we come on one of the best organized of the peninsula's mercenary armies. Yet Sforza soldiers were so poorly paid, and often partly paid in bales of cloth, that they were allowed to top up their earnings with plunder and contraband. The dukes complained about this, but it was also in their fiscal interest to look the other way.

In the early sixteenth century, on paper at least, the German Landsknecht seemed able to have a more comfortable material life than many journeymen: craftsmen who were not their own masters. Volunteer recruits came forward in numbers. But their initial expenses for kit put them immediately into debt. Costs ran to something like

one *gulden* for a long pike, three *gulden* for a helmet, three and a half
gulden for an arquebus in the latter part of the century, and all of
twelve *gulden* for simple armor. Meanwhile they paid for their own
food, clothing, and shoes out of their monthly wage of four *gulden*,
the value of which was whittled down by the extraordinary inflation of the sixteenth century. In due course, when going into a
company of Landsknechts, German youths were likely to be enticed
by the promise of loot alone. Their plan was to live on booty.

THE INABILITY OF STATES TO keep paying the wages of their mercenaries was far from being the whole story. We have seen that military entrepreneurs could ply their trade only in the shadows of war,
and that their regiments were organized to bring in—like business
firms—as much profit as possible. A lesser tale now comes up, linked
to the individual companies and to the captains who regarded them
as their property.

Owing to the scantiness of government cash, rulers often assumed—
or wanted to believe—that captains would have enough capital on
hand, when the need arose, to pay recruitment bonuses, to lend money
to soldiers for equipment (not seldom even for shoes), and to pay for
food and fodder when the due funds failed to arrive. Regimental
bosses (colonels), who might own several companies, were also seen
in this light, and not seldom they were titled men with landed estates.
Yet in meeting the needs of their men out of their own pockets,
captains and colonels turned themselves into moneylenders, and
so they sought to collect interest on their loans. But they also expected a return on the primary business ventures: their companies
and regiments.

In this jigsaw of operations, always anxious about delayed government payment, our military enterprisers looked for every profitable angle, particularly officers in pursuit of higher place, more
servants, better dress, a more generous table, or a surplus for the needs
of family and land back home. Some of them, indeed, had incurred
debt for the initial outlays of capital, so as to pay for dress, food, and

horses, or even to buy a company of soldiers. Every coin that came into their hands raised the question: Was it one that could be kept? The same consideration went into the sums that they paid out in wages, and for food, arms, pack animals, and other needs. These were the occasions when the hands of captains might engage in sleight of hand. Sources abound in comments about starving soldiers standing next to well-fed officers dressed to the nines. At the peak of France's wars of conscience and religion, officers were capable, as we have seen, of galloping off with the wages of soldiers. Fighting for God did not necessarily reinforce honesty. Not surprisingly, recruits were known to desert en masse, as occurred in Spain, when a group of them saw that their captain was crudely seeking his own profit at their expense.

Fraud among army officers was most glaringly connected with the mustering of troops for review by a government official. A specific sum—the soldier's wage—would then be due to the company commander for every foot soldier and horseman present at the muster, as confirmed by the official inspector. Almost everywhere, it seems, impostors (*passe-volants*) checkered the mustered ranks: men fetched in and paid a tiny sum for the walk-on part. The Germans had a saying, "Not all men who carry pikes are pikemen." Rulers knew all about this trickery, knew it was rife, but were unable to put a stop to it; and the commanding officers battened. When possible, such as on campaign or after skirmishes and battles, officers were also likely to submit muster lists that included dead men and deserters; and if they owned their companies, this temptation became urgent.

Many other forms of fraud also flourished, as we may glimpse in one of the most detailed inquiries ever made of soldierly corruption in early modern Europe: a study of Milan's garrison during the early 1580s.

Milan was headquarters for the troops of Spanish Italy, although its great fortress, the *castello*, held a garrison of only little more than one thousand men, of whom just over six hundred were soldiers. Favoritism and bribery were rampant in that tight community.

Guard duty was de rigueur, but not for favorites. Food in the fortress was dearer than in town and not nearly as good, in spite of being free of excise taxes. But since their wages were nearly always far in arrears, most of the soldiers had to buy their food on credit and hence in the *castello*. They were in debt perpetually. A sum was regularly deducted from their wages for a hospital in the city, but most of that money was pocketed by the castellan. First arrivals at the fortress, arriving with a weapon of their own, were forced nonetheless to buy an overpriced second one, often touched up to look like new. Soldiers even had to buy monthly amounts of gunpowder, sold at a profit, to be used in gun salutes for the arrival and honoring of important people.

The villains of the scene were the castellan, Don Sancho de Guevara Padilla, and Lieutenant Bartolomé Palomeque. The lieutenant had even forced the *castello* taverner to borrow 200 gold *scudi* from him at 30 percent interest, payable monthly. Alas for justice, at the end of the inquiry (1586), the castellan was found not guilty of corruption, and the lieutenant died before he could suffer penalties, so much time had passed before judicial proceedings were finally complete.

We cannot say that conditions in the Milan garrison were typical. But with the galloping inflation of the sixteenth century, and the cost of bread sometimes on a seesaw, conduct at the *castello* reveals the hard cynicism and abuse of a time and place of dearth. Milan itself was not even directly in a war zone. Still, officers everywhere were driven to sniff out opportunities for dishonesty, and ruling elites, manipulated by privileged castes, were unable to block the avenues to temptation.

And yet there was something to be said for the officers—a mitigating word, above all in wartime, when government funds ran out fast. For all their finery, officers too could go hungry in the field, and even find themselves reduced to poverty by the state's inability to honor its contracts with them. France especially, in the seventeenth century, had cases of captains and colonels whose heavy investments in their units carried them toward ruin and encouraged fraud if, as they saw it, they were to save themselves financially. The cancer of corruption thus went back, to a large extent, to the failures of the emerging tax–and–power state.

THE MILITARY ENTERPRISER WAS PASSING out of the picture by the late seventeenth century. But the quest for private gain from the finances of regiments and companies ran through the eighteenth century. Modest Prussian noblemen, as army officers, built careers and attained wealth on that coveted income. Noblemen in France bought and sold companies for the sake of gain. And Spanish colonels in the Low Countries turned the cushier positions in their regiments into places for clients, relatives, retainers, friends, and servants from back home.

3

SACKING CITIES

T HE ROOT METAPHOR here, in the word *sack* (Latin: *saccus*), is in the notion of putting a city into a sack and going off with it. An extravagant image. Yet the sense of it was close enough to the essential reality. At Brescia in 1512, Antwerp in 1576, and Magdeburg in 1631, as we shall see, soldiers left the scenes of their violence with as much booty as they could carry or transport by cart, wagon, and horse.

To sack a city, however, was not only to loot it, leaving behind a spoor of destruction, but also to murder at will, to violate women, and to batter inhabitants until they revealed the whereabouts of their concealed valuables—money, jewelry, plate, silks, and prized furnishings. Another source of rich plunder—often the most lucrative—was in ransom moneys squeezed from as many people as possible, particularly the rich and well connected.

Looking back to Renaissance Italy, we find that the peninsula fell victim to four extraordinary sackings. The most notorious of them ripped through papal Rome in 1527, when unpaid soldiers, mostly Spanish and German, paid themselves with the wealth of cardinals, noblemen, bankers, ambassadors, and rich citizens. But up in Lombardy, Brescia, fifty miles east of Milan, was the first big city to be stormed after 1500. Next came Genoa, on the Ligurian coast, in 1522. And princely Mantua would suffer a similar fate in 1630, in an assault that dispersed the remains of one of Europe's most famous art collections, assembled over more than two centuries by the ruling Gonzaga family.

But lesser sacks, though not for the victims, invested other places: Ravenna and Prato in 1512, Lodi in 1516, Como in 1521, and Pavia in 1528. Italy's luminous cities seduced Europe's leading monarchs. And the peninsula was turned into the main "theater of operation" for the territorial claims of the Valois kings of France and the Habsburg princes of Spain and of Germany's Holy Roman Empire.

BRESCIA (1512)

The makings of Brescia's nightmare went back to January 1512, with a conspiracy organized by Brescian noblemen and directed against the occupying French governor. The aim of the conspirators was to return the city to the control of the Venetian Republic. Prominent local noblemen had never ceased to figure in public life, and now they were about to plunge the city and themselves into horror.

An old city, with roots reaching back to ancient Rome, Brescia had long known how to prosper. And with a population of about thirty-five thousand souls—London then had about sixty thousand—it was one of Europe's largest urban centers, home to busy cloth, iron, and metal-working industries. The Visconti dukes of Milan had ruled Brescia until it was torn away from them by the Venetians in the 1420s. The city's new link with seafaring Venice proved to have trade advantages, and while one of the noble factions accepted the regime change, the other, being high-profile and anti-Venetian, turned in favor of the French.

In the tale before us, Brescia had passed to the hands of the French only three years before, in the spring of 1509, when a remarkable European alliance against Venice briefly dismantled the Venetian mainland empire. French armies grabbed Brescia, Bergamo, and Cremona, then restored these cities to the puppet government of the duchy of Milan, which was now in the grasp of the king of France.

The French got wind of the 1512 plot a day before the planned assault on them. They fanned out at once, on January 21 and 22, to arrest, interrogate, and behead scores of plotters, while also confiscating their properties in the process. The leader of the conspiracy, an old warrior, Count Luigi Avogadro, managed to escape. Fleeing from the city, he rushed to meet his Venetian accomplices and his own mercenaries, who were already on their way to Brescia. The plan had been to open one of the gates of the city in the middle of the night and to let Venice's soldiers and the other mercenaries steal in to catch the defending garrison by surprise.

Knowing that the French had reduced their troop numbers in Brescia to a mere nine hundred men, Avogadro and the Venetian commander, Andrea Gritti, decided to press on to the city, despite having lost the benefit of a surprise attack. They were then joined along the way by several thousand peasants. Alerted, the governing French official assembled the Brescian nobility and made a plea for their help to defend the city. He seems to have been met mostly with silence, whereupon the pro-French families urged him to provide them with arms, but he turned down their request, no longer trusting even them.

To the sound of drums and trumpets, Avogadro's own mercenaries, backed by volunteers, made the first attack on Brescia on February 2 and were afterward joined by Venice's troops. Peasants scaled the city walls after two hours of fierce fighting, and the plotters broke into Brescia, while the French retreated to the *castello*, the upper fortress overlooking the city. Avogadro's supporters now assaulted and sacked the houses of Milanese merchants and of the pro-French Gambareschi, noble satellites of the Gambara counts. So it was now civil war as well. Gritti's cannons, however, did not have the firepower to silence the upper fortress, from which the French now used their artillery to rain terror on the city.

In Bologna, meanwhile, the supreme commander of French forces, the young Gaston de Foix, getting word of the debacle, moved his army out at once and made a race for Brescia. Stung by the humiliating coup there, in the midst of a war with Spain's army in Italy, and resenting the Italian propaganda campaign against the "barbarian"

French, de Foix was in no mood to be merciful. On the sixteenth of February, he was already outside the walls of Brescia, laying waste to the suburbs and killing about eight hundred men on the Venetian side. He waited two days, then sent a trumpeter into the city with a call for its surrender and the promise of security for life and property. The invitation was spurned in the belief that a Spanish army, commanded by Raimondo Cardona, was on its way to engage the French forces. A fatal mistake, for in the customary rules then governing the conduct of war, if a city rejected the terms of surrender and was then taken by storm, it was liable ipso facto to a sacking.

During the night of February 18 and 19, more than six thousand French, Swiss, and German mercenaries, using an emergency stairway and moving two abreast, climbed slowly up into the upper fortress. Dawn found five hundred French cavalry positioned just outside the Gate of San Nazzaro; but all the gates were now surrounded, and the soldiers had been given license to sack and kill, sparing only the "Ghibelline" (pro-French) families. Ghoulishly, it was the week of carnival.

Four hours later, French fighters, bearing "the flag of death," started their descent into the city from the *castello*. Meeting heavy arquebus firing, they pushed forward anyway. Some of them fought their way to the Torlonga gate, opened it, and let in a new wave of French mercenaries. Picking up the scent of defeat, the light cavalry of the Venetians, crossbowmen from Dalmatia, panicked, whereupon they made for the Gate of San Nazzaro, forced it open, and a few of them managed to escape. But the waiting French horsemen now waded in, slaughtering many of them at will. Avogadro and his fighters fought on bravely, only to be overwhelmed, while Gritti and his men were surrounded on three sides. The battle was soon over. Prisoners were taken; the "gentlemen" and officers on the Venetian side, including the rich Andrea Gritti, were picked out to be held for ransoming. But Avogadro and the other Brescian "traitors" were not about to be spared for money. They were beheaded, along with two of Avogadro's sons, and then quartered—each body hacked into four parts. The parts were fixed to the city gates and to prominent points in the government square, low enough, however, to be got and torn at by dogs. An express reminder to traitors.

Meanwhile, the entire city was a tumult of cries and screams and the swooping attacks of poorly paid foreign soldiers, speaking a mélange of tongues, their ranks already thinned out by casualties. Confronting a rich and rebellious city with a license to kill, they threw themselves on the civilian population.

The sack lasted three days, from Thursday to Sunday. Eyewitness accounts report horrific scenes of torture, rape, butchery, and violent theft. A citizen from Bologna, Cesare Anselmi, who was with de Foix's troops in Brescia, put together one of the fullest accounts, although here and there, in his reporting, he gave way to exaggeration and fiction.

> My soul all but leaves me when I think about it. There was no security in convents or other holy places . . . One saw armed men dividing the money and jewellery among themselves, while still wearing their helmets . . . In those three days they inflicted every kind of torment on the wretched inhabitants, men and women, to force them to reveal the hiding places of their money and valuables. Every dishonourable violence was used on women, and throughout the city, day and night, one heard nothing but the most wretched cries of the miserable . . . or of women resisting those who were trying to rape them, and many were seen to throw themselves from windows, seeking to die that way, rather than to satisfy with their bodies the wild lust of those who had killed their fathers, husbands, sons, and brothers, and who were still pillaging and burning and ruining their houses. Many women killed themselves with knives. Others, pretending contented acceptance, killed their ravishers, in many cases in bed, caring nothing about then being cruelly killed by others . . .

Some, finding a dead loved one, would be there for hours, crying or tearing at themselves or praying over the corpse. And it was horrid to see many of those vile soldiers who, on catching sight of a good-looking woman weeping desperately over the body of a loved one, would go up to her, hike up her skirts, and try to dishonour her right then and there over the corpse.

Observing again that many women were killed, disfigured, or had their garments ripped away, Anselmi concluded: "I swear to you [he was writing to a friend] that finding myself in that city, although loved by the French, being from Bologna, and having come along with them to see, to inform myself, and to write about the operation . . . I passed into such an anguish of the soul that not only did I deeply regret having come, I regretted ever having been born." For a time, he claims, he wanted to die, because in any house he entered, "day and night, I would see nothing but desperate gentlemen and citizens, stripped of their clothing, tied, beaten on their genitals, placed with their feet over fire, with bits of wood driven between their teeth, or having their mouths poked into with a stick or a knife above the tongue and under the palate, until, unable to talk and using signs, they would show themselves ready to disclose the places of their hidden valuables."

When taking Brescia in battle on February 2, Avogadro's men had peeled clothing and belongings away from dead and wounded French soldiers, and this had not endeared the people of Brescia to de Foix's men.

Everywhere in Europe, when a city was faced with the danger of a sack, the custom was for inhabitants to hide their prized possessions in churches and convents, in the desperate hope of finding security there. But soldiers were familiar with this dodge. An account written by the nobleman Innocenzo Casari, prior of the Convent of St. John the Baptist, tells us that the French killed more than one hundred people, both priests and laymen, in the cathedral, including three penitents and a priest directly in front of the main altar. Soldiers also charged into some of the parish churches, where they bloodied the floors with beatings and torture, determined to lay hands on the hidden jewelry, money, and small valuables of parishioners. The rector of the church of St. Agatha was brutally kicked about until he came out with the desired secret, and then "everything was stolen." Casari himself, accosted by a French officer who seemed to choke with anger as he snarled out his demands, had to borrow one hundred pieces of gold to buy him off. But the sum provided no guarantee of protection, as he had hoped, for after the officer departed, a group of German soldiers broke into the convent and began to smash cabinets and chests, grabbing everything of value that they could carry away. They even tried to ransom some of the monks. In the end, they settled comfortably into the convent for seven days, "living it up," bringing in prostitutes and other women, including "honorable girls," and "violently forcing them to satisfy their disgraceful appetites."

Casari goes on: "The [charitable] Bank of the Monte di Pietà was robbed of more than 100,000 gold pieces." The inmates of every monastery were beaten into paying a ransom for the house, with death otherwise as the penalty for some of the monks.

A number of priests were burned alive. The nobleman Cristoforo Guaineri had his arms cut off and died on burning coal. A rich merchant named Antonio [del Sacro Fonte] was flayed alive. Two of my brothers, Ottobono and Girolamo, and Ottobono's son Angelo, were strung up by their hands and feet and only escaped death by paying out 90 gold pieces . . . Rich in people, with wealth and amenities of all sorts, and second in this respect to no other city in Italy, at a stroke this flourishing city was reduced to something vile and squalid and abject and deserving of pity. The patricians and grand folk who used to be seen in the streets and squares, decked out in fine dress and with a train of servants and dependents, but now despoiled of everything, were ashamed to appear in public and would hide at home, locked away in their empty and ruined *palazzi* . . . The streets, once busy and full of people, the expressive image of the city's prosperity, are now barren and empty of living souls.

For some days, in the wake of the sack, "the city and its suburbs were cemeteries. Unburied and stinking corpses lay everywhere." This claim by Casari was echoed by a Venetian soldier: "You couldn't walk through the streets save by stepping on corpses." A third witness provided the segue: "The dead were taken out of Brescia like dung on carts."

The numbers of dead in wartime and in catastrophes, even in our day, are often the stuff of speculation. Estimates put the dead—how to count the maimed and the mutilated?—at from six to sixteen thousand, although the second estimate, offered by the famous Venetian diarist Sanudo, purported to include the casualties on the French side. But if we must have a sum, a figure of eight thousand dead, nearly one quarter of the city's population, stands out as the most reliable number.

We come to the question of plunder, always a matter of considerable guesswork. When the French army raced to Brescia from Bologna, the officers had little reason to be thinking of plunder, and anyway there was no time to collect carts or wagons for the transport of loot. Soldiers would find these, along with pack animals, in and around Brescia. And they would reportedly leave the city with about four thousand vehicles, all loaded with booty. Most of the loot seems to have gone up for sale in towns along the way of their next march. Churches, convents, and houses, as we have seen, were despoiled of their hidden treasures. Ransoms brought in huge sums of cash. The officers, entitled to the lion's share of the booty, had picked out all males over the age of eight, putting a price on the heads of those believed to be worth something. Victims were judged by their dress, but above all by where they lived.

A week after the sack, French commanders capped their doings with a little more blood by executing another group of Brescian conspirators, and again their quartered remains were put on show at prominent points, until "the dogs ate most of them."

THERE IS A STRONG WHIFF of something literary in Cesare Anselmi's claims concerning the heroism and willing martyrdom of Brescia's women when threatened with sexual violence. It is not that suicide, or that the crafty killing of rapists, was impossible in the circumstances. Such action, however, was exceedingly rare. And no other source that I know of, when reporting similar events elsewhere in Italy or in other parts of Europe, provides instances of heroic suicidal resistance. Hence many of Anselmi's claims must be taken with a grain of salt.

But a tale of pathos may rightly close our events of 1512.

One of the most brilliant mathematicians of the sixteenth century, Niccolò Tartaglia, ironically also an expert in the field of military engineering, was twelve years old and in Brescia on the day of the exploding sack. Seeking cover and protection, he and his mother and sister, like many other Brescians, rushed to the cathedral. "Our house had been pillaged, though there was little to take." He was tiny for a twelve-year-old, and there is no knowing what he did to provoke a cruel incident, which must have occurred just after the soldiers burst into the cathedral. Was it a simple act or word of resistance? His account is silent about this. He cuts straight to the violence:

> In my mother's presence, I was dealt five very grave wounds, three on the head, in each of which you could see my brain, and two on the face, such that if my beard failed to hide them now, I would seem a monster. One [blow] passed through my mouth and teeth, splitting the jaw-bone and upper palate in two, and the same in the lower jaw. Because of this wound, not only could I not talk, except deep down in my throat like a magpie, I also could not eat, inasmuch as I could not in the least move my mouth or my

jaws, everything there being shattered. I had to be fed with liquid foods only and with great labour. But more serious still was the fact that not having the money to buy the needed unguents, not to mention calling in a doctor, my mother had to tend and treat me with her own hands, and not with ointments but just by keeping my wounds constantly clean. She copied the example of dogs, which, when they are wounded, heal themselves by licking the wound clean with their tongues. With this care and prudence, my wounds healed after a few months.

For some time after, when trying to speak, he used to stammer. Neighboring children gave him the nickname *Tartaglia* ("Stammerer"). Later, he would take this epithet as his surname, springing, as he did, from such humble circumstances that his father, Micheletto ("Little Michael"), had been without a family name.

There was something fabulous about Niccolò Tartaglia's brilliance. In all his life, he had only fourteen days of schooling with a tutor who taught him how to read. Yet he was the first Italian to translate Euclid's *Elements* into the vernacular.

ANTWERP (1576)

In the 1560s and 1570s, northern Europe experienced a new wave of religious fervor. Calvinists—revolutionary Protestants—had entered their most combative period. Having edged France into religious civil war, they were stealing over borders into Germany and the Low Countries, aiming to root out "popery" and the "whore of Babylon," the old Church. The king of Spain, Philip II, having inherited the Netherlands from his father, the Habsburg Emperor Charles V, had sworn that he would rather lose his kingdom many times over than be the ruler of "heretics." His vow would turn into suffering for millions of people.

Some of the glories of early modern Spain—*conquistadores*, political muscle, ambition, a global empire—were to find their first cemetery in the Low Countries. That graveyard was the Eighty Years War (1567–1648), fought on the one side to keep rebellious peoples under the rule of Spanish kings, and on the other to be free from foreign domination. At the critical moments, the royal share of all the gold and silver from the Indies would not suffice to pay for the armies raised against the "disobedience" of the Walloons, Flemings, and Dutch. Indeed, when converted into wages for soldiers, that fabled treasure hoard faded into paltry sums.

The drawn-out tragedy of the Eighty Years War, though often interpreted in a political key by historians, was also in part propelled by a powerful social fuel: religion. In the early years of the war, it was a case of evangelical Calvinists in an all-out battle against Catholics who came—both leaders and rank and file—from a religious frontier: the Iberian peninsula. Here Spaniards had banished Jews and defeated Muslims, peoples who reject the use of images in religious worship. Now, suddenly, in the Netherlands the Spanish had to confront an image-smashing fury that broke out on the tenth of August, 1566, and seemed to spread like wildfire.

Calvinist sermons in the countryside around cities, often attended by men with pikes and swords, preceded the iconoclastic assaults. But the fury began in little towns in western Flanders, swept east and then north to Antwerp, and passed on to neighboring cities, reaching Amsterdam, the Hague, and other urban centers by late August. Hundreds of churches and chapels were attacked, scarred, and ransacked by spearheading gangs of thirty to forty iconoclasts—a minority everywhere. But they were organized and skillfully led. In many cases, the workingmen amongst them were paid to use clubs, axes, knives, and hammers to destroy or deface statuary, altars, painted images, baptismal fonts, books of all sorts, vestments, and other objects. Laws, dating back to 1523, had identified the nascent heresies as capital crimes, but no one now dared to invoke them against the iconoclastic furies. Local authorities blanched, retreated, or were paralyzed by division. During the previous forty years, about thirteen hundred "heretics" had been executed, but most of them, Anabaptists, had been looked upon as "low-born" troublemakers. Calvinists, instead, were a different sort. Too many of them came from the respectable classes. Yet in law, the war on images constituted flagrant civil disorder and rebellion, a fusion of politics and religion. These would be indivisible for the next three generations.

The image breakers took inspiration from events in neighboring France, where a civil war between Huguenots and Catholics had erupted in 1562 and where, in the space of a year or so, the evangelical reformers seized temporary political control of more than twenty cities. In fact, in the 1560s the Huguenots looked at times as though they might sweep across all of France in a wholesale victory for the cause of Calvinism. They were ready to let armies clinch their cause.

WHEN THE NEW SPANISH GOVERNOR of the Netherlands, the Duke of Alba, reached Brussels in August 1567, his plan was to impose political and religious obedience. His enforcers? The ten thousand Spanish and Italian soldiers who had arrived with him; and he now began to hire thousands more by recruiting mercenaries from Germany and the Netherlands. Over the next fifteen months, Alba's troops defeated four different armies and the inchoate breakaway state of Prince William "the Silent" of Orange, a moderate Protestant who then crossed over to an intransigent position. The Council of Troubles, appointed by Alba, would order more than one thousand executions as punishment for rebellion and treason. Most disturbing in that deferential world was the capital punishment of sixteen noblemen and the beheading of two Catholic counts, Egmont and Hornes. Their severed heads were affixed to the gallows on pikes. The revolt had transcended religious convictions and was now dominated by a political stance.

A "grandee," says the historian Israel, "well versed in Latin, French, and Italian, who also spoke some German," Alba was removed from his post in 1573, a victim of court intrigue in Madrid. He legacy in the Low Countries was a swirl of anger over taxes, executions, brutal soldiers, and the merciless slaughter of civilians in the rebellious towns of Naarden, Zutphen, and Mechelen.

Brussels was the capital of the Spanish Netherlands. But Antwerp, a flourishing port with a population of about ninety thousand inhabitants, was the largest city in the Low Countries and the hub of commerce. It handled about 75 percent of all trade there.

The bloody events that would unfold in Antwerp were set off by the death of the governor general, Don Luis de Requeséns, in March 1576. King Philip II had declared bankruptcy the year before, with the result that most of the unpaid Army of Flanders disintegrated. Units verged on mutiny, ready to launch attacks on citizens; anxieties flared; and the Council of State in Brussels assumed full powers, purporting to speak for the king, until the arrival from Madrid of the next governor general.

With only a single Spaniard, Gerónimo de Roda, serving on the Council of State, the Council and the army clashed. Late in July 1576, a contingent of Spanish soldiers—their wages unpaid for years—mutinied, passed into Brabant, and sacked Aalst, a little town not far from Brussels. Branding them outlaws and rebels against the king, the Council decreed that they could be killed on sight, while also encouraging the local (Brabant) estates to raise soldiers to protect the province from the angry rebels. But Spanish officers in other garrisons, acutely short of men and fearing armed attacks from the estates, refused to turn their backs on the mutineers. The split between Council and army became a chasm.

As the weeks passed, the actions of the Council began to strike the zealous supporters of the Prince of Orange as too moderate, too tame, with the result that on September 4, soldiers of the local estates suddenly struck. They arrested the members of the Council and raised a call for a meeting of all the states of the Low Countries. The more ambitious aim now, passing beyond religious differences, was to rid the Netherlands of Spain's armed forces. Regiments of

Walloons (French-speaking Belgians) deserted the army, passing over to the states, and efforts were also made to woo German mercenaries away from the royal ranks by offering them down payments on their wages.

The lone Spanish Councillor, Gerónimo de Roda, escaped the arresting soldiers of September 4, alerted by the fact that his house had been plundered and a servant killed. Fleeing to Antwerp, he took refuge in the citadel, the city's new fortress, which was occupied by two hundred Spanish soldiers. Hatred and resentment colored relations between the commander of the citadel, Sánchez d'Avila, and the governor of Antwerp, the Lord of Champaigney (Frederic Perrenot), himself a Catholic and a soldier. The Spanish financial crisis had brought about a near collapse of the Army of Flanders, reducing it, in the course of three years, from 54,500 troops to a mere 8,000. And now, in late September, all these men were being treated as "traitors" to the king of Spain by a fractious Council of State. In October, the boats of the Prince of Orange's Protestant forces sailed into the Scheldt River, facing Antwerp, stood by for many days, and lobbed some cannon shot at the citadel.

The Army of Flanders was at this point about one quarter Spanish. Most of the others were Germans and Walloons; the rest were Italian, English, French, and even Albanian mercenaries. When the unpaid Germans, summoned to Antwerp, reached the city in late October, they arrived shouting, "Money! Money!" Their commander, Count Otto Eberstein, dithered between Sánchez d'Avila on the one side and Champaigney on the other. At the last minute he chose the latter, whereupon early on the third of November, contrary to a previous agreement, Champaigney allowed the troops of the estates to enter Antwerp. Feeling betrayed, some of Eberstein's officers and men marched into the citadel and joined the Spaniards.

That day, a Saturday, in thick fog and in the face of light cannon shot from the citadel, about eleven thousand citizens worked on defensive trenches and ramparts, all dug or erected in a day, and stretching along the ends of the three streets that led to the esplanade in front of the fortress. Cannons, their muzzles pointed at the citadel, were also put into place. The temporary ramparts were raised to the height of pikes, fifteen to eighteen feet. Roda and Sánchez d'Avila, meanwhile, had been in touch with soldiers at Lier, Maastricht, and Breda; and some of those men were already in the citadel or on their way. A summons went out to the Aalst mutineers, Walloons mainly, and a forced march of six to seven hours had these men in Antwerp by nine o'clock on the morning of Sunday, November 4. A ghastly lack of foresight among Champaigney's men allowed the soldiers of the Army of Flanders, using an upper gate, to steal into the citadel from the eastern side of the city.

As we look back to those events, our democratic sympathies go out to the people of Antwerp. Their leaders had put the necks of all inhabitants into a noose by in effect inviting a sack, unless they could engage and defeat the tiny but thoroughly professional army up in the citadel. Champaigney's forces numbered eight to ten thousand troops, including one thousand horse. Many were veterans, seasoned in the Army of Flanders. Furthermore, a local militia of fourteen thousand men stood by. Figures for Sánchez d'Avila's troops in the citadel put their number at nearly five thousand men, about one fifth of them being cavalry. The fortress's two hundred men had been joined by more than four thousand other mercenaries—a mix of Germans, Spaniards, Walloons, Italians, Englishmen, and others.

Once they had their desired men, the commanders in the citadel struck almost at once. The Aalst mutineers were the most ardent about making the first attack, and they charged out of the fortress before noon, their "blasphemous" flag—says a nineteenth-century Protestant historian, M. P. Génard—showing the Virgin and Child on one side and Christ crucified on the other. On reaching the new trenches, where their captain was killed, they were momentarily forced to slow down. Yet an English witness, George Gascoigne, noted, "It was a thing miraculous to consider how trenches of such a height should be entered, passed over, and won, both by footmen and horsemen." A unit of German soldiers from the citadel, in the next wave of assault, was already on the heels of the Aalst mutineers.

On Champaigney's side, a regiment of Germans now threw down their weapons, while others simply passed over and joined their former comrades. The militiamen were nowhere to be seen, although many must have been among the firing arquebusiers and musketeers at the windows of the Town Hall. Some of the Walloons and Eberstein's Germans, the ones who had chosen to fight for the city, put up a fierce battle for fifteen or twenty minutes, before they were overwhelmed.

Many of Champaigney's mercenaries must have regarded the speed and spirit of the assault from the citadel as unstoppable. But they were also prey to disorder and lack of planning, caused partly by the fact that some of them had spent the night drinking and carousing. They even robbed and abused citizens, forcing Champaigney, sword in hand and in danger to himself, to step in among them. He wanted them in the trenches. Count Eberstein, moreover, a heavy drinker, was possibly drunk on that fatal morning.

The pitched battles, including cavalry charges, took place around the great town hall, the Bourse, in the main marketplace, and on several streets. Heavy firing from the town hall windows provoked the Spanish commanders to order the building set on fire. It was seriously damaged, and the fire spread to the adjoining grand houses. In just over two hours, the defeat of Champaigney's army was complete. He and others escaped by making for the Scheldt to board one of the Prince of Orange's waiting boats. Eberstein, however, weighted down by armor, drowned in his efforts to get on board.

From this point on, the sources—already thin in their descriptions of the fighting—offer conflicting accounts of the atrocities in the days following. Although Antwerp was a Catholic city, it was in revolt; hence priests and religious houses were not spared. Roda ordered an end to the sacking after a day or two, and then renewed the order more effectively on November 8—too late. The violence of the human storm peaked in the first three days. Some accounts see the conduct of English mercenaries, former soldiers in the Duke of Alba's army, as the most savage. But it would be folly to try to apportion blame among the different groups of soldiers. Citizens were bludgeoned into revealing hidden valuables. Women and girls, some taken into the citadel, were sexually assaulted. Houses were ransomed, not just people. But we get no palpable sense of the scale of violence. And accounts vary sharply as to the numbers of people killed (from seventy-five hundred to eighteen thousand) and the houses or dwellings destroyed by fire (from six to fourteen hundred).

Although we may take for granted that the value of the plunder was colossal, estimates of the "spoil" of Antwerp are best treated with some degree of skepticism. The most important commercial center in the Low Countries, with a large colony of foreign merchants and bankers, Antwerp was one of the four or five richest cities in Europe. Consequently, in their looting orgy, the Spanish and German captains seem to have picked and worked separate parts of the city. George Gascoigne, an eyewitness, testified that three days after the storming, Antwerp had "no money nor treasure to be found therein, but only in the hands of murderers and strumpets. For every Don Diego must walk jetting up and down the streets, with his harlot by him, in her chain and bracelets of gold." One account held that the soldiers got their hands on two million florins in gold and silver coin, in addition to more than again as much in gold and silver objects, plus furnishings. The lot added up, conceivably, to more than two years of Spain's royal revenue from the wealth of the Indies, as recorded in the late 1570s. An official report of the *Magistrat*, now lost, relied on notes that put the comprehensive value of the Antwerp plunder at five million florins. No house, it appears, was spared in the sack. The spoils from Champaigney's house alone were reportedly worth—in a different coin—about 60,000 crowns.

For many of the looters the take was fairy gold, a delusion, inasmuch as gambling and carelessness among mercenaries were rife, especially in the face of a cascade of coin. In the first few days of the sack, enormous quantities of money and valuables passed very probably through many hands.

We touch here on a Europe-wide pattern. Wherever towns and cities were sacked, goods of all sorts quickly went up for sale cheaply, because plundering soldiers wanted cash first and foremost, or jewelry and precious objects that could easily be sold or traded. Hence merchants and pawnbrokers from the larger region, amongst them local tradesmen, would close in at once on such treasure. They knew that most of that spoil, even when snatched from their own homes, would flood markets nearby or in more distant towns. And although foreigners in Antwerp were also despoiled, Spanish and Portuguese merchants amongst them, they too were in on the take, along with Florentines, Genoese, and others. Precious tapestries seem to have passed out of Antwerp through the hands of a Spanish merchant. In short, once the shock of the first days of violence began to pass—on November 7 baptisms were already being recorded all over the city—lots of men were prepared to recoup their losses by trading in loot. They found themselves in a moral climate that had been suddenly and dramatically altered.

If rich traders and moneylenders trafficked in plunder, poor people—laborers, maidservants, artisans—also succumbed, in some cases by helping to expose the wealth of neighboring acquaintances. Marie de Soeto, a Flemish maidservant in a Spanish household, led a troop of soldiers in the systematic pillage of certain houses. She may even have cooperated in the use of torture, applied to get confessions regarding hidden valuables. Kinks to one side, her behavior—disloyalty and cruelty—smacks of revenge, of a settling of scores. It belongs to a world of underlings, beatings, obedience, and servitude, and to a gulf between rich and poor.

HUNGRY SOLDIERS ARE ANGRY SOLDIERS, ready to vent their temper on innocent civilians. In Antwerp, the citadel was well stocked with provisions, and the soldiers were not hungry. They were, however, unpaid, and such men wanted loot. With their lives in danger, they wanted their wages, but with as much interest—plunder—as possible. The license to sack meant that they were ready to kill, but not in the first instance, not if victims were ready to blurt out their secret hiding places. And the people of Antwerp knew that their attackers, headed by the Aalst mutineers, sprang from the ranks of an unpaid army.

Modern scholarship finds that the so-called "Spanish fury" in Antwerp resulted in about twenty-five hundred deaths, although Leon Voet and Jonathan Israel put the numbers of those murdered in the "hundreds." Voet, again, having studied historical maps of the city, believes that "probably just over a hundred" dwellings were destroyed by fire.

Champaigney and the Council of State in Brussels made alarming political and logistical mistakes. Moreover, in the days leading up to the sack, Orange's Protestant fleet of a hundred boats, floating on the Scheldt and looking on, deepened the anxiety and anger in the citadel. Yet those boats did nothing to assist the city. It was as though the Protestant commanders wanted to teach that Catholic city a lesson.

MAGDEBURG (1631)

It was the spring of 1631. The Holy Roman Empire of the German Nation, the geographic heart of Europe, had been plunged into the middle of a religious and political blood storm, the Thirty Years War (1618–1648). A frugal backdrop may do for us here.

The war broke out in a clash between the Habsburg Emperor Ferdinand II, an arch-Catholic who was claiming the kingdom of Bohemia (today's Czech Republic), and a leading prince of the Empire, the Elector Palatine, Frederick V. This hardy Calvinist had grabbed at the Bohemian kingship when it was offered to him by the country's nobility. Religious differences between emperor and elector now turned toxic for the Empire. Frederick's allies were defeated at the Battle of White Mountain (1620), a catastrophe for the

Bohemian nobility, and there was next an astounding land transfer. About half of all landed property in Bohemia, wartime booty, passed into the hands of Habsburg courtiers and the leading officers of the Habsburg army.

But the need to pay and feed soldiers fast became the most nerve-racking of all matters. The chief banker of the war, Hans de Witte, lender to Wallenstein, the great Imperial general, would end in bankruptcy and commit suicide; and the general himself would be assassinated by colleagues, with the approval of the emperor. Wallenstein's flair for keeping armies together by means of ruthless financial expedients had rendered him independently dangerous.

Issued in March of 1629, the Emperor Ferdinand's infamous Edict of Restitution would hang like an evil star over northern Germany. Looking back to the famous Peace of Augsburg (1555), the edict called for the restitution to the Catholic Church of all the ecclesiastical properties and rights that had been seized—illegally was the presumption—by Protestant princes and towns, stretching back to 1552. The document posed a particular threat to Germany's great prince-bishops of the north.

In the early spring of 1631, the Lutheran city of Magdeburg, once the seat of a major bishopric, came under fire. Recently thinned out by plague, but still a dominant commercial center of twenty-five thousand inhabitants, "Maiden" Magdeburg (local wordplay) was extremely proud of having resisted two previous sieges, first by the Elector Moritz of Saxony, back in 1550–1551, and then by Wallenstein in 1629. When the Protestant Lion of the North, Gustavus Adolphus, king of Sweden, entered the war in July 1630, Magdeburg was the first free city to side with him, thereby breaking the rule which barred all the Empire's princes and free cities from entering into alliances against the emperor. Gustavus was now leading an army through Brandenburg, wanting to press southwest into Saxony, just as the Imperialist and Catholic League generals, Tilly and Pappenheim, rounded on Magdeburg in April and May 1631, laying siege to it with an army of more than twenty-five thousand foot and horse. The Swedish king already had a military governor there, the iron-willed Hessian nobleman Dietrich von Falkenberg, who had entered Magdeburg in the autumn of 1630. One of the many rumors held that he had sworn to see the city in ashes, rather than turned over to Catholics.

In 1629, at the time of Wallenstein's attack on Magdeburg, political schisms in the city had the upper class calling for loyalty to the emperor. A party of moderates rather went along with this call, but a militant constituency of radical Lutherans wanted a break with the Catholic emperor, and they seem at first to have found a good deal of support among the populace. By the spring of 1631, in the shadow of the Edict of Restitution, and with Gustavus Adolphus not far away, loyalist sympathy for the emperor had faded. Or his sympathizers had fallen silent. And the city's restructured ruling council—now in Falkenberg's grasp—was able to hold out to the very end against Tilly's pleas for a negotiated surrender.

In the early morning of May 20, even as Pappenheim's troops, primed with good wine, were storming the northeastern face of Magdeburg's great walls, grappling their way up four hundred ladders, the town council, unbelievably, was still debating the question of holding talks with the Imperial general Tilly. One of Pappenheim's officers, Jürgen Ackermann, described the assault: "There was such a thunder and crack of muskets, incendiary mortars and great cannon that no one could either see or hear, and many supporting troops followed us, so that the whole rampart was filled, covered and black with soldiers and storm ladders . . . After several hundred men had fallen, we broke in over the defences, putting the remainder to flight."

In the face of Dietrich von Falkenberg's menacing presence, the town councillors had scuppered all talk of a surrender. But now, suddenly on that fatal morning, it was a case of sleepers waking on the precipice. The tocsin had been sounded from St. John's spire, and when the councillor, Otto von Guericke, rushed into the town hall to cry out that Croats were already in the city, running down Fischergasse, plundering, the council reacted with shock and wonder.

Only then did Falkenberg break away from the meeting and race out to his horse to take command of the defense.

Something had gone wrong, calamitously so, though not because of treason or the work of spies. In the predawn hours, the night watch had failed to pick out the final preparations of the besiegers before their all-out assault, despite the protective presence of Swedish officers in Magdeburg, in addition to twenty-five hundred troops and a local militia of five thousand men. The city's great moat had been partly drained, and Imperial engineers had got the army to coerce local peasants into filling parts of it with solid materials, with a view to easing the push to the city walls and the emplacement of scaling ladders. Even so, many of the Imperial foot soldiers would break into the city drenched with the moat's waters.

The siege had started in early April, with a gradual blocking of the Elbe River and a cutting off of the flow of supplies into the city. This had been done at the cost of bloody skirmishes and the death— in the Imperial camp too—of hundreds of mercenaries. In the first weeks of May, to aggravate the animosity already caused by the losses on both sides, lashings of hatred and resentment were added at Magdeburg's walls, as Catholic soldiers and evangelicals hurled insults at each other over parapets and ramparts, with one side abusing the Virgin Mary and the other promising, once they got into the city, to rape and enjoy the wives and daughters of the besieged. Insults of this sort were the stuff of sieges. Looking down from their walls, the civilian militia had also used gunfire and missiles to maim and kill besiegers.

The suburbs, meanwhile, had suffered bombardment. Day and night too, for two or three days in May, the city itself was battered by thirty big guns and six mortars, spewing forth some eighteen hundred missiles every day and inflicting heavy damage on certain houses, churches, and steeples. The defenders themselves used very little cannon fire. They had run grievously short of gunpowder.

Now, as the Empire's polyglot mercenaries—hungry, angry, unpaid—broke into Magdeburg, they bounded in with a license to kill and sack because the town council had repeatedly rejected Tilly's call to surrender, in the belief that Gustavus Adolphus would come to their rescue. And for this, as for the ensuing carnage, Falkenberg, the city's military governor, carried much of the responsibility. For although suspecting and fearing that the Swedish king might not be able to come to the rescue of Magdeburg, he had plied citizens and council with promises about the king's imminent arrival, he himself possibly hoping that the Imperial army would despair and abandon the siege. The city's chorus of die-hard preachers and evangelicals had thus won his support when they argued that it was a far better thing to resist and to die heroically than to be yanked under the "papist yoke." In the meantime, the city had resounded with conflicting rumors and claims, many based on alleged signs and portents regarding Magdeburg's history and destiny. Some of the claims promised salvation, while others hinted at the possibility of a cataclysm; and there was a bounty of references to Troy, Babylon, Thebes, Jerusalem, and other supposed ancient parallels.

Mortally wounded in the first hour of the street fighting, Falkenberg tried bravely to conceal the fact in order to keep from spreading panic in his ranks. He was soon dead. Once in the city, Pappenheim's soldiers fought their way to the Kröcken Gate, opened it to their horsemen, and in rode the Imperial cavalry, followed by more companies of foot soldiers. From windows and in the streets, the defenders fought back with startling spirit, killing hundreds of the attackers. And now, it seems, either Pappenheim's men or fighters in the Protestant ranks set fire to several buildings, possibly hoping that the blaze would distract the others from the fighting. The maneuver, however, had no effect on the raging street battles. Within two hours or little more, Pappenheim's troops had triumphed over the city's defenders, and a unit of Imperial cavalry rode down Lackenmacherstrasse to the sound of drums and trumpets.

Otto von Guericke, an eyewitness, described the actions of plundering soldiers: "When a band of looters broke into a house, if the master of the household was able to give them something, this served to rescue him and his family from harm, but only until another soldier turned up, also making demands. In the end, after all the house's things [valuables] had been handed out and nothing else remained, that's when the woes really began. Now the soldiers would start to assault and terrify [their victims], shooting, hanging, and hacking at them," and insisting that valuables had been hidden. The result was that in about two hours, thousands of "innocent" people, "men, women, and children were pitilessly murdered in different ways . . . and words can simply not do justice to what took place."

The looting and killing were under way when a wind started up, gusting into the city. No one bothered to try to tame the fire, and it was now blown into and over the mass of clustered buildings. Twelve hours later, most of Magdeburg lay in smoldering ashes. The cathedral, a monastery, houses near the New Market, and a scatter of buildings somehow survived, but out of nineteen hundred buildings, only about two hundred remained. The town hall and all the churches of the old city were leveled by the flames: St. John's, St. Ulrich's ("the most beautiful of the churches . . . with its splendid paintings"), St. Catherine's, St. Jacob's, St. Peter's, and three other parish churches.

In the ardor of religious bias, historians have pinned the blame for the fire on one side or the other. Common sense would argue that plundering armies do not seek to destroy the fruits of their conquests. They want booty; they have a vested interest in the safety of the goods they covet. In the case of Magdeburg—and there was much talk about this at the time—the fire was more likely the work of local residents, determined to distract the enemy and, in their fanaticism, to keep the city and its wealth from falling into the hands of the hated Imperialists and Catholics. Some evangelicals even saw this as a kind of heroic martyrdom. But if, as was also claimed, Pappenheim called for a few houses to be set on fire, he was undoubtedly thinking of a swift and limited operation.

Even as the city burned, the "victors" raced through it in search of loot. And some of them, it seems, were driven by such a frenzy of greed that they ended by being trapped and killed in cellars, as burning houses caved in on them, all their pillaging now in vain. Along with money and goods, women too were taken—as concubines. Death from starvation had already raked through the ranks of the poor. The entry of foodstuffs into the city had been cut off for weeks, putting the prices of basic victuals beyond the reach of the destitute. Hence the victors would not look for ransom money among the poor. These, instead, were pressed into the service of the rampaging looters and made to pick out the rich, or to help them gather and cart their plunder out of the city. But all people in Magdeburg who could be ransomed were, including the city councillors and the surviving Swedish officers. Armed with pikes fifteen to eighteen feet long, pikemen broke them in half to be able to search out booty with more ease. And in that many-tongued Imperial army, the officers were no less avid for booty than the common soldiers. Some of them helped whole families to get out of the city safely, but only at a price. There were also cases in which officers, as well as "low born" mercenaries, were able to show pity and to offer their help.

About twenty thousand people, including besiegers, perished in and around Magdeburg on May 20 and in the days that followed: "For a full fortnight the Elbe was choked with the corpses of victims." Many were slain in battle or murdered. Many more perhaps were the victims of smoke and fire. The city's population seems to have plummeted, almost overnight, to something like five thousand inhabitants. Despite the fact that many of the dead were soldiers and other outsiders— such as neighboring villagers who had streamed into Magdeburg when the Imperial army began to surround the city—the catastrophe may have been even more devastating than hinted at in my extrapolation. A census of 1632 found only 449 residents on the ravaged site, "and a large part of the city remained rubble until 1720." In the work of rebuilding, during the months following the sack, as survivors and others dug into the foundations of houses to get at burned-out cellars, they came on bodies and human remains, even those of entire families. These had apparently collected there, seeking to die together or to escape the violence of pillaging mercenaries.

Days after the tragic assault, pitchforks were used to spear and collect the parts of bodies torn apart by the havoc of angry soldiers or by collapsing buildings. The many random and scattered dead were put on carts, to be hauled to the river and dumped into its purging flow. But the Elbe—if I may so apostrophize—was not always a ready accomplice, for a few of the corpses seem to have floated about in a display of gruesome postures, with limbs or heads poking up out of the water.

LOOKING BACK

I have focused on Brescia, Antwerp, and Magdeburg for the following reasons. The Brescian tragedy, overshadowed by the famous Sack of Rome (1527), is almost never discussed by historians, despite the fact that sources for Brescia are rich. It therefore seemed right to highlight the city on the map of European warfare. Antwerp and Magdeburg suffered the most destructive sackings of early modern Europe, and yet military historians skip over these too, usually by treating each to brief descriptions in a paragraph.

Looking back to the sack of the three cities, we can see that surviving victims might easily be drawn to exaggerate the evils of soldiers run riot, particularly when religious or linguistic divisions played a part. It is therefore well to be suspicious of reported numbers of casualties, as in a statement claiming, for example, ten thousand dead, when, on the grounds of demography, three thousand had to be closer to the true mark. Much more difficult to weigh are reports of the impaling or burning of children. Criminal action of this sort was not common, even if a good deal of evidence survives alleging that rural fortresses and village houses were sometimes set on fire, in full knowledge of the fact that entire families, children as well, were about to be incinerated. Then we remember that the popular culture of early modern Europe gave its approval to gory public executions, to torture as a matter of ordinary judicial procedure, and to the display of pictures that depicted the torn bodies of martyred saints. Such exposure and official validation was likely to make people more prone to extremes of violence.

Polyglot armies were the occasion and ground for tragic misunderstandings. Menaced by a foreign tongue, victims were bound to call forth more violence by their muddled reactions. Yet the many-tongued army was a regular feature of war in Europe until the end of the eighteenth century.

Casting back to Brescia, Antwerp, and Magdeburg, we come on a pattern of angry soldiers, blundering political authority, violence run out of control, and horrendous mistakes by the governors of the assaulted cities. Unpaid soldiers pointed to the ruthless (and often unnecessary) policies of political leaders: the kings of Spain and France, Ferdinand II, Gustavus Adolphus, and the ministers around them. Wedded to the employment of massive military force, they were soon confronted, in any decision to go to war, by the fact that their resources were too meager, too desperate, too easily misappropriated, to pay the costs of mercenaries. They were thus more than complicit in the universal practice of preying on civilian populations. Their empty purses imposed it.

War in the three cities also shows that it was a mistake to rely on civilian militias and guardsmen. They were no match for professional soldiers in armed combat. Religious fanaticism (Magdeburg), internal party divisions (Brescia), and botched planning helped to thrust the three cities into their suicidal nightmares.

4

WEAPONS AND PRINCES

NEW WEAPONS

A state which acknowledges no superior in the conduct of its affairs: this was sovereignty in Roman law. Such a state did not truly exist in Europe at the beginning of the sixteenth century, and the tide of European politics would take another century to bring it fully forth. Although complexities and cavils may nag at this claim, it comes with the following second part, bearing even greater significance.

The ability to conduct major warfare was the decisive force in the making of the modern state. But this force, in turn, was predicated on the power to levy taxes and to command credit: that is, on the capacity to pay for war. We may reverse the claim by saying that the power to raise and increase taxes, or to conjure up new ones, called for a widening apparatus of officials, even when these were taken on as contractors. By these means the state was acquiring more foreign and domestic clout and becoming more invasive. Not surprisingly, then, in England, by the end of the seventeenth century, Parliament's control of the purse strings made it, in many ways, the decisive force in the state.

These are points to be borne in mind as we consider the new weapons of the Renaissance world. And consider them we must, for they would have sinister consequences for civilian populations.

THE USE OF GUNPOWDER IN European warfare was first seen in the fourteenth century. Two new weapons appeared on the scene: the cannon and the small firearm. But the early history of explosive powder was joined mainly to artillery, particularly for use in the besieging of the coveted centers of wealth and action: cities. These were inevitably hedged in by great walls and defensive towers, unless they were flanked, like Venice or Antwerp, by protective waters. In sieges, giant catapults, epitomized by the trebuchet, had long been deployed against them. They could lob stones that weighed up to half a ton, but their usual load was closer to two or three hundred pounds, and they could cast seventy-five-pounders over a distance of some two hundred meters. The use of trebuchets was common until the early fifteenth century, when the irresistible spread of explosive artillery began to edge them out of action. They were pretty much gone by the end of the century.

The making of gunpowder—a mixture of charcoal, saltpeter, and sulphur—improved in the later fourteenth century, and there were later refinements, with the result that production costs fell by 80 percent in the fifteenth century, but never enough for the purses and taxes of kings and free cities. All the same, explosive artillery took wing, and a different kind of terror began to ghost through Europe's urban centers, as the puncturing blast of the new weapon—a sound that carried for miles—came to be heard more and more often.

At the start of the fifteenth century, bombards, the earliest big guns, emerged as rivals to the mammoth five-storied trebuchet. They were made of great wedges of wrought iron, clamped together by iron bands: hence "hooped bombards." Weighing up to five tons or more, bombards fired carved or shaped stones. However, if inexpertly handled, the detonation could cause them to burst and kill the cannoneers. A half century later, they were being replaced by safer, muzzle-loading guns cast entirely in bronze. A new form of shot was also introduced: the iron ball, brought in by the French in the 1440s. This missile was denser but lighter, with a longer range and a more destructive impact. Yet with rulers trying to control expenses, stone shot continued in use and would be seen as late as the 1580s.

After 1450, the making of artillery began to zero in more selectively on the question of sizes and calibers, of lighter field guns or of heavier ones for siege batteries. Experts also started to design them with a view to their fitting more mobile gun carriages. The point here, of course, was to be able to move artillery trains more swiftly. Interestingly, as an item in the culture of the age, the lightest guns came to be known as sakers, falcons, and falconets—names drawn from one of the signature pursuits of noblemen: falconry. Ranging in weight from five hundred to twenty-five hundred pounds, they shot cast-iron balls weighing from one to six pounds. The prince of heavy cannons, the royal or double cannon, with a payload of one hundred pounds per shot, could weigh up to twenty thousand pounds. Another heavy piece of artillery, the culverin, came in lighter versions and was to be much used on the battlefield. Having a small bore and a superior targeting range, the culverin was a long-barreled gun with a thicker tube; hence its name was rightly rooted in the Latin for snake, *colubra*.

Terrain, weather, circumstances, supplies, tactics: all these determined the varied use of artillery in warfare. And field generals often held conflicting views about when and how to deploy the different guns. Although efforts were made to standardize calibers in the interests of efficiency, remarkably, not much came of this. Combat in the Thirty Years War would see every kind of weapon in use. William Guthrie, one of the leading authorities on the battles of the war, found that its artillery was "a morass that no amount of research can clarify." For "all weapons were essentially handmade and varied to a greater or less degree." In effect, every gun was likely to be different, each "a unique work of art." Europe had yet to enter the machine age.

The coming of heavy artillery added many more wagons and draft animals, oxen as well as horses, to the winding columns of armies. Yet the new weapons and technology, including the casting of bronze guns, were taken up everywhere and had reached the Russian steppes by 1500.

But if soldiers and horsemen could move no faster than artillery trains, then the pace of armies was now greatly slowed down, particularly in muddy or hilly terrain. And this could lead to disaster or sudden hardship for innocent populations, because it meant that soldiers were more likely to prey on the civilians whose lands they were crossing.

If artillery determined the early career of gunpowder, small firearms—and first of all the arquebus, a microcannon—soon made their appearance. Once it was known that an explosive charge could eject a deadly missile from a tube, metalsmiths were able to make a handheld firearm. Right around 1430, Bohemia's Hussites, alleged heretics, were already using tubes with a powder charge in their victorious battles against German armies. In 1453, in the Battle of Castillon (near Bordeaux), the last of the Hundred Years War, the master gunner, Jean Bureau, seems to have deployed about three hundred such guns to help annihilate an English army of ten thousand men.

In 1496, the new arquebus turned up in the ranks of Spanish foot soldiers at the battle of Atella, and then, a few years later, at Cerignola. Joining a powder charge to a mode of ignition, the operating system of the matchlock arquebus was built around a small flash pan, a triggering device, and a slow-burning cord (the match) which had been saturated with saltpeter. The gun was fired by lowering the match into the flash pan or priming tray.

All early handheld firearms were unwieldy, heavy, and highly inaccurate at distances. But they were lethal at close quarters, or even at a distance if they happened to make direct hits. Field commanders therefore found them effective enough for use on the battlefield, and armies began to rely on them in large and ever-increasing numbers.

The true arquebus, a muzzle loader, seems to have been fashioned by German gunsmiths sometime after 1450. It was thirty-six to forty inches long, mounted on a heavy stock, and weighed around ten pounds. Firing iron or lead shot of about half an ounce in weight, its effective range was in the region of one hundred to two hundred yards.

While the arquebus was gripped with both hands and could be

fired from the shoulder, its immediate descendent, the matchlock musket, a heavier and more destructive weapon, was usually mounted on a forked prop and then fired. It was first used by Spanish troops in Italy at the outset of the sixteenth century, as early as the Battle of Cerignola in 1503. In 1591, an English observer reported "that a lead musket ball could penetrate the best armour at 200 yards, ordinary armour at 400, and kill an unarmoured man at 600." But this advantage was offset by the fact that soldiers could fire the light arquebus—a kind of early carbine—from horseback, and so it was swiftly adapted for use by entire units of cavalry.

Meanwhile, right around 1500, enterprising German gunsmiths devised a proper handgun, the wheel-lock pistol. They must have had links with craftsmen of the sort who were doing meticulous metal work and who just then were making small clocks with coiled steel springs. First seen in Nuremberg, the pistol, about a foot long, was developed to be used against besiegers from the tops of city walls and parapets. Its mechanical workings were relatively simple. A wound-up spring, released by a trigger, would cause a serrated disk (the "wheel") to spin against a piece of clamped flint, giving off sparks and igniting the powder charge. Since this weapon could be fired with one hand, it was soon taken up by horsemen, mounted pistoleers (*Reiters*) who carried at least two such pistols, and more often three or four, strapped or tucked away about themselves, as they rode into battle. By the middle of the sixteenth century, rulers were hiring large mercenary units of German pistoleers. Here at once we see an aspect of the changing face of cavalry, no longer the exclusive arm of noblemen.

But the fast-growing numbers of light horsemen, armed with arquebus or pistol, were not a mere fact of military science, locked away from people in town and country. In the wide vicinage of sieges and skirmishes, the new units also moved more swiftly over the countryside, where they killed and plundered with greater ease. In the Italian Wars, in France's religious civil wars, and in the Thirty Years

War, thousands of villages and little towns would feel the muscle of that rapacious cavalry.

ALL BULLET VELOCITIES OF THE early handguns broke the sound barrier. Tests have shown that the bullets of the wheel-lock pistol approached the speed of their modern equivalents. But the arquebus, like the musket, fired missiles at speeds about half as fast as those from the assault rifles of the late twentieth century.

Only one other innovation need be mentioned here: the flintlock pistol and musket, a muzzle loader. Not much used until the late seventeenth century, when the bayonet was also introduced, the flintlock had a more effective triggering device. As a "fusile" or musket, it doubled the previous rate of fire, could be easily fired from the shoulder, and was lighter and more accurate. But it was really an eighteenth-century weapon.

IN EUROPE'S VAST AND UNPOLICED rural world, where brigandage was at times common, small firearms and gunpowder soon found their way into the hands of civilians. Many a French and German farmer possessed an arquebus by the late sixteenth century. Brought back from the wars by relatives or by other local men, firearms could be readily put up for sale, although the foot-long pistol, being more expensive and trickier to operate, would not be seen regularly for some time to come. Despairingly, doctors observed that gunshot wounds were uglier and far more difficult to treat than the punctures or gashes of the edged and pointed weapons of tradition: pike, arrow, and sword. Civilians, too, would come to know this by experience.

CHANGES IN OFFENSIVE WEAPONS AND tactics necessarily elicited changes in methods of defense, most especially in the defense of cities. Almost as soon as the heavy cannon became the cardinal wrecker of walls and ramparts, military architects turned to defensive needs and designed fresh modes of fortification. They found that a fortress with "angled" bastions constituted the most effective new form. It relied on lower and thicker walls, together with a great buildup of earthwork and sloping ground just outside and around the walled ring. The format included an encircling ditch, but also crucially, for crossfire, polygonal or angled defensive emplacements on the outside of the walls. On the inside, out-of-sight platforms were erected for defensive artillery, and this was a fundamental new addition: a battery of guns intended to fire back enough shot at the besiegers to neutralize or silence theirs.

The men in command of cities soon realized, however, that the new styles of fortification were extraordinarily expensive, not only because of the costs of materials but also because of massive labor costs, despite the fact that humble manual labor—digging, hauling, breaking stone, masonry—was extremely cheap in Europe. Here again we touch on a change in technology that had a dire impact on rural populations. For any war or military emergency was likely to produce decrees that forced the peasantry around cities to labor without payment: coerced into tearing down trees, razing suburbs, or toiling to improve the defensive emplacements and earthworks that girded the curving sweep of city walls. Inevitably, too, enemy armies, intent on sieges, were also masters in the business of dragooning squadrons of neighboring peasants into hard labor.

Owing, at any rate, to the enormity of costs, few cities were ever fully protected by the new forms of construction. Antwerp, Lille, and Turin would press far in that direction, but at the end of the sixteenth century, not one of Europe's biggest cities "could boast a completed and fully bastioned enceinte." As a result, defending them from sieges often became hellish; and in many cases, when seriously threatened by an army, towns would simply open their gates and surrender, to avoid being sacked.

Medieval Europe already knew, and knew only too well, that war was never cheap. The twelfth and thirteenth centuries were the great age for the walling in of suburbs, as more small armies took to the field. By about 1275, military costs had started to shatter the political hopes of scores of would-be princes, independent cities, and regional warlords. In Italy, the outcome was a scourge of local tyrants and several aristocratic republics. But after 1500 the costs of war again leaped, in payment for gunpowder weapons, the rebuilding of defensive structures, and the swelling demand for professional soldiers and their longer periods of service. Now, with few exceptions, only the stronger states—Spain, France, Habsburg Germany, and then the Dutch Republic and England—could successfully keep to the new direction of war. Nor was it enough for a prince, if he had little else, to concentrate on his artillery park and to build up a train of superior guns. The Duke of Ferrara, Alfonso d'Este, did just this in the early sixteenth century; but his artillery, in that changing world, gave no true independence to Ferrara. The Este dukes became the hirelings of popes and of the rulers of Spain, France, and the Empire, because it was impossible for them to field armies large enough to back up their guns. In the grasp of out-of-control princely ambitions, a Europe at war would require more manpower; and professional soldiers were exceedingly expensive, even—weirdly enough—when they went unpaid, as we shall see. If the old infantry arms, such as the longbow, the pike, the sword, and the crossbow demanded special skills, so too did the new weapons.

In the fourteenth century, archers and other foot soldiers had already started to challenge the primacy of lance and heavy cavalry, the distinctive arm of the old warrior nobility. In his classic stance, the nobleman required a horse, armor, and a lance. His glory lay in shock combat: the charging cavalcade. The later stages of the Hundred Years War (1337–1453), however, saw the passing of the heyday of the knight, like that of the trebuchet. He was having to get down from his horse more and more often, and to fight alongside foot soldiers. The turn in the composition of armies, with the center of gravity slowly shifting from horse to foot, was flagged in 1476 at the battles of Grandson and Morat, which pitted Swiss pikemen against the horsemen of Charles the Bold, the Duke of Burgundy. Disciplined blocks of Swiss mercenaries, using pikes eighteen feet long, defeated a renowned cavalry and the duke's gunpowder artillery. Evidently, then, the new artillery could not in itself bring victory in battle. It had to be successfully combined with sufficient numbers of foot soldiers and horsemen.

With their lands as the arena of "the Italian Wars" for France and Spain, Italians were the first people to suffer the new style of warfare over many years (1494–1559). The best fighting forces of the sixteenth century were the Spanish *tercio*, the huge and dense squares of Swiss pikemen, and regiments of German Landsknechts. Like the selling of Swiss pikemen, "marketing" German mercenary pike (Landsknechts) was a flourishing business in the sixteenth century. The sound of their drums, to which they might march in step, could be thunderous enough to distress the ears; and townsfolk possibly felt at times that it was an eerie echo of the double cannons employed to batter the gates and walls of cities.

All professional infantry units soon began to combine pike with shot. Well before the end of the sixteenth century, a company of Swiss fighters might consist of two hundred pikemen, thirty musketeers, and thirty arquebusiers. Mercenary units of Swiss and German pikemen attained celebrity by fighting for different princes—French, Spanish, Danish, Swedish, and German, but also, after 1570, for the new Dutch Republic. The feared arm of the king of Spain, the infantry regiment known as a *tercio*, saw its most sustained action first in Italy, then in the Netherlands and northern France.

It was only in France that the mounted nobleman, heavily armored and with a lance, survived into the second half of the sixteenth century. Elsewhere he had disappeared almost entirely. In Spain, even before the Low Countries became a theater of martyrdom for Spanish troops, noblemen (some *hidalgos* apart) abandoned cavalry units except as officers. And in Germany, as we have seen, combat from the backs of horses passed into the hands of arquebusiers and pistoleers.

Aside from the tactical use of artillery, the overall direction of change for infantry, now the decisive arm in battle, had mostly to do with the proportions of pikemen to musketeers. Approaching parity—meaning one to one—around 1600, by 1635, in the midst of the Thirty Years War, the ratio was sometimes two muskets for every pike. Yet even late in the century, Vauban, marshal of France and a leading military engineer, wanted infantry regiments to be made up of 25 percent pike, for the simple reason that musketeers, when not fronted by formations of pikemen, were too easily overwhelmed by charging, saber-wielding horsemen and pistoleer cavalry.

Military historians have a good deal to say about the merits of the "old-fashioned" battle formations (dense blocks of infantry) versus the newer "linear" tactics of the Dutch and the king of Sweden, Gustavus Adolphus. Seeking mobility, the newer approach to battlefield tactics employed longer lines of foot soldiers and fewer ranks in depth. Armed with the arquebus or light musket, the front row would fire a volley and then peel off to form a new row at the back of the formation while also reloading. But the implicit debate here, with all of its ifs and buts and possibilities—pitting, say, the *tercio* against the linear arrangement—is food for the battle experts and amateur tacticians.

One point, however, regarding the shape and makeup of armies should be clarified, because it had an immediate impact on civilian populations. Wherever war was turned into raids and skirmishes, as in regions with acute scarcities of foodstuffs, armies stepped up their reliance on cavalry. Horsemen—dragoons and pistoleers— could more easily round up supplies. For this reason, after the devastating Imperial victory over the Swedish army at Nördlingen in 1634, the use of cavalry in the Thirty Years War rose from a figure of 30 percent to 50 percent or even more of the armies in action. As an engine of warfare, in short, cavalry remained absolutely fundamental.

While it was true that master gunners faced the great walls of towns and cities with new powers, it was also true that the new fortifications, with their defensive artillery batteries, were able to hold off attacking armies. La Rochelle, Paris, Augsburg, Vienna, Turin, and many fortress towns, such as Metz and Casale, hurled back the attempted escalades of besiegers. These successes, however, were by and large the facade of events. In their surrounding, unexamined shadows lay the effects of starvation: the mass dying of the besieged civilians, as well as the deaths of many of the besiegers themselves, felled by epidemic diseases and even by hunger. In Flanders, the Spanish siege of Ostend (1601–1604) issued in eighty thousand casualties for Spain and sixty thousand for the Dutch defenders. In 1573, the royal siege of the great Protestant port of La Rochelle ended with the death of about ten thousand besiegers. But in the annihilating siege of 1628, some fifteen thousand *Rochelais* perished, mostly from starvation, out of a population of eighteen to twenty thousand inhabitants. And we shall see the results of the horrific siege of Mantua in 1630.

THE MAKING OF WEAPONS, EVEN in preindustrial Europe, imposed a good deal of specialization, particularly because many of the required tasks called for precision work with metals and a range of operations involving mines, foundries, and workshops. These were enterprises, or their management, based in cities such as Augsburg, Nuremberg, Brescia, and the busy urban centers of the Low Countries. In Italy, the big arms buyers looked to Milan, Brescia, and Bergamo, the peninsula's best producers of armor and weapons. But by the beginning of the seventeenth century, leadership in the manufacture of firearms and other weapons had passed to the Netherlands.

The Dutch—those early stalwart republicans and enterprising merchants—made every type of weapon for the open market, from pikes, swords, and halberds to the wheel-lock pistol, hand grenades, the matchlock arquebus, and the full range of artillery. Wealthy Amsterdam was the foremost producer. Some of the lesser towns had their own specialties, such as Gouda for match, Utrecht for armor and grenades, or Delft and Dordrecht for small arms and gunpowder. Arms makers in the United Provinces also produced parts of weapons, such as gun barrels and firing mechanisms, and the guns would then be assembled elsewhere. But the Dutch also imported parts, among which sword blades from Germany.

Everywhere in Europe, rulers and armies were buying weapons "off the shelf." And two experts note, for example, that "as Siena prepared for war in the 1550s, arquebuses were purchased in lots of 500 at a time." Although probably made in one of the north Italian cities, the five hundred guns are likely to have arrived in Siena via the agency of Venetian middlemen. But by 1590, they could easily have been purchased from the Dutch, who had gone on to develop an extraordinary export trade in arms. Their list of buyers was striking. They sold weapons of all sorts to buyers in Portugal, Poland, England, Russia, Denmark, Venice, even in Morocco, and of course in Sweden, France, and Germany. The range of their wares may be gauged from an Amsterdam sale of 1622:

> Count Christian of Brunswick bought everything to fit out a small army of 7000 men, to wit, 3000 muskets, 3000 suits of armour, 3000 pikes, 1000 suits of armour for cavalry, 1000 harquebuses with bandoliers, 10,000 pounds of gunpowder, 20,000 pounds of match and 10,000 pounds of musket balls at 20 per pound, totalling 200,000 balls, and also 1000 hand grenades.

If we add that the market value of all this hardware exceeded 100,000 guilders, we are speaking of a sum which amounted, in 1620, to the monthly wages of more than three thousand skilled craftsmen, or, in other terms, to about 8.5 percent of the annual tax receipts of Friesland, the Dutch Republic's second-richest province or ministate.

EUROPE HAD EDGED ITS WAY into a new political world, a world made by the wars of aggressive princes and a few hustling but powerful cities, Venice and Amsterdam most notably. But first of all, for the principal war makers, it was a world which required that they be able to rely on credit or borrow money fast, great chests of it. Revenue from taxes and princely domains—the prime sources of income for German rulers and the crowned heads of Spain and France—always added up to a fraction of the sums needed to field and supply the armies of their bloated ambitions. Troops on campaign had to pay out ready cash for food and supplies. Local vendors demanded the sight of gold and silver coin, unless, relying on ironclad guarantees, they agreed to offer credit.

So exit political posturing and enter the bankers: the gentlemen who could raise and lend the immediate cash. Their far-flung networks were the arteries for the transfer of money or credit from one part of Europe to another. They had the contacts and could reach out to depositors. But of course they were motivated by the promise of profit. Their loans were secured by the future income from varieties of taxes, by the sale of bonds, by the spoils of office, or, as in the case of the Fugger banking house in southern Germany, by lucrative rights over silver and copper mines.

The ability to move money and credit across the face of Europe had a fundamental importance. Armies ranged far: French troops were dispatched to Italy, Germany, and Spain; Spanish regiments went to the Netherlands, to France, Italy, and Germany; Venetian and Dutch mercenaries were assigned to Germany and even sent into combat on the high seas; Swedish armies fought in Poland, Russia, and Germany; the mercenaries of the German Habsburgs found themselves in Italy, but also along the frontiers of Poland, France, and the Netherlands. And as soldiers trekked over long distances, their supply trains could not provide all they needed in the way of food and fodder. Local towns and villages became the suppliers.

The nascent "sovereign" state was developing muscle and showing it along the way, pushing far beyond its frontiers with soldiers and keeping this up for years. Payment of the ensuing gigantic debts was then spread out over generations, as we shall see in some detail later. No medieval state had managed to do this. But neither had there been one which could rely on the resources of continuing fear, coercion, and degrees of loyalty. Early modern Europe had more than one such state, with France and Spain leading the way. Relying on just enough anxiety and loyalty among their subjects, these states were able to levy new rounds of taxes again and again. Indeed, their moneyed subjects got into the habit of investing in the "sovereign" debt by purchasing government bonds. Huge war debts could thus be borne for years.

THE RIGHTS OF PRINCES

A view of early modern Europe used to be glimpsed in what the old histories of the period called it: "The Age of the Renaissance and Reformation." The implication was that two events had shaped the sixteenth and early seventeenth centuries: a) the rebirth of the arts and secular learning, along with a passionate new interest in the world of antiquity, and b) the Protestant revolt against the Roman Catholic Church, heralded by the breakaway Augustinian friar Martin Luther in 1517.

Our view of that period has changed. Historians now situate the Renaissance and Reformation in a more comprehensive, densely woven narrative. In this reorientation, at least for some historians, the primacy of change belongs to the rise of sovereign states. War, debt, and unprecedented taxation loom up to overshadow the European scene.

The matter of sovereign states may be approached through the question of coinage and currencies.

Europe in 1500 was a wilderness of different currencies. I refer not only to a cascade of coins in gold, silver, copper, billon, and other alloys, but also to lines of coins minted and issued by myriad territorial governments. The Italian peninsula alone had more than a score of different currencies, coined in Venice, Milan, Genoa, Florence, Rome, and Naples, as well as in Lucca, Siena, Ferrara, Mantua, Bologna, Urbino, Perugia, and lesser places. Spain and France were crisscrossed by a variety of currencies, and Germany, under the Empire, minted scores of them. Lower Saxony alone, in the early seventeenth century, had thirty different mints. In the Low Countries, where circulating foreign coins were carefully tabulated, ordinances carried "engravings of upwards of 1000 different pieces." The aim was to provide identifications.

This bewildering diversity of moneys was a nightmare for travelers but a boon for money changers, some of whom, astute traders, journeyed hundreds of miles to ply their trade. Such a one was Lippo di Fede del Sega, a small-time money changer who came from a little village outside Florence and spent years in France, pursuing profit.

Wherever there was a legal title to mint coins, there, too, was a lawmaking authority and local arrangements to dole out justice—in other words, the rudiments of a state. The authority in question was also bound to have "foreign relations" and a little body of soldiers for defense. Here then was a micro half-state, as in all those places where the German emperor had granted or sold the rights of coinage to a city or a petty prince.

As Europe emerged from the late middle ages, the course of change cut a path through a thicket of "statelets," or microstates. Political fragmentation—and the movement or trend away from it—may be tracked in upper Italy, which teemed with bustling urban communes in the twelfth and thirteenth centuries. Cities such as Milan, Pisa, Genoa, Padua, Pavia, Verona, Florence, Lucca, Perugia, and Siena had broken away from a nominal subjection to the Holy Roman Emperor of the German Nation. But by the early fifteenth century, war and conquest had seen most of them incorporated into the territories of the biggest regional powers: Venice, Milan, Florence, and the papal monarchy. The pulling together of scattered authority went on in Italy right through the sixteenth century.

If we turn to France, we find a process of parallel incorporation, as the French crown reclaimed a series of autonomous provinces (old fiefs of the kings of France): Normandy in 1358; Guyenne in 1451; Burgundy (and Artois briefly) in 1477; Provence, Anjou, and Maine in 1481; Orléans in 1499; Angoulême in 1515; Auvergne and Bourbon in 1527; and Brittany in 1532. France filled out.

Spain knew a similar trend in the uniting of Castile and Aragon, and in the Spanish conquest of Navarre and Granada. The expulsion of the Muslim emirate from Granada was completed in 1492, at the end of a pitiless ten-year war, for which the monarchs of Castile and Aragon "kept an army of 50,000 men and 13,000 horses on a permanent footing."

In Germany, on the other hand, the swing toward consolidation was foiled by regional princes. They claimed to be acting in the name of "German liberties" and local customs. Emperors had to compromise or give way to their demands, including the demands of Imperial cities and of numerous lesser lords of the Empire. These, too, like the dukes of Bavaria or the electors of Saxony and Brandenburg, governed their territories as autonomous or independent rulers. They consulted the privileged in representative assemblies (Landsstände), levied taxes, raised small armies, administered justice, passed laws, minted currencies, and conducted their own foreign policies. The Thirty Years War (1618–1648) would exhibit in blood the perils of Germany's fragmentation.

War-making was an obvious characteristic of sovereignty. The costs of war, however, could hobble rulers, because war, as we have seen, had to be paid for primarily out of tax moneys, and taxes required the approval of the "estates"—representative diets made up of noblemen, urban elites, and clergy. There was no way around these, except by means of executive thuggery, and this was a recipe for trouble or even rebellion. Moreover, the need to obtain the fiscal consent of the upper classes was as obligatory in the kingdoms of Spain, France, England, and the Baltic countries as in the urban republics of Genoa, Venice, and the Netherlands. Kings were far from being absolute: Their right to tax, and even to legislate, was ringed in by limitations.

In the face of an invasion or unprovoked aggression, all rulers had the obligation to defend the lands they governed. Hence any military crisis gave them the right to arm and assemble soldiers—either a local militia or fighters brought in from afar. Local militias satisfied customary defensive needs almost everywhere, but in the early modern world, they were too often inept and of little use in sustained warfare.

An old feudal prerogative, the princely right to summon the military arm of vassals survived, ghostlike, into the seventeenth century, despite the fact that princes and self-governing cities began to hire professional mercenaries as early as the twelfth century. This expedient, the hiring of mercenaries, sprang from the need to meet the expanding scope of wars, as these broke out and became more frequent during the twelfth and thirteenth centuries, in the trail of Europe's explosive economic energies. By the early fourteenth century, the best troops were always mercenaries. In a Europe of war and more war, a prince's obligation to defend his lands faded into the right to assemble armies more and more often, even for aggressive purposes. Such action could be passed off as defensive. The distinction, passive or active, was nudged into subtleties, and bold or clever princes found ways of getting what they wanted.

But princes also had assistance from another quarter: in their claims to be hereditary rulers, that is, dynasts. This line of legal argument took on the raiment of a sacred right, especially when the claim concerned disputed territory, including, therefore, the possible need to use armed force. If early modern European political thinking accepted a hard axiom, it was in the idea that dynastic rights were somehow embedded in "natural" law. Accordingly, in a Europe of spirited economic energies, as rulers regarded their boundaries with more zeal, the banner of dynastic rights was carried to the forefront of international relations, and there it would remain until the nineteenth century.

Princely bloodlines ran through marriages and offspring, spreading out, fanlike, to provide the legal substance for claims to territory. Marriage was the agency that made dynasties. But when a prince had muscle and loftiness enough, his bastards too moved in the shadow of majesty, married brilliantly, and could be centrally engaged in matters of war. This was the destiny of Margaret, Duchess of Parma, governor of the Netherlands (1559–1567), the daughter of a servant and of the Habsburg Emperor Charles V.

At the dawn of modern times, when the king of France, Charles VIII, led twenty-five thousand soldiers down the length of Italy to lay hands on the kingdom of Naples, he was calling on a distant connection and a thirteenth-century claim of the dukes of Anjou. When Louis XII, his successor, invaded Lombardy in 1499, intent on seizing the duchy of Milan, the basis of his claim went back more than a hundred years to the marriage of a Visconti princess, Valentina, and Louis d'Orléans.

Europe's elites hearkened to the dynastic claims of the kings of Spain and France, of German princes and Habsburg rulers, and of lesser lords as well, even when the claimants jockeyed to bring new lands under their political sway. A dynastic claim to territory always pivoted on a question of legal rights, of honor, of duty, and even of squaring things with "divine and natural" law.

Diplomacy itself was governed by assumptions about the rights of dynasties. Never mind the ways of rulers. King Charles VIII—a living caricature: short with skinny legs, a big head, and a funny beak of a nose—was publicity for the assumption that royal blood could raise the strangest men to the pinnacle of powerful states. In a decision that was altogether his, the astonishing invasion of Italy (1494–1495), he was really seeking adventure and glory, and dreaming of a heroic crusade against the Ottoman Turks. His successor, Louis XII, also turned his face and soldiers to Italy, urged on by predatory noblemen, and attracted not by the nonsense of chivalric dreams but by the visible wealth of Italy's northern cities.

A king inherited not only a personal domain but also a state and its lands, as though these had about them something of private property. If nationality, language, and religion in his territories happened to be different from his, this cut no ice. The essential point turned on a dynastic right, the legal grounds alleged by the kings of France and Spain in their wars (1494–1559) to be masters in Italy.

Meanwhile, were dynastic claims doing something for the subjects and citizens whose taxes paid for the wars? Or something even for the rule of law? Very little, if anything. War, anyway, like diplomacy, was the business of princes and courtly elites, not a topic for the twitter of subjects in town and country. Yet war, as we know, wanted money, tax money, and this compelled princes to turn to the high representatives of the nobility and rich bourgeoisie. These had to be consulted; there had to be discussions. Now every kind of ploy on both sides, menacing and silver-tongued, was borne into the key forums. Solutions varied, but a strong prince usually got some of the wished-for funds, then proceeded to rush into debt. Later, this too—managing the debt—would have to be negotiated.

A GENEALOGICAL CHART OF THE Habsburgs—the most dominant dynasty in the history of western Europe—reveals nothing but the bare bones of a vanished animal. The real creature appears only when we clad the chart with inherited dominions, wars, public debt, and taxes, along with appalling mistakes and tragedies. There were the salutary things, of course, such as donations to monasteries, convents, and churches, and the commissions made to many leading artists. But these take us away from the motors of Habsburg dominance.

The high fortunes of this dynasty began with the Duke of Austria, the Emperor Maximilian I (d. 1519). His marriage to Mary of Burgundy brought the Netherlands and parts of France as inheritances to their son, Philip the Handsome. Philip, in turn, was married to Joanna, who inherited Castile and Aragon. And their son, Charles V (d. 1559), was heir to the Spanish crown, the Netherlands, Austria, Franche-Comté, and in Italy the kingdom of Naples: "all kingdoms and territories"—he noted in his memoirs—"given to him by God." In 1519, with gold borrowed from German bankers (850,000 florins), Charles bought the Imperial crown from the Empire's seven electors, and this enabled him to claim the duchy of Milan, an ancient and nominal fief of the Empire. The bribe money would have sufficed—by cutting corners—to cover the wages for a year of about twenty-four thousand foot soldiers in the Venetian and other armies.

An "impresario of war," as one historian has called him, Charles now attempted to exercise political control over much of western Europe. He ended by abdicating in 1555–1556 and dividing his dominions, but he also bequeathed prodigious debts to his heirs. Spain, the Netherlands, Franche-Comté, and his lands in Italy went to his son, Philip II (d. 1598). The German lands he willed to his own brother, Ferdinand I, who succeeded him as Holy Roman Emperor.

War became the métier of the leading Habsburgs. Almost continually on the move for more than thirty-five years, traveling by horse, boat, and carriage, Charles V spent much of his reign and resources fighting the kings of France for the control of contested lands in Italy. His son, Philip II, and the next two Habsburg kings of Spain pushed Castile to the brink of economic ruin with their wars in the Netherlands. In the 1580s and 1590s, Philip's armies were also marched into the French Wars of Religion. Thereafter, two Habsburg emperors, Ferdinand II (d. 1637) and Ferdinand III (d. 1657), would be leading actors in an Empire bloodied and depopulated by the Thirty Years War.

FROM THE MOMENT THEY COULD touch bankers for enough money to field an army, princes took their lands into war with relative ease.

But once the enterprisers had mustered the ambulant city—that is, the desired army—cascades of additional cash and credit would be needed to keep it together, to move it, and to pursue the war. Now was the time for princes and their counselors to exhibit their vaunted leadership.

SIEGE

IN DEGREES OF violence and bloodletting, the sacking of cities would seem to be the fiery edge of war. For all its trauma, however, a three-day hurricane of torture, theft, and rape was not necessarily the measure of the utmost cruelty. Long sieges touched every aspect of war, including food supplies and the use of artillery. A prolonged attack on a city—adding the horrors of starvation to death by shot and sword—could turn into an even more murderous operation than a sacking.

Siena, our point of departure, provides a remarkable entry to the horrors of famine in the midst of sieges. Sancerre, a little French town (and home of that wine), will come next, borne into the chronicles of Europe by the pen of a brave Calvinist minister. But Paris was to be the scene of the deadliest siege of the age. And Augsburg, one of the chief victims of the Thirty Years War, lost more people to starvation than any other German city.

SIENA (1554–1555)

The Italian Wars (1494–1559) were dynastic conflicts between the kings of France and Spain. Each side claimed the rich duchy of Milan and the crown of Naples, but they were fighting in effect for political dominion over the Italian peninsula. The wealthy and populous cities of Italy, with their harvests of taxes and commercial know-how, were scintillating prizes. And a peninsula divided into minor states was an open road—all but an invitation—for the mercenary armies of the Valois (French) and Habsburg (German-Spanish) royal houses. No Italian state—neither the proud Venetian Republic, nor the fragmented Papal State, still less Medicean Florence—could stand up to the armed might of the royal contenders, with their armies, when combined, of twenty-five to forty thousand foot soldiers, ten to fifteen thousand horsemen, and long artillery trains.

In the 1550s, Tuscany turned into the peninsula's flash point. Seeing the little republic of Siena, a client state, as a weak node in his web of controls against French designs, the Emperor Charles V decided to build muscle there by constructing a new fortress on the city's highest point. A hugely expensive operation, it was to be paid for by Siena itself, with its diminished population of twenty thousand people. They were fiercely opposed. Against the will of the city, nevertheless, construction of the fortress began at the end of 1550 and was relentlessly pursued. But in late July, 1552, with help from the French, the Sienese broke out in rebellion against the small garrison of Spanish soldiers and forced them to abandon the city. The rebels at once turned to obliterating the new fortress. It was war. And now Charles V's deputies in Italy scrambled to find the money for it.

Fearful of passing soldiers, peasants and other rural folk began to pour into Siena, nearly doubling its population. By late December, the city was also host to 10,500 defending mercenaries (five hundred of whom were cavalry), for a total amounting to roughly half of Siena's ordinary population. These numbers put tremendous strains on daily food supplies and raised the question, almost at once, of Siena's "unwanted" or "useless mouths" (*bocche inutili*): a pointed reference to the begging poor who would be a drain on foodstuffs once the enemy mounted the expected siege. The town council took steps to have new flour mills constructed and to lay in stores of grain, salted meat, and cheese. But keeping the enemy, too, in mind, the defenders also combed the country for twenty kilometers around

Siena, seeking to sequester or destroy all edible goods, with an eye to denying future provisions to the enemy soldiers, who would certainly be foraging for victuals.

Always short of money in his grand war aims, Charles V and his envoys forced a protégé, Cosimo I, Duke of Florence, to raise and pay for a small army of ten thousand men to assist in the assault on Siena. To do so, Cosimo had to break a secret agreement with the king of France, Henry II. More, he had to come out candidly in favor of Spain and the Empire, borrow large sums of money in different parts of Europe, and ramp up Florentine taxes. An extra spur for Cosimo lay in the fact that he feared and hated the small throng of Florentine republican exiles who were now gathering in Siena, in zealous support of the revolt against Charles V. They were aiming to bring Cosimo himself down, and to succeed his overthrow with the reestablishment of the Florentine Republic. In its lines of ramification, the battle for Siena stretched from bankers in Antwerp, Augsburg, Genoa, and Venice down to the Spanish viceroy in Naples. German mercenaries would soon be joining the Italian and Spanish troops directed against the French in Siena.

By March 1553, the Imperial forces in Tuscany had been raised to nearly twenty thousand foot and horse, and operations against Siena's territories were soon under way. Posted to serve as military governor of French forces in Tuscany, Piero Strozzi, one of Duke Cosimo's most bitter enemies, reached Siena on January 2, 1554. The new commander of troops in the city itself was to be a French nobleman, Blaise de Monluc; but he was very ill and did not arrive in Siena until mid-July. Under Strozzi and Monluc, everything was done to prepare the city for a prolonged siege. The sale of bread, for example, was put under strict controls, and all people without a store of flour had to apply for a special permit, allowing them to collect two small loaves of daily bread from a specified baker. Soon this ration was reduced to one loaf. Meanwhile, the Marquis of Marignano, the commander of Imperial and Medicean troops in Tuscany, was conducting a scorched-earth policy designed to choke off any leak-age of victuals into Siena. His troops were also assaulting and taking Sienese towns and villages. Anyone who dared to resist their advances was executed without further ado.

The summer of 1554 turned into a disaster for Strozzi. His fifteen thousand troops, mostly unpaid, were running short of food and even water; desertion was thinning his ranks; and he lost a major battle, near Marciano, at the beginning of August. Marignano's mercenaries, on the other hand, seemed to become more robust; they received daily bread supplies from Cosimo's territories. All the while, too, on both sides, the war in the countryside was turning more savage.

In Siena, for civilians as for soldiers, the tightening blockade continued to reduce the daily rations of the all-important foodstuff, bread. Looking at moments as though it might end in violence, bitter wrangling broke out between civil and military authorities over the matter of whether or not to expel the "useless" mouths from the city. What did "useless" mean? Were the mouths in question those of the mendicant poor only, or those of all children, women, the sick and the old? What about upper-class women: Were they "useless" as fighters or defensive workers against the besiegers?

Military theory, as represented, for example, by Bernardino Rocca's *De' discorsi di Guerra* (1582), did not touch fine points on this matter. Its ruthless assumption was that when a city came under siege and food supplies were short, you put the so-called useless or unnecessary mouths outside the great curtain of walls. Who the useless were exactly was evidently a decision for local authority, civilian and military. With equal ferocity, however, military theory also called for the besiegers, the army outside the walls, to kill or somehow drive back into the embattled city all the expelled refugees.

In August 1554, it was decreed that all people not from Siena had to get out, or face brutal punishment: the women with whips and scourging, the men by being dropped from pulleys (*strappados*), arms tied behind their backs, and then stopped with a jerk, which often resulted in dislocated shoulders. The city was sliding toward a harrowing food crisis. Some of the well-off, taking along their valuables, were buying their way out of the city, in some cases even securing safe-conducts from Duke Cosimo. By now, too, sneaking food into Siena could earn fortunes. But anyone caught at this was liable to an on-the-spot penalty of death. The Marquis of Marignano had nearby trees "festooned with the [hanged] bodies" of men caught breaking the blockade.

Not knowing how long they might have to hold out against the siege, Strozzi and Monluc were thinking of food for their soldiers. They insisted that all the useless mouths be expelled from the city. For the civilian Council of Eight, however, this meant only the poor, all the more so in view of the fact that the armed escorts assigned to accompany the unwanted out of Siena were unable to prevent besieging soldiers from killing, maiming, torturing, and shaming the cast-out victims. And the terrible fear of the civilian bosses in Siena was that Strozzi and Monluc meant their purging of useless mouths to include "honorable" mouths: namely, the wives and children of men from the political and propertied class.

Having met on this question, a special council of 150 of "the most honorable" Sienese citizens came back with a resounding reply. Strozzi's blanket command, they declared, could not be accepted, "first from love of country, and next for the honor of their women and families . . . and if it be said that this is the way to ensure the security of our native land, and thus to be put above and before all other things, let the reply be that our fatherland is not the walls [of the city] but rather our families and their honor." For the rest, they were all in favor of expelling "the dirt poor" (*la poveraglia*), who had neither honor nor a fatherland to safeguard and defend.

The dispute went on as food supplies continued to dwindle. Muted voices soon began to talk about cutting a deal with the besiegers. But Strozzi and Monluc, professional soldiers and officers of the king of France, were in Tuscany to defend a city against the king's enemies; and they were in no mood to compromise. Monluc was still rather ill. Worse still, in a battle at the beginning of August, Strozzi had lost four thousand men and as many more had been seriously wounded, including the general himself. Soldiers began to desert the French ranks, some, it seems, passing over to the Imperial side for food and money. The first commitment of the French commanders had to be to their men, and food stocks had to be at the top of their considerations. Which is why they kept returning to the rebarbative problem of ridding the city of its useless mouths.

In the third week of September 1554, in spite of painful scenes, about twelve hundred poor folk were got out of the city. But the horror of a new round of expulsions soon halted the purge. Religious orders and large charitable foundations, in Italy as elsewhere in Europe, often kept their own grain supplies. Not surprisingly, then, thinking about the city's famous Hospital of Santa Maria della Scala and its rich stores of grain, Strozzi had been calling for the ejection of the hospital's orphans and poor people. On the night of October 5, about seven hundred of its inmates were led out of the city by escorts who were intended to guarantee their safety. Near the town of San Casciano, however, a company of Spanish and German mercenaries pounced on one of the convoys and its charge of more than 250 children, ranging in ages from six to ten. More than one hundred men, women, and children were killed. The Marquis of Marignano later claimed that he had sent them back to Siena.

Scipione Venturi, the head of the hospital, now seems to have faced up to Strozzi, vowing that he would allow no other inmates to leave his premises until he could be absolutely certain of their safety. In the ensuing clash with the urban patriciate, Strozzi and Monluc, demanding more authority over the city, finally laid hands on part of Venturi's stock of grain. They even tried to expel the hospital's last forty-five boys and girls, aged ten to fifteen. But the screaming children were driven back into the city. In November, the daily bread ration in Siena fell to 250 grams for civilians and 400 for soldiers. Every house battered by cannon fire was stripped and turned into firewood for heating and cooking.

Although Monluc's forces in Siena were now down to twenty-

eight hundred foot and three hundred horse, the city was well fortified and resisted another bombardment in December. On Christmas
night, Monluc's men threw back the assault and scaling ladders of two
thousand Germans. But the end must already have been in sight, for
early in the second week of January, Monluc, getting up from his bed
of pain, concealing the pallor in his cheeks with a smear of red wine,
and flaunting fancy dress, addressed the city's civilian authorities,
urging them to ignore Duke Cosimo's ultimatum and blandishments.
Later on in January, a covert night operation underlined the food
crisis in the city. In a move to reduce the number of "mouths," eight
hundred German soldiers slipped out of the city to join Strozzi in the
fortress of Montalcino—a costly operation, for many of them were
ambushed and killed on the way. And no wonder. Imperial and
Medicean forces in the region greatly outnumbered the French, who
were dispersed and numbered no more than five thousand foot, plus
a few hundred horse. War, meanwhile, had reduced Siena's rural hinterland to a waste where hungry, scavenging dogs gnawed at human
corpses.

Serious surrender talks with Cosimo—dealings at this point were
with him, not with Charles V's emissaries—began shortly after March
10. Yet there was no letup in the efforts to expel useless mouths from
Siena, and those driven out were driven back to the walls in ugly,
loathsome scenes. Ambassadors, meanwhile, stepped up the wheeling
and dealing; vows were made; and on the night of April 5–6, in a
secret agreement with the Marquis of Marignano, Monluc slipped
out of the city with a large band of Florentine republican exiles and
Imperial rebels—men who had been marked for execution, though
not Monluc himself. Cosimo signed the surrender document on
April 17, and four days later the remaining French troops marched
out of Siena. Out, too, went 242 noblemen and their families, plus
another group of 435 armed citizens, together with their families and
servants. Making their way to the little Tuscan town and fortress of
Montalcino, home of the Sienese Republic in exile, they were escorted
by a squadron of horse and a company of Imperial infantry. From a

population of about twenty thousand, not counting the outsiders or *forenses* who had flooded into the city, only six thousand people now remained in Siena. Some had perished in the fighting, but most of the rest had either fled or died of starvation.

Marignano entered the supine city to the sound of trumpets, drums rolling, and flags waving.

MONLUC'S MEMOIRS PROVIDE AN INSIDER'S view of happenings in Siena during the siege. He dictated his *Commentaires*, as he chose to call them, more than fifteen years after the events, and though he was something of a poseur and braggart, he offers fresh details.

On his arrival in Siena, or soon after, he had a garrison of eight to ten thousand soldiers but ended with fewer than eighteen hundred men, most of the rest having been killed, like the German mercenaries, after their departure, and some (deserters) having taken to their heels. In the final weeks of the siege, Monluc's daily food ration was a small loaf of bread (nine ounces), some boiled peas, a little bacon, and mallow (a leafy herb with hairy stems). So we can imagine what the food rations of most civilians must have been. Monluc saw people drop dead in the streets, felled by starvation.

On the matter of expelling useless mouths from the city, he was as hard as Strozzi. Given dictatorial powers for a month, sometime after the first week of January 1555, Monluc went to work with a commission of six men and drew up a list of the "useless," numbering forty-four hundred or more people. The vile job of expulsion was given to a Knight of Malta and a platoon of twenty-five to thirty soldiers. By rounding up the unwanted in groups, they got that weeping, wailing throng out of the city. Nearly all of them were poor folk "who lived by the sweat of their brows." Monluc admits that he was never again to witness so much misery. For time and again the besieging soldiers appear to have kicked, clubbed, and punched the unwanted "mouths" back to the walls in a pitiless and bloody seesaw that went on for eight days, their victims fighting to stay alive by eating herbs and grass. In the end, about three fourths of them starved or were killed, some dying without ears and noses. Of those who actually survived and got away, Monluc reveals, the large majority were the women who had been grabbed and taken by soldiers at night "for their own pleasure" and then secretly allowed to escape. "These are the consequences of war. To thwart the designs of the enemy, we are sometimes forced to be cruel. And so God has to show mercy to men of my sort [soldiers], who are guilty of many sins and cause so many miseries and ills."

He claims—and the claim has the support of the European experience of war—that Marignano's troops also ran short of food. He means, I suspect, that they suffered moments of privation. Bread for them had to be delivered from afar. Mule trains with provisions from Florence and other points took five to six days to reach the front lines, and bad weather or mistakes easily delayed deliveries. For twenty miles in all directions around Siena, the countryside had been ravaged and mills destroyed. There was no fodder for horses. Cavalry units were paralyzed. The few horses for the use of leading officers had to be fed with forage hauled in from many miles away. That the Marquis of Marignano had lost more than a third of his men by the end of the siege, as Monluc alleges, is entirely credible—lost to desertion, disease, and death in battle. The claim is fully in line with wartime casualties in the sixteenth and seventeenth centuries. Siena's citizens and his own men, Monluc asserts, had long since started to eat the city's pets and stray animals. Even rats were prized, and dear when put up for sale.

He concluded: "Nothing in nature is so dreadful as famine."

The impact of costs and horrors was finally too much for the debt-ridden Duke of Florence; and from sometime in January 1555 he became almost as eager for peace as the Sienese themselves. Still, not until the end of March was he able to push negotiations hard enough to bring combat to a halt. The agreement—it turned out—displeased Charles V, who felt that the losers had been indulged.

But Cosimo met the charge by correctly declaring, among other things, that hunger and the sword had killed ten thousand people in Siena.

With the support of Piero Strozzi and the French, a Sienese Republic was now set up at Montalcino, where it claimed an existence until the Peace of Cateau-Cambrésis in 1559. Siena and its territories were formally handed over to Duke Cosimo in 1557.

SANCERRE (1572–1573)

Eighteen years after the battle for Siena, in a blistering moment of France's Wars of Religion, the hilltop town of Sancerre would suffer an even more agonizing siege. It was a Huguenot stronghold, walled in and built around a fortress. Overlooking the Loire, the town was located about a hundred miles west of Dijon. The siege came at the end of a chain of murders involving the slaughter of more than three thousand Huguenots in different parts of France. But the killing orgy had started in Paris on August 23–24, 1572, the Eve of St. Bartholomew's Day, with the massacre of about two thousand people.

That autumn Sancerre took in five hundred Huguenot refugees—men, women, and children. The town's remaining Catholics fell to a small minority. In late October, a prominent nobleman from the region, Monsieur de Fontaines, turned up suddenly, hoping to enter and seize control. Refusing to promise the Huguenots the right of worship, with the claim that he had no such charge from the king, he was refused entry to the town, whereupon he replied that he knew what he would have to do. It was war. Less than two weeks later, a tempestuous attack on the citadel was repelled.

Now, fearing a siege, the *Sancerrois* began to examine their stocks of food and other resources. I draw the following narrative from one of the most remarkable eyewitness chronicles in the history of Europe: Jean de Léry's *Histoire memorable de la Ville de Sancerre,* published in the Protestant seaport of La Rochelle less than two years after the siege.

Born in Burgundy, at La Margelle, Jean de Léry (1534–1613) became a Protestant at the age of eighteen and spent the better part of two years (1556–1558) as a missionary in Brazil, about which he published a famous account, *Histoire d'un voyage fait en la terre du Bresil, autrement dite l'Amerique*. Later, after a second stint of study in Geneva, he returned to France to preach the word of God as a Calvinist minister. Fearing for his life in the wake of the August massacres of 1572, he fled to Sancerre in September. And here Léry would become one of the foremost leaders in the Huguenot campaign of resistance.

Since the kings of France were prime movers of the Italian Wars (1494–1559), Italy became a school of warfare for thousands of French noblemen, with the result that France's religious wars would be captained by seasoned officers on both sides of the confessional divide. Sancerre had more than enough of these in November 1572, in addition to 300 professional soldiers and another 350 men who were being trained in the use of arms. There were also 150 small-time wine producers who would serve as guardsmen along the town's defensive walls and gates. At the peak of the fighting, the night watch would even include a number of bold-spirited women armed with halberds, half pikes, and iron bars. They concealed their sex by wearing hats or helmets to hide their long hair.

From November onward, the countryside around Sancerre rang out with frequent and bloody skirmishes, provoked mostly by the Huguenot defenders, who made daring sorties into the surrounding country to fight the enemy, seize supplies, or gather provisions for the coming siege. By December they were stealing grain and livestock in night raids. On the night of January 1–2, for example, they broke into a neighboring village and returned to Sancerre with "the priest of the place as their prisoner and four carts loaded with wheat and wine, plus eight bullocks and cows for feeding the town." Raids of this sort went on right through the winter, but became bloodier, less frequent, and more dangerous as the gathering royal army swelled and tightened its ring around Sancerre. Meanwhile, the town itself would know internal wrangling as the mass of refugees provoked disagreements, or blaspheming soldiers offended Huguenot ears, and the pride of competing officers clashed.

By the end of January, the enemy forces massed around the base of the Sancerre "mountain" numbered about sixty-five hundred foot soldiers and more than five hundred horsemen, not counting volunteer gentlemen and others from the surrounding area. By January 11, the people of Sancerre had resolved, in a general assembly, "that the poor, a number of women and children, and all those who could not serve, apart from eating, should be put outside the town." But the men charged with this repugnant task failed to carry it out, "partly because of giving way to the outcry raised. And so they put no one outside the town gates." This, Léry observes, was a grave error, because at the time the unwanted could easily have departed and gone wherever they chose, "which would have prevented the great famine . . . and which [later on] caused so much suffering."

The *Sancerrois* did not even bother to answer the regional governor's call to surrender, made on January 13. Claude de La Châtre informed them that his troops were there to subjugate Sancerre, in accord with the king's orders, so he and his men now began to dig in seriously, both by building a network of trenches and fortifying the houses in the village of Fontenay, at the foot of towering Sancerre. They hauled in artillery early in February and soon began a daily bombing of the Huguenot fortress. In four days, from February 21 to 24, the town took more than thirty-five hundred cannon shots. Léry speaks of "a tempest" of bombs, debris, and house and wall fragments "flying through the air thicker than flies." Yet very few people were killed—it was God's doing, he opines—and the attackers were dumbfounded.

That winter, Léry points out, the weather was dreadfully cold, with a great deal of ice and snow, and for this the Huguenots praised God, because it was especially hard on the encamped enemy soldiers. La Châtre, nonetheless, was already having Sancerre under-mined, with an eye to planting explosives and blasting breaches in the town walls.

Léry's comments on the weather were revelatory. In the Europe of that day, there was an all but universal feeling in towns under attack that time destroyed besieging armies by working through hunger, painful discomfort, disease, and desertion. Living in squalid conditions, mercenaries were likely to succumb to malnutrition, wounds, and sickness; and desertion was a tempting solution, particu-larly when men stole off in pairs or in small groups. One thing was almost certain: Though a besieging army might begin with money in its pockets, as the weeks passed, that money ran out and desertion became more and more enticing. So, when not negotiating an im-mediate surrender, the best hope for a besieged town was to hold out for as long as possible until, in despair, the ragged remainders of the besieging army pulled away. To hold out, however, the besieged had to have ample stores of food.

WARNED BY A PRISONER, the *Sancerrois* were ready to receive and re-pel a major assault on March 19, preceded by mine explosions and a furious bombardment. The assault was repelled, and Léry, in his description, touches fleetingly on a girl who had been working near him, carrying loads of earth for the defenders, when she was hit by a cannon shot and disemboweled before his eyes, "her intestines and liver bursting through her ribs." Dead on the spot. His own sur-vival, he felt, was God's work. The defenders lost seventeen soldiers and the girl, but enemy casualties amounted to 260 dead and 200 wounded.

The bombardment of Sancerre continued, but always, Léry ob-serves, with little loss of life in the town. When the royalists erected two towering, wheeled structures near the walls, with arquebusiers on the top, aiming volleys at the defenders on the walls, groups of Hu-guenot soldiers made stealthy nighttime attacks and set fire to them. Throughout their many armed engagements, seeking to maintain unity and to keep up their spirits, the besieged Huguenots sang hymns, flagging their evangelical bent. Yet all the while a silent enemy was slowly taking shape, and it was to be more fatal than the daily cannonades of the royalists. It was taking form around their dwindling food supplies. There was wine galore, but beef, pork, cheese, and—most important—flour were running out, with the remaining stocks turning, in value, to gold.

The *Sancerrois* sent messengers to Protestant communities in Languedoc to plead for military help, but there, too, the Huguenots were at war. Step-by-step, in the teeth of shrill complaint, Sancerre's town council was forced to commandeer all wheat still in private hands and to put it into central storage for communal bread.

In March and April, they slaughtered and cooked their donkeys and mules, used for transport up the town's steep rise of more than 360 meters, until all had been eaten up by the end of April. Later, as the siege continued, they would regret having consumed their pack animals with such greedy abandon. In May, they began to kill their horses, the council ruling that these had to be slaughtered and sold by butchers. Prices were fixed at sums that were lower than would have been allowed for by the tightening pincers of supply and demand. But in July and August, as Sancerre went to the wall, prices for the remaining horse meat soared, despite strict policing; and every part of the horse was sold, including head and guts. Opinion held, Léry observes, that horse was better than donkey or mule, and better boiled than roasted. He was coldly reporting, but also, possibly, adding a sliver of gallows humor.

Then came the turn of the cats, "and soon all were eaten, the entire lot in fifteen days." It followed that dogs "were not spared . . . and were eaten as routinely as sheep in other times." These too were sold, and Léry lists prices. Cooked with herbs and spices, people ate the entire animal. "The thighs of roasted hunting dogs were found to be especially tender and were eaten like saddle of hare." Many people "took to hunting rats, moles, and mice," but poor children in particular favored mice, "which they cooked on coal, mostly without skinning or gutting them, and—more than eating—they wolfed them down with immense greed. Every tail, foot, or skin of a rat was nourishment for a multitude of suffering poor people."

June 2 brought a decision to expel some of the poor from the town, although their numbers had already been reduced by starvation and disease. That very evening "about seventy of them departed of their own accord." And the essential ration was now lowered to one half pound of daily bread per person, irrespective of rank or social condition, soldiers included. Eight days later this ration was reduced to a quarter pound, then to one pound per week, until flour supplies ran out at the end of June.

But the imagination of the starving *Sancerrois* found more to eat than any of them could ever have dreamed of, and it was in the leather and hides that came from "bullocks, cows, sheep, and other animals." Once these were washed, scoured, and scraped, they could be gently boiled or even "roasted on a grill like tripe." By adding a bit of fat to the skins, some people made "a fricassee and potted pâté, while others put them into vinaigrette." Léry goes into the fine details of how to prepare skins before cooking them, noting, for example, that calfskin is unusually "tender and delicate." All the obvious kinds "went up for sale like tripe in the market stalls," and they were very expensive.

In due course, the besieged were eating "not only white parchment, but also letters, title deeds, printed books, and manuscripts." They would boil these until they were glutinous and ready to be "fricasseed like tripe." Yet the search for foods did not terminate here. In addition to removing and eating the skins of drums, the starving also ate the horny part of the hooves of horses and other animals, such as oxen. Harnesses and all other leather objects were consumed, as well as old bones picked up in the streets and anything "having some humidity or taste," such as weeds and shrubbery. People mounted guard in their gardens at night.

And still the raging hunger went on, pushing frontiers. The

besieged ate straw and candle fat; and they ground nutshells into powder to make a kind of bread with it. They even crushed and powdered slate, making it into a paste by mixing in water, salt, and vinegar. The excrement of the eaters of grass and weeds was like horse dung. And "I can affirm," Léry asserts, all but beggaring belief and alluding to Jeremiah's lamentations, "that human excrement was collected to be eaten" by those who once ate delicate meats. Some ate horse dung "with great avidity," and others went through the streets, looking for "every kind of ordure," whose "stink alone was enough to poison those who handled it, let alone the ones who ate it."

The final step was cannibalism, which must already have been taken, sooner than Léry himself could know. He turns to the subject by first citing Leviticus 26 and Deuteronomy 28, with their references to the starving who ate their children in sieges, and then says that the people of Sancerre "saw this prodigious . . . crime committed within their walls. For on July 21st, it was discovered and confirmed that a grape-grower named Simon Potard, Eugene his wife, and an old woman who lived with them, named Philippes de la Feuille, otherwise known as l'Emerie, had eaten the head, brains, liver, and innards of their daughter aged about three, who had died of hunger." Léry saw the remains of the body, including "the cooked tongue, finger" and other parts that they were about to eat, when caught by surprise. And he cannot refrain from identifying all the little body parts that were in a pot, "mixed with vinegar, salt, and spices, and about to be put on the fire and cooked." Although he had seen "savages" in Brazil "eat their prisoners of war," this had been not nearly so shocking to him.

Arrested, the couple and the old woman confessed at once, but they swore that they had not killed the child. Potard claimed that l'Emerie had talked him into the deed. He had then opened the linen sack containing the body of the little girl, dismembered the corpse, and put the parts into a cooking pot. His wife insisted that she had come on the two of them as they were doing the cooking. Yet on the very day of their arrest, the three had received a ration of herbal soup and some wine, which the authorities had regarded as enough to get them through the day.

Looking into the life of the Potards, the town council found that they had a reputation for being "drunkards, gluttons, and cruel to their other children," and that they had lived together before they actually married. It was found, indeed, that they had been expelled from the Reformed Church, and that he, Simon, had killed a man. The council now took swift action. He was condemned to be burned alive, his wife to be strangled, and l'Emerie's body was dug out of its grave and burned. She had died on the day after their arrest.

Lest any of his readers should think the sentence too harsh, Léry remarks, they "should consider the state to which Sancerre had been reduced, and the consequences of failing to impose a severe penalty on those who had eaten of the flesh of that child," even if she was already dead. "For it was to be feared—we had already seen the signs—that with the famine getting ever worse, the soldiers and the people would have given themselves not only to eating the bodies of those who had died a natural death, and those who had been killed in war or in other ways, but also to killing one another for food." People who have not experienced famine, he adds, cannot under-stand what it can call forth, and he reports a curious exchange. A starving man in Sancerre had recently asked him whether he, the unnamed man, would be doing evil and offending God if he ate the "buttocks" (*fesse*) of someone who had just been killed, especially as the part seemed to him "so very pleasing" (*si belle*). The question struck Léry as "odious" and he instantly replied that doing so would make the eater worse than a beast.

In the meantime, there had been another purge of poor folk. Many of them had been ejected from the town in June. As expected, how-ever, the besiegers blocked their passage at the siege trenches, killed some, wounded others, no doubt mutilating the faces of a few, and then, using staves, battered the rest back to the walls. Unable to re-enter Sancerre, the outcasts lived for a while by scrounging about for grape buds, weeds, snails, and red slugs. In the end, "most of them perished between the trenches and the moat." But the inner spaces of the town itself offered no guarantees. There, too, people died at home and in the streets, children more often, and those "under twelve nearly all died," their bones sometimes "piercing the flesh."

Murmuring was to be heard by late June. The rabidly hungry, their voices rising, wanted Sancerre to surrender. The town, however, was in the clasp of religious hard-liners, of the better-off, and of soldiers. Hence the complainers were ordered to shut up or get out of town. Otherwise, came the warning, they would be thrown from the town's soaring walls. Sancerre was an island in a vast countryside of hostile Catholics. Yet the starving kept stealing away, passing over to the enemy even when threatened with death, knowing, in any case, that they faced a sure death in that walled-in fortress. As late as July 30, seventy-five soldiers paraded through the streets in testimony of their will to hold out for "the preservation of the [true] Church." But they were a minority, for at that point Sancerre still had at least another 325 soldiers. Then, on August 10, affected by rumors about Huguenot losses in other parts of France, the despairing garrison captains announced that the army was ready to surrender, that they preferred to die by the sword rather than hunger. A debate in council ignited passions, differences broke out, tempers flared, and men drew out swords and daggers. But by the next day common sense had prevailed.

Informal negotiations with the enemy, already broached, revealed that the commander of the siege, La Châtre, was ready to spare all their lives. Talks went on for over a week. The countryside was a waste for thirty miles in all directions around Sancerre. Surrender terms were finally fixed and approved on the nineteenth.

In a changed climate and in accord with the king's new mandate, the *Sancerrois* could go on worshipping as Huguenots. The honor and chastity of their women would be respected. They retained full rights over all their goods and landed properties. There would be no sequestrations. However, they had to face a fine of 40,000 *livres*, intended as pay for the besieging army. It was a sum that would undo the well-off families; hence residents were given the bitter right to sell, alienate, or remove any or all of their goods.

On the twentieth of August, bread and meat began to arrive from the outside. And now, in the moving about of people, Léry was the first man to be let out of Sancerre. Although he had negotiated the surrender agreement for the besieged, he was provided with a special pass and accompanied by several soldiers, because La Châtre feared that he might be assaulted, owing to his office as pastor. The enemy also maintained that he was the one who had taught the *Sancerrois* how to survive on leather and skins. Léry was followed out of Sancerre by the Huguenot soldiers, some of whom were accompanied by wives and children.

La Châtre seems to have offered his surrender terms in good faith. But he was rushing off to a royal assignment in Poland, and in the furies of the time, it was going to be next to impossible for the king's ministers to guarantee the terms. Hatreds were intense, and Sancerre presented a chance for plunder.

Priests and monks entered the town at the end of August. Catholics began to dismantle walls and defensive points. They removed the town clock, the bells, "and all the other signs" of a busy municipality, in effect reducing Sancerre to the level of a mere village. Many houses, especially the empty ones, were robbed and stripped of their furniture. In due course, residents who sought to leave Sancerre were compelled to pay ransoms. And those who remained, although seeing some of their possessions confiscated, had to pay special taxes, leaving them, in the end, all but destitute. In time their church was suppressed. The destiny of Calvinism in France would be hammered out in Paris, La Rochelle, Rouen, and other cities.

Once it was published, Léry's memoir transformed the siege of Sancerre into an event of legendary resistance, particularly among Huguenots. But the strange foods of the famine intrigued all who heard about them. Had the eating of "powdered slate" actually taken place? Some of the foods seemed to lie beyond the utmost limits of the imaginary. Paris was to learn a thing or two from Léry's recipes.

SINCE THE HUGUENOT PASTOR SOON rushed his memoir into print, it is likely to carry moments of exaggeration and even of fiction, particularly with regard to the scale of the cannonades directed against Sancerre. His general outlines of the siege, however, and of the wild workings of hunger, are perfectly in accord with the consequences of sieges in the sixteenth and seventeenth centuries.

PARIS (1590)

The ferocity of religious conflict could prolong wars, but it could not alter the technical nature of warfare. A siege remained just that, as in the noose that was thrown around Paris in the spring and summer of 1590.

France's Wars of Religion had turned by then into a struggle over the question of princely bloodlines, because King Henry III had been assassinated the year before and the rightful claimant to the throne, Henry of Navarre, was a Protestant. About this claim, however, the rival Guise and Bourbon families, and the chieftains of the mighty Catholic League, were saying, in effect, "Over our dead bodies." And so it might have been, as a result of the war being waged against them by a Protestant Henry IV, in command of an army of twenty thousand troops.

Fresh from recent victories at Ivry and Mantes, Henry led his army to the outskirts of Paris in April 1590, proposing to lay siege to it and to impose a blockade. This would be no easy matter. For even with three to five thousand horsemen, he was looking at a great loop of about thirty miles, not to speak of the obstacles that would be raised by efforts to patrol the region during the hours of the night, by soldiers taking bribes, and by Paris's stubborn determination to resist. Henry therefore cut off traffic on the Seine by placing artillery on facing banks of the river at different points, from where he could target attempts to float foodstuffs into the city.

With its 220,000 inhabitants, Paris prepared to hold out. There were wheat reserves for a mere month and only about fifteen hundred great barrels of oats. Food prices began to rise dizzily almost at once, and certain bakeries, in different parts of the city, were appointed to sell bread to the poor at cut prices. Soon three thousand Landsknechts were hired and brought in to help lead the defense. Buildings in the suburbs were demolished, to eliminate cover for the enemy; and the Duke of Nemours, commander of the defense, distributed sixty-five pieces of artillery along the city walls to thunder back at Henry's guns. In a stern move to prolong the resistance, as noted by an eyewitness, the authorities next ordered the expulsion of "30,000 peasants, useless mouths, and beggars, people whom the enemy had more or less forced into the city." But they neglected to keep an eye on the assigned enforcers, who simply did nothing, and later fell back on excuses, alleging Paris's "honour and grandeur," in spite of "the fact," reports the witness, "that in all other well-policed cities, it has always been the practice on such occasions to do the same." As a result, the city was pitched into an acute food scarcity.

Raids, skirmishes, robberies, and artillery volleys became the anxious stuff of everyday life in the suburbs and country around Paris. As May and then June passed, the lack of money to pay soldiers and buy provisions turned into acrimony and hardship on both sides. Henry's troops, seen increasingly in ragged clothing, would on occasion go hungry. In Paris, the nobility, the rich, and the array of wealthy foreign ambassadors and provincial bishops had to dig into their pockets to pay the soldiers hired to defend the city. The rectors of churches were also pressured to donate their dispensable silver, again to help pay for the wages and food supplies of mercenaries. Bernardino de Mendoza, the Spanish ambassador, began to provide great cauldrons of gruel made from oat bran for more than two thousand shamefaced or respectable poor on a daily basis. The religious orders, from Capuchins to Jesuits, although not happy about it, had to submit to having their stocks of food checked and inventoried. This did not blunt their readiness to take up arms against "a heretic" pretender to the throne, Henry IV.

For all their notoriety, the well-known sieges of Sancerre and Siena had failed to convey a fundamental lesson. When faced with the prospect of a long-term blockade, no large European city, with the possible exception of Turin in 1706, seems ever to have stocked enough food to achieve the planned resistance of local authority. And the scantiness of public funds was the primary reason. Urban revenue could not afford the charges; the tax base was too thin and porous; debt was also a likely barrier; and the haves could be shamed into paying out only so much, but no more, to help feed the have-nots.

In July, having somehow managed to get his hands on extra funds, despite his ragged and murmuring troops, Henry was able to add two thousand foot (Gascons) and eight hundred horse to his besieging army. These helped to tighten his noose around the capital. On July 9, his soldiers captured a major suburb and Catholic League garrison, St. Denis, where the effects of starvation had obliterated resistance. Here was the determining force, hunger, not Henry's siege guns, which were too sparsely distributed, too far from the important targets, and doing little serious damage inside the city.

Paris's hungry throngs had begun their lamentations ten to twelve days from the start of the siege, hence not later than early May. The ruling elite realized at once that flaring anxieties should be met with religious processions, all-night public prayers, and special services in the parish churches. As hunger turned into keening famine, there was no retreat from the compensations of litany and ritual. And we are informed by an anonymous witness that the ambassador Mendoza, a pillar of the Catholic League in Paris, took to minting large quantities "of half-pennies, stamped with the arms of Spain, which he then had thrown into crowds at street crossings, causing the populace to cry out, 'Long live the king of Spain!'" To stiffen resistance, the papal legate in Paris, Cardinal Gondi, began to grant generous indulgences and remissions of sin.

The hard-liners, meanwhile, had to suffer embarrassments. When the Jesuit College was ordered to open up its store of food supplies for the compiling of an inventory, the head of the school went to the papal legate to request an exemption. Whereupon the top official of the society of merchants, quickly confronting the Jesuit, objected: "Why should you be exempted from the inventory? Is your life of greater worth than ours?" The priest relented. And it was discovered that the Jesuits had enough wheat and biscuit for a year. Their stores also contained "a large quantity of salted meat which had been dried, the better to preserve it, despite the fact that they had more food supplies in their house than the four best houses in Paris." In fact, says the reporter of these details, every religious house in Paris had enough biscuit for at least a year. This included "even the Capuchins, who are alleged to live strictly on what they are given every day and who save nothing for tomorrow, because they [supposedly] distribute all their surplus to the poor. Well, they were found to be well-supplied, which astonished lots of people."

Once clergy and religious houses were roped in to help feed the starving, officials looked into the condition of the poor. They found and counted two sorts of poor households: seventy-five hundred with some money, but unable to find bread cheap enough to buy, and five thousand without a penny. Now, for a period of fifteen days, the clergy agreed to feed the utterly destitute once a day, and to subsidize the others, those with a modicum of money, to help them buy a daily pound of cheap bread, also for fifteen days. But the cheap bread was to be stamped with "the arms of the city." The poor, in other words, were meant to be thankful to the city's ruling council too.

And here all of a sudden we touch on pets, on the city's cat and dog population. All the poor—those about to receive the handouts—were ordered to take their cats and dogs to a given depot three days before the start of the food distributions. "A certain number were then killed and cooked with herbs and roots in large pots . . . and the soupy stew was doled out to the poor. To each a little piece of dog and cat meat, plus an ounce of bread. To the less poor one pound of common bread for six *sols* each, for as long as it lasts, and after that was finished, then biscuit for eight *sols* the pound. When the fifteen days expired, the clergy had met their obligations in the matter."

This grudging account is offered by an observer who sympathized with King Henry and was critical of the Catholic Leaguers. But there was nothing distorted about his outline of events. July had come, and Paris was in the grip of an existential crisis.

Police agents were sent to the city walls to meet with Henry's officials and "really to plead with his majesty that it please him to let some of the poor people out of the city." The king rejected the plea and declared that "not a single person was to come out." Later, however, moved by what he saw and heard, he authorized the exit of three thousand people, instead of which about four thousand of the starving pushed their way out. The besiegers had to use violence to stanch the flow of refugees.

Pierre Corneio (Cornejo), a resident Spaniard and strong supporter of the League, reported that the "comfortable rich" also suffered. Instead of their usual "delicate meats," they were now eating "oatmeal bread, donkey, mule, and horsemeat, although there was little of this and very dear." By late July or early August, as the depleting of food stocks quickened, "all the city's glory and triumph, beautiful tapestries, silver plate, jewels and precious stones, handsome carriages, coaches, and horses of the sort for taking gentlemen and ladies about: these had been exchanged . . . for kettles of porridges, for cooked grass and weeds without salt, and pots of horsemeat, ass, and mule, on which these poor Christians now lived. The skins themselves and the hides of the said beasts were sold cooked, and they ate these with as much appetite as if they were the best meats in the world."

The men in command of Paris carried their fight into the second week of September, so that they and their defending mercenaries, at least, had enough food to hold out against Henry's harassing troops. By now, however, many who had once been well-off were also the victims of famine, and this extreme was splintering the will to resist. Grass and weeds had long since vanished from that great urban space, ripped up to be eaten; and private gardens had either been stripped of their greenery or were being protected—we may assume—by armed men. Reflecting on the hardships of the rich, Corneio remembers Léry's memoir and the claim that the people of Sancerre seem to have eaten even powdered slate and stone mixed (he adds) with wine. But "they were few and nearly all were fighting folk and soldiers."

Wailing for bread, the poor broke out in noisy street demonstrations. But as what they really wanted could only be got by capitulating to Henry IV, they were brutally dispersed. Another popular outburst on August 9 was also put down, and participants were accused of being seditious heretics. They were beaten, jailed, ransomed, and some were hanged. Paris's prayers multiplied, but so did the numbers dying from starvation, especially after the clergy's fifteen days of special relief expired. And now, says Corneio, "Some mornings there were 100, 150, and at times as many as 200 dead of hunger in the streets."

The starving had taken to eating horrors. On June 15, the Spanish ambassador, who had witnessed strident hunger among Spain's soldiers in the Netherlands in the 1570s, made a remarkable proposal to the city council. Thinking of food for the needy, he recommended that they mill and grind the bones of the dead in the Cemetery of the Innocents, mix the bone meal with water, and turn it into a breadlike substance. No one present appears to have objected to the recipe. It was also on this occasion, probably, that Mendoza spoke of a recent incident in which the Persians had reduced a Turkish fortress to the eating of a substance "made of ground-down and powdered bone."

With so many of the city's poor having already eaten cooked animal skins, grass, weeds, garbage, vermin, the skulls of cats and dogs, and every kind of ordure, Parisians now ate the bones of their dead in the form of bone-meal bread. Reports of cannibalism surfaced insistently. The anonymous witness gives an account—one of the most detailed—of a Parisian lady whose two children, despite her wealth, had starved to death. She dismembered, cooked, and ate them. The moral temper of the city had some men openly willing to discuss the question of cannibalism. Pierre de l'Estoile observes that "toward the end [of the siege] . . . the most barbarous . . . began to chase children as well as dogs in the streets . . . and three were actually eaten." And he claims to have heard it argued "by a well-known Catholic . . . that there was less danger [in the hereafter] by eating a child in such circumstances, than by recognizing . . . a heretic [Henry IV]."

With views borne to such extremes by the fears and furies of Catholic Leaguers, how were any rational decisions possible, and how could the diehards reach any understanding with Henry IV?

SINCE THE CITY APPEARED TO verge on suicide, with religious intransigents still in control, the end had to come soon, and it turned out to be in the twists of international politics.

Opposed to the "heretic" king and in favor of France's Catholic Leaguers, the king of Spain had ordered his general, the Duke of Parma, to march the Army of Flanders down into France to engage Henry's forces. Unwillingly, because of his Sisyphean labors in the north, Parma at first dispatched three to four thousand men to assist the Duke of Mayenne (Charles de Guise), whose Catholic League army was too small to be pitted against the troops encamped around Paris. Giving way to more insistent appeals, the Duke of Parma finally crossed into France about the middle of August, at the head of a fourteen-thousand-man army, and on the twenty-third he was at Meaux, where Mayenne met him with his ten thousand foot and two thousand horse. Suddenly, therefore, Henry IV had to pull away his tattered noose of twenty-seven thousand men from around

Paris, although they were longing to sack the city. He moved out fast to engage Parma, hoping for a swift encounter and intent on then rushing back to the siege. Seeing Henry's troops drawing away, Parisians bolted out of the city to look for foodstuffs, only to be shocked by how little they could find, because the entire region, for many miles around, "had been eaten bare by the four months' sojourn of the besieging army."

Henry realized that he had met more than his match in the scion of a famous papal family (the Farnese), the Duke of Parma, the most brilliant general of his day. This man refused to do battle unless he believed that circumstances would enable him to deal out a crushing defeat. No contact between the two armies ensued. And by the first of September, the king saw that he would have to give up his dream of taking Paris. But with two thousand scaling ladders still in his baggage train, he could not refrain from making a desperate final attempt at an escalade. Striking between the gates of St. Jacques and St. Marcel on September 9, his assault was repelled. Dramatically, Henry's army was met by a resisting front line of thirteen hundred armed priests, Jesuits, "and the ramparts soon swarmed with resolute defenders." The king drew away in retreat, and Paris could now begin to count its dead. A few years later, in the wake of his public conversion to Catholicism (1593), Henry would get the allegiance of longed-for Paris; and France's other cities, too, would soon fall into line.

In the course of the siege, no fewer than thirteen thousand people had starved to death. But the overarching casualty rate reached a figure, very probably, of thirty thousand or even more.

Generally speaking, in early modern Europe, 18 to 25 percent or more of people in cities lived from hand to mouth and were ranked as poor or destitute. In Florence in the fifteenth century, one fifth of the city's population was listed as "wretched" (*miserabili*) in the urban tax records. Lübeck and Hamburg, in about 1500, had 20 to 25 percent of people living on public assistance. In 1618, Augsburg's tax officials put 48 percent of residents into the class of the penniless.

And in the Low Countries—as elsewhere in Europe—we have seen about "half the income of the average poor family" was likely to be spent on bread alone. In our day, by contrast, the poor in the United Kingdom spend about 20 percent of income on all their foods, while in the United States, this expense for the "average" American is closer to 7 percent of income.

But from the moment a city was subjected to a siege, bread and food prices climbed crazily. In a week or two, the poor could double in numbers as hunger reached out to turn shamefaced craftsmen and burghers into mendicants. With a population in the region of 220,000 people, Paris, in a siege, was ideal ground for thirty thousand casualties: the results of starvation, malnutrition, sickness, and the violence of soldiers outside the city gates, where the starving often scurried about in search of something to eat.

AUGSBURG (1634–1635)

In September 1634, when an Imperial army began its siege of Augsburg, King Gustavus Adolphus was already dead. His twenty-nine-month spree over the face of Germany had been stopped on the battlefield of Lützen, near Leipzig, in November 1632. Tilly and Pappenheim were also dead—Wallenstein as well, coldly assassinated in February 1634.

Several of the most brilliant generals of the Thirty Years War had thus disappeared halfway through the stretch of those years. It was a conflict that would be the graveyard of many generals and thousands of noblemen from all parts of Europe. How, therefore, could it have been anything but an abattoir for "little people"? In 1635, Louis XIII had taken France into the war, seeking to obstruct German and Spanish Habsburg ambitions by contributing subsidies to the free-booting Swedish army—the chief defender of the Protestant cause in Germany and enemy number one to the Holy Roman Emperor, Ferdinand II.

A city of about forty-five thousand people at the beginning of the war, Augsburg had lost more than fifteen thousand inhabitants by the time of the siege, victims of widespread crop failures, dearth, and disease. But it would take a stunted imagination to believe that the survivors had therefore got used to their woes. They had not. They gritted their teeth, fought their way, and showed immense human reserves.

A sharp divide between rich and poor ran through the city, with most of the population—petty craftsmen in the cloth industry—living on the margins of subsistence and tipping over into hunger when crops were poor. They kept an eye on the size of bread loaves, on changes in the weather, and on crop yields. Bread riots in January 1622 had led to the storming and plundering of bakery shops. In fear of serious civil disorder, the city council had taken to making occasional handouts of grain.

Despite the fact that the city was predominantly Protestant, Catholics had enjoyed a certain freedom of worship until the Edict of Restitution (1629) planted anxiety among Protestants by seeming to pose a menace to the property rights of Augsburg's Lutheran churches. This anxiety was dispelled—only to be replaced by others—when the Swedish army seized the city in April 1632 and introduced a garrison of soldiers. The fist of military authority quickly brought in restrictions against Catholics. On April 23, they were removed from the city council by a Swedish royal order. On May 3, Swedish forces confiscated all arms from "papists." In July, Catholics were ordered to stay at home until further notice, and anyone pursuing studies with the Order of Jesuits was given two days to get out of Augsburg or face the penalty of death. A few months later, in November, came a decree forbidding Catholics, on pain of death, to attend church, whatever their social condition. In other words, the rich and noble must also beware.

Meanwhile, the Swedes decided to reinforce the walls and defenses of the city by adding ravelins and other outworks. Some four thousand troops arrived on May 15, all to be quartered on citizens.

Their wages would be used to pay for food and drink. Three days later, the new bosses began to arm Protestants and to organize all able-bodied men into a militia. In July, to speed up the work on the city's defenses, they decreed that one person from every household had to go out daily to work on the construction sites. Here was a testament to the hustling ways of Swedish armies in Germany. In action so far away from their native land, Swedish officers knew that most of their soldiers and all their material resources, money or payment in kind included, had to come from wherever they found themselves. And if subsidies came in from abroad, such as from France, so much the better; but subsidies would not suffice to meet the needs of the Swedish-led armies.

The fact that the newly arrived soldiers would be spending their wages in Augsburg did not mean, therefore, that they were bringing in any kind of wealth. On the contrary, what they spent would be coming from increases in local excise taxes, from a new poll tax, from abuses in the system of billeting, and from the plundering of castles, houses, villages, and farms in the outlying districts, including towns as far as Memmingen, about fifty-five miles away. This booty, however, would slowly work against Augsburg's benefit, because the theft and destruction of rural wealth led to spikes in the price of foodstuffs. The damage to crops and livestock added still more melancholy to the fact that war and bad weather, during the early 1630s, had already slashed the production of cereals in that part of Bavaria and eastern Swabia. So to have six thousand horsemen making a stop in the villages around Augsburg—as happened on May 27, 1632, to be billeted there for nearly a week—simply aggravated the district's yawning poverty. In short, for two or three years before the siege of 1634–1635, famine, the stealthy destroyer, had been edging its way toward Augsburg, and those in command were turning the city itself into a little garrison state.

The link between hunger and the occupying soldiers is highlighted by a military command of July 26, 1632, which ordered the local peasantry to cut down the thousands of trees, many of them fruit-bearing, that formed a thick circle of greenery outside and around Augsburg. Logistically, their removal would deprive the Catholic enemy of protective cover, while also providing lumber for the work on the city's defensive perimeters. The bitter resentment of the peasants over the destruction of so many trees was swept aside. They had to do as they were told. And then on January 3, 1633, out went a town cry ordering all refugee peasants to get out of the city. But if any chose to labor on the defensive works around the walls in return for one and a half pounds of bread per day, they were permitted to remain. Eight days later, this order was overruled by the command that all foreign or refugee peasants leave Augsburg at once and go back to their lands. The shrinking food supply was creating anxieties. With four to five thousand soldiers quartered on citizens, the claims on foodstuffs—on grains in particular—had become fierce, now that 20 percent of the city's population was made up of soldiers.

By April 1633, with the endless to-and-fro of troops, Augsburg's rural hinterland had lost large numbers of horses and cows to pillaging Swedish troops. Many fields lay fallow. And though the sale of booty in the city had been outlawed, the ordinance was ignored, first of all by army officers. Augsburg's streets and open spaces teemed with plundered horses and cattle, and with numerous carts and wagons, all loaded with copperware, pewter, bedding, linen, clothing, and heaps of personal items. Much of this spoil, now "selling for wretched, paltry sums," had belonged to the peasantry. But there was more. Because of the rural violence of soldiers, a large number of peasants, fleeing danger to life and limb, had managed to steal into Augsburg, despite the decrees and town cries against their doing so. They arrived in wagons, carrying their families and all possible foodstuffs; and there they lived, parked in cramped spaces, in horrendous circumstances, straining to survive. Over the coming year or two, many of them would meet death inside or outside the city walls.

No wonder, then, that in the larger picture of southern Germany, military violence in villages provoked peasant uprisings against mercenaries and local officials, such as in upper Austria in 1626 and 1632–1636; in Swabia, Breisgau, and Sundgau in 1632 and 1633; and in Bavaria, closer to Augsburg, in 1633–1634. But all were violently suppressed. One such outburst in Austria ended with the massacre of four hundred women, children, and old people.

THE CHIEF CHRONICLER OF LIFE in Augsburg in the 1630s was Jakob Wagner, the son of a wealthy merchant. In his early sixties at the time, he was a close observer of daily events and in a position to gauge the growing tensions between soldiers and burghers. Billeting, new taxes, "contributions," nocturnal guard duty, and the endless toil demanded for defensive works at the city walls had generated angry resentment among the people of Augsburg. The soldiers, in turn, and especially their Swedish commanders, seeing themselves more and more harassed by Imperial troops, were unrelenting in their demands. A mutiny in the Swedish army had erupted late in April 1633, led by officers and caused by the fact that the army had not been paid since 1631. Nor had soldiers received the promised bounties for the famous battles of Breitenfeld (1631) and Lützen (1632). To settle the mutiny, Oxenstierna, the head of Swedish forces in Germany, found a solution in the conveying of conquered territories and lordships, by deed and legal title, to his generals. The generals could then pay their officers, who would seek, in turn, to satisfy the demands of their soldiers. Meanwhile, even before the outbreak of the mutiny, there was no controlling a soldiery which had been invited, in effect, to grab whatever it took to stay alive.

The wages of soldiers in Augsburg thus turn out to have been mostly payment in kind: food, plus loot from outside the city, or anything they could squeeze from the hosts on whom they had been quartered.

By the summer of 1634, in war's annihilation of rules and civilian supply lines, trade in Augsburg verged on collapsing. Many of the neighboring lands had been stripped of foodstuffs by traversing armies, and certain places had not seen bread in more than a year. Yet taxes and the bullying requests of the soldiers never let up. To satisfy war taxes, citizens were driven to sell assets, and rich merchants began to file for bankruptcy in the looming face of financial destruction. Jakob Wagner records the names and losses of the main bankrupts. Some of the amounts were enormous—in one case, for example, 169,764 florins, and in another 163,909 florins: each sum large enough for the purchase of dozens or even scores of houses in Augsburg. Such losses sufficed to pitch families of patricians into the ranks of the near destitute, for if they depended on returns from investments, those too had come to an end.

Worse was to come. On September 6, 1634, Imperial, Spanish, and Bavarian forces destroyed the Swedish army at Nördlingen. Some of the victorious units were now ordered to take Augsburg. And there, outside the walls, they would harry a city council which had already resolved to make a live-or-die defense at the expense, if need be, of "all their God-given earthly goods." Croats and other Imperial dragoons rode into the region to plunder any remaining cattle and to set fire to mills, while also killing, in their raids, passing burghers. With the help of other units, they blocked the Lech River on October 3, diverting its waters away from the city. On the fourteenth, local peasants, on higher ground, managed to unblock ditches and to get the waters flowing toward Augsburg again. Fearing that the river would again be cut off and thus disable their grain-grinding facilities, the burghers began to construct eighty human- and horse-driven mills.

Inhabitants now turned against the city council. Eager to avoid the death and ruin of a drawn-out siege, the poor favored a negotiated surrender, knowing well that they would be the first to die of hunger. In the clashing of fears and angers, the city was treated to seditious lines and verses. This angry output circulated furtively, or was passed on by word of mouth, in response to an urban council that was determined to crush public opposition to its evangelical stance against the besiegers.

If the city had previously struggled to lay in food reserves, by the end of October it was impossible to bring in anything in quantities because of the tightening blockade. And efforts to cut through the ring of soldiers were punishable—as we have come to expect—by mutilation, death, "merciless beatings," or even by the tearing down of the houses of smugglers. Food prices leaped. The poor began to plead for work on the city's line of defenses, asking only for bread as payment, in spite of the fact that those labors had recently been completed. City councillors tried to meet the pleas, making more defense plans, and soon "loaves of bread" were being "cut into pieces every day and distributed among the poor. Now more work was being done for bread than previously for money, and it is a wretched thing to behold."

Once firewood ran out, soldiers broke into empty houses, stripping them of rafters: wood to be burned for heating and cooking. When they started to come down with dysentery late in the year, they became an even more serious worry for the authorities. But one rule was always axiomatic: Soldiers had to be fed and kept at least minimally contented, for in the end—thus the reasoning—only they could keep Augsburg from the hands of the Imperial forces. Being ready, presumably, to give up their lives at the walls and ramparts, they had to be among the first in line, along with the city's leading families, for the vanishing stocks of food. The "useless" poor—useless in the economy of any resistance to a long siege—had to be sacrificed. Yet the savage irony was that unless they were cut down by a malady, soldiers were among those who were most likely to survive a siege that ended in a negotiated surrender. Famine, on the contrary, always did away with the poor.

When Siena's patricians argued, in 1554, that the city was in the survival and honor of its patrician women, not in its physical walls, they were saying, in effect, that lives (some at least) were more important than those walls.

In January 1635, as Augsburg edged toward the limits of its food reserves, the urban council lived in some fear of a popular revolt and even feared that the soldiers, seeking to escape the gnawing spread of famine, might reach a secret agreement with the Imperial besiegers. But the control of the military and civilian bosses held. Indeed, on January 8, they voted unanimously to hold out for their Protestant cause as long as possible. This turned out to be bravado, for twelve days later, in an about-face, the council voted to negotiate "with the Papists," although even then the evangelicals, supported by the army officers, succeeded in slowing up the pace of negotiations.

Soldiers continued to claim a bread ration of one and a half pounds per day, more than double the ration for civilians. They had no doubt insisted on this, for the public sale of bread had ended by late December. Thereafter, when citizens picked up bread allotments at the few well-guarded bakeries, they sought to steal back home, casting eyes in all directions, to avoid the risk of being assaulted for their bread by soldiers. Pack animals, horses, and pets had disappeared from streets and houses. Eaten. Animal skins had gone the same way. All eatable greenery must also have disappeared before the onset of that icy winter, when the waters of the encircling moat, outside the city walls, froze over. As for eating carrion, some time earlier, the famine-stricken had been seen to gnaw at dead horses rotting in the streets.

The eating of human flesh was inevitable. And the subject now broke into reports and conversation. Grave diggers complained that many bodies were brought to them missing breasts and other fleshy parts. What to make of this was only too obvious. "To his horror . . . a Swedish soldier who had stolen a woman's shopping basket discovered flesh from a corpse." When citizens found that bits of bodies had been cut off, they began to throw the dead into the river. Wagner believed that the desperate countryside was more given to the atrocity of cannibalism than the city. But commenting on its incidence in Augsburg, Johann Georg Mayer, a neighboring village pastor who had found refuge there, hauntingly declared that "the bodies of the living had thus become the graves of the dead."

In the meantime, some of the poor were also freezing to death.

WHY WERE THE CITY COUNCILLORS so determined to let the siege go on? What were they hoping for in negotiations that lasted two murderous months? In January and February, many hundreds of people died of hunger in the streets or froze to death. The will to rebel against the council was broken by the enervating effects of famine, and starving civilians were likely to be all but worthless as guardsmen at the walls. The danger of a revolt had passed. Then what about the hope of succor from Swedish forces? That army had been cut to pieces at Nördlingen; its remnants fled north into Saxony and Hesse, pursued or reconnoitered by the Catholic enemy. The siege of Augsburg was a mopping-up operation, around a city expected to fall to the juggernaut of starvation, not to thundering guns or a storming.

Yet the resisting hard men held their course. Lutheran preachers of an evangelical bent stepped up their reassuring words: God would come to the help of this godly city. Wanting a humane capitulation, opponents jumped on this litany but gave it an ironic twist and posed a rhetorical question: Was the council expecting citizens to become brave martyrs?

In view of the thousands of soldiers garrisoned in Augsburg, we must assume that Sweden's officers had a decisive voice in prolonging the stubborn defense, while at the same time seeking every kind of concession from General Matthias Gallas, the commander of Imperial forces. That the Swedes were able to keep this up for so long was remarkable, for if, as threatened, the city had been taken by storm, the entire garrison could have been put to the sword and only the officers ransomed—a mercy intended to secure the same kind of treatment for captured Imperial officers.

What were Gallas and the Imperial forces getting in return for their lenience? They expected to march into an intact Imperial city and a peaceful situation. Besides, Augsburg was the home of many "papists." But more concretely, Gallas was perhaps seeking to save the lives of hundreds of his men, who would have perished at the walls and just after scaling them. The sack of Magdeburg was fresh in the German public mind, a thorn now lodged in memory. And since Imperial officers were perfectly aware of the nightmarish conditions inside Augsburg, they would have had no trouble envisaging the consequences of bursting into the city in a wave of violence and blood.

THE SURRENDER TERMS OF THE Löwenberg agreement, March 22–24, 1635, confirmed the right of the city's Protestants to practice their faith. But this article, tellingly, had long been on offer. After the Catholic victory at Nördlingen, moderate Protestant princes crossed back to the support of the Habsburg Emperor Ferdinand II, and this change was soon clinched in the Peace of Prague (May 20). The question therefore has to be raised: Was Augsburg's fierce resistance to the siege worth the sacrifice of thousands of lives? Army officers and a dominant group of city councillors would perforce have said yes, whereas most residents would have said no.

In fact, the Löwenberg articles show that the officers had good reasons to insist on a stubborn resistance, for the articles throw a mantle of remarkable protection over the Swedish garrison. They authorize the soldiers to leave Augsburg with all their flags, weapons, wagons, and camp followers. They guarantee their safe departure from the city, along with anyone else who chose to leave with them. In addition, the departing soldiers would be allowed to march to their destination, Erfurt, at their own pace, to make stops where they wished, and to carry all their own food and fodder, inasmuch as the entire region lay in a sea of waste and scarcity. But if they managed to pick up any food or forage along the way, there was to be no payment for it. Any soldier who had previously served in the Imperial or Bavarian armies could now go back to them; and any other soldier who wanted to pass to that side was also free to go. There would be an amicable exchange of prisoners. Finally, soldiers forced to remain in Augsburg out of injuries or illness were to be cared for until they could return to their regiments.

There was a certain comradely spirit among soldiers, and sometimes it crossed battle lines. Indeed, that sense of affinity grew stronger during the Thirty Years War, especially when it became the norm, from 1631, to press captured soldiers into the ranks of the winning side. When the Swedish army was shattered at Nördlingen, the victors found that many of their prisoners had previously served in the Imperial army. They were promptly taken back into the Habsburg and Bavarian ranks.

The Swedes had been hands-on witnesses to the effects of starvation, and they had known about the claims concerning cannibalism. Yet when they and the troops under their command left Augsburg, they could say that all things considered, affairs had gone well for them.

The people of the city could say no such thing. In the course of the war, the numbers of their dead climbed grimly. Credited with a population of about forty-five thousand souls at the beginning of the war in 1618, seventeen years later Augsburg had a mere 16,500. The city was still there physically, unlike Magdeburg, but it would have struck merchants and diplomats—travelers who had known it previously—as a specter, a pale eminence.

WAR WENT TO PEOPLE, to food, to supplies; it moved inevitably to the points where these abounded. Not surprisingly, then, all European cities and large towns came out of the late middle ages flanked by defensive walls, enabling them to repel marauding armies. The "laws of war"—and they were nothing more than custom—laid it down that a successful siege would be followed by a sack, unless preceded by a negotiated surrender. But a sack was unlikely, unless there had been sustained combat beforehand, as occurred even in Antwerp.

Yet all the unwritten rules could be broken, and a town might be sacked or spared, despite negotiated arrangements or stubborn resistance. The outcome hinged on the condition of the besieging forces and their officers. In the face of fragile, unruly armies, custom itself held a fragile status.

6

ARMIES: AMBULANT CITIES, DYING CITIES

Loaves of bread are the face of God.
Lazarillo de Tormes (1553)

THE CITY MOVES

In the mid-seventeenth century, an army of twenty thousand men, with their tail of ten to twenty thousand camp followers, had more people than most European cities. Hamburg, Germany's biggest metropolis, had fifty to sixty thousand inhabitants. So if we raise army numbers to thirty or forty thousand foot and horse, adding next their followers in the baggage train, we have a multitude that would have swamped all but Europe's six or seven largest urban clusters: London (with nearly 400,000 people), Paris (250,000), Naples (250,000), Amsterdam (135,000), or Seville and Rome (125,000 each).

In 1600, Europe already had 220 places of more than ten thousand souls each. Leipzig, for example, had fifteen thousand, Turin and Bristol twenty thousand, La Rochelle more than twenty thousand, and Ghent thirty thousand. All were walled in, and the same was true, at least in Germany, of some 40 percent of towns with populations of less than a thousand residents. Most of the rest, little towns and large villages, lay open to the battering of armies.

The numbers explain the title of this chapter. Even a small army, such as the ten thousand mercenaries who marched into Florence in

November 1494, was a walking city. The ten thousand were a moving community in daily need of bread, drink, and other foods; and on campaign they would include wagoners, smiths, carpenters, bakers, and other craftsmen. The people of Florence lined the streets to stare at that soldiery and at the king of France, Charles VIII, who rode into the city, "lance on hip and bare sword in hand." The sound of drums and pipes heightened the strangeness of the scene, as the French crossed the city to receive a blessing in the cathedral. Visibly awed and internally terrified, Florentines knew that they would have to feed and lodge those invaders for days—ten, as it turned out. But the occupation might have lasted for weeks, and this prospect— an experience that would have required close physical contact—was simply unimaginable. The king's men were to be billeted in the city. Days before, many hundreds of houses, now marked up with chalk, had been carefully picked out to host the soldiers. To remove the marks was a capital crime. The matter was evidently serious. Apart from demanding the best beds—in accord with the known behavior of soldiers—that flood of strangers was very likely going to eat Florentines out of house and home. They had already been in the field for more than three months.

When Charles and his soldiers finally left the city on November 28, their hosts turned to intone grateful prayers. But what prayers of gratitude would theirs have been if, instead, they had managed to fend off, keeping it outside their city walls, an army like the one raised by the Emperor Charles V for his invasion of France in 1544? Here was a truly ambulant city: forty-seven thousand men in all, including eighteen thousand Landsknechts, ten thousand Spanish foot soldiers, another ten thousand foot from the Spanish Netherlands, five thousand heavy German cavalry, and another four thousand light horsemen drawn both from Italy and the Low Countries. This moving colony also included fourteen hundred pioneers, two hundred supply wagons with eight horses each, sixty-three large guns pulled by thirty-five hundred horses, and seventy river boats borne on wagons. The boats were designed to be turned into a bridge, and their crews, too, were in the train. The supply wagons were probably for ammunition and food stocks. Officers and soldiers had their own hundreds of other wagons. And we have yet to mention teamsters, smiths, and camp followers. Moreover, all the men and camp followers to one side, we must not forget the great multitude of horses: twenty thousand at least, since heavy cavalry usually involved an extra two or three horses per knight.

Without detailed descriptions by close witnesses, no historian can turn the spectacle of that Imperial army into accurate historical images. The task passes from history and historians to fiction: the imagination of the novelist.

In the unsanitary conditions of preindustrial Europe, our ambulant cities readily picked up and transmitted epidemic diseases such as plague and typhus. Now they became dying cities.

When an army passed through a village like a flood in, say, southern Germany or northern France, the event—depending upon numbers—might go on for a day or two. The soldiers moved no faster than their baggage and artillery trains, the latter often pulled by oxen. If the local peasants had not already fled in fear, they would never forget the sights and sounds and stink of that endless horde. And if it was an army stricken by disease, the sight would perhaps have struck some witnesses as a thing unearthly, a procession out of hell.

In its pressing search for food and billets, an army could also scatter. When on campaign in the winter, the ambulant cities of the Thirty Years War might have their troops spread out over many miles and, like Ambrogio Spinola's army of 1620–1621, wintering along the middle Rhine, near Mainz, be quartered on more than fifty little towns and villages.

In the late spring of 1704, France was at war with three adversaries: England, the Dutch Republic, and the Empire. The initiative had passed into the hands of the Duke of Marlborough. From a point just northwest of Cologne, he cut a path of 250 miles to the Danube

With its flashing white horse, circular bridge, and plumes of smoke, Philips Wouwerman's vision of war here removes us from the immediate carnage of battle.

Copy after Philips Wouwerman (1619–1668): Cavalry Battle on a Bridge, 1665–1668 (© Veneranda Biblioteca Ambrosiana/De Agostini/Getty Images)

Louis XIV surveys his men, who look like an army of ants as they cross the Rhine.
Louis XIV, King of France, known as the Sun King, and the French army crossing the Rhine, June 12, 1672, engraving (©Getty Images/Leemage)

Although this scene is cast around frozen postures, it manages to convey the violence of St. Bartholomew's Night, August 23–24, 1572. In Reformation Europe, religion added to the intensity of conflict.

François Dubois (1529–1584): St. Bartholomew's Night *(De Agostini/Getty Images)*

In Dürer's *Death Riding* of 1505, the horse itself is dying of starvation. For all the carnage of warfare in this period, famine and disease took more lives.

Albrecht Dürer (1471–1528): Death Riding, 1505 (Private Collection/The Bridgeman Art Library)

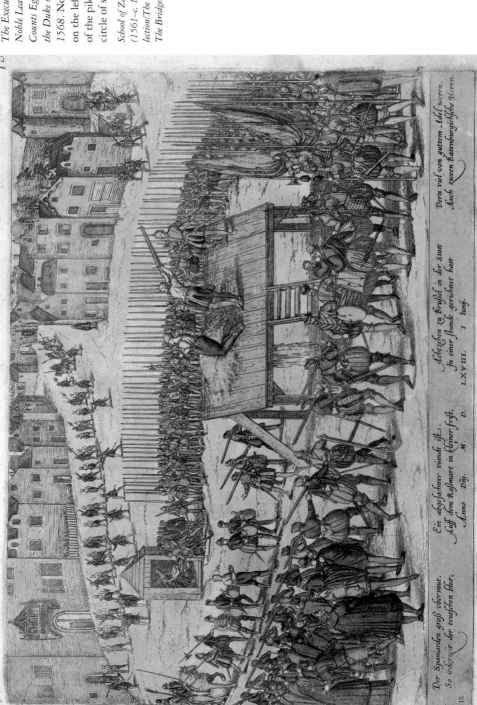

The Execution of Twenty Noble Leaders including Counts Egmont and Horn by the Duke of Alva in Brussels, 1568. Note the muskets on the left and the length of the pikes in the semi-circle of soldiers.

School of Zacharias Dolendo (1561–c. 1604) (Private Collection/The Stapleton Collection/The Bridgeman Art Library)

The resistance of walled-in Naarden ended in the town's being stormed and barbarously sacked. The savagery in Europe's wars often peaked when long-besieged cities fell to invaders.

Franz Hogenberg (1540–c. 1590): Massacre in Flanders during the Government of Fernando Alvarez de Toledo, Duke of Alba, 30th November 1572 (Bibliothèque Nationale, Paris, France/Giraudon/The Bridgeman Art Library)

NAERDEN.

Fire and smoke attest to the conquest and burning of Magdeburg (May 1631), as Imperial soldiers break into the city through a breach in the walls.

German school (seventeenth century): The Sack of Magdeburg by the Imperial Army, November 1630–20, May 1631, between 1726–27 (Deutsches Historisches Museum, Berlin, Germany)/© DHM/The Bridgeman Art Library)

Eroberung Magdeburg 1631.

P. 1809.

Homicidal assaults on villages, farms, and country folk constituted a universal aspect of war in Europe.

French school (seventeenth century): The Pillage of a Farm *(Musée Bargoin, Clermont-Ferrand, France/Giraudon/ The Bridgeman Art Library)*

Apres plufieurs degaft par les foldats commis
A la fin les Payfans qu'ils ont pour ennemis

Les guettent à l'efcart et par une furprife
Les ayant mis à mort les mettent en chemife.

Et fe vengent ainfi contre ces Malheureux
Des pertes de leurs biens, qu'ils ne viennent que deux. 17

Peasants ambush and massacre soldiers in revenge for what soldiers had done to them. *Engraving by Israel Henriet after Jacques Callot (1592–1635): The Peasants' Revenge; plate 17 from The Miseries and Misfortunes of War, 1633 (Grosjean Collection, Paris, France/The Bridgeman Art Library)*

A picture of the wartime rape and murder that might go on in the countryside. The mounted soldier in the foreground is clearly an officer.

Sebastian Vrancx (1573–1647): Pillage of a Village (Louvre, Paris, France/Giraudon/ The Bridgeman Art Library)

A battle scene showing Landsknechts (mercenaries) with a halberd, a two-handed sword, an arquebus, and a dense array of pikes.

German school (sixteenth century) c. 1550 (Deutsches Historisches Museum, Berlin, Germany/© DHM/The Bridgeman Art Library)

Despite his fancy dress, the cannoneer has a gunpowder pouch hitched to his waist. Gunners were nearly always commoners, not noblemen.

German school (sixteenth century): Loading a Cannon through the Breech, *illustration from* L'Art de l'Artillerie *by Wolff de Senftenberg, late sixteenth century (Ministère de la Défense—Service Historique de l'Armee de Terre, France/Giraudon/The Bridgeman Art Library)*

Death here is ennobled as allegory by the dramatic foreshortening of the soldier, and by the highlights on the skull, leg, huge hand, face, armor, and sword handle. The suggestion is that although war brings death, there is something noble about it: a viewpoint that could belong only to Europe's military and political elites.

A Dead Soldier (*seventeenth century*) (© *National Gallery, London/ Art Resource, NY*)

Murderous scuffles between soldiers and civilians fighting over loot, as war and a burning town light up the background.

Gillis Mostaert (c. 1534–1598): A Scene of War and Fire, 1569 (Louvre, Paris, France/Photo: Erich Lessing/Art Resource, NY)

War envelops a city. The scene is titled *Titus' Conquest of Jerusalem*, but the painting shows settings and bloodshed that might well have been seen in the artist's homeland, northern Europe.

Vienna Master of Mary of Burgundy (fl. c. 1470–80): Titus' Conquest of Jerusalem (Museum voor Schone Kunsten, Ghent, Belgium/© Lukas—Art in Flanders VZW/Photo: Hugo Maertens/The Bridgeman Art Library)

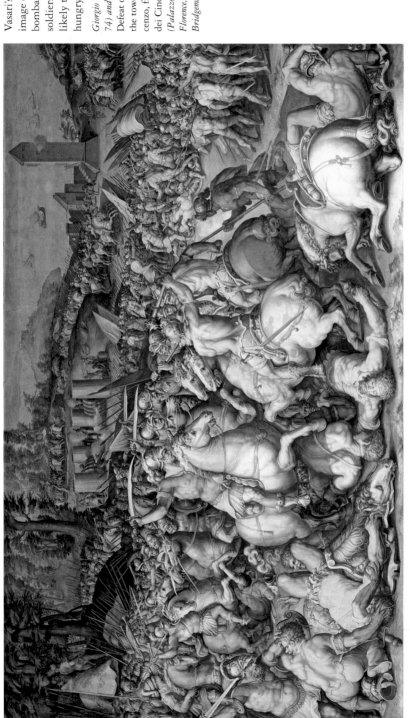

Vasari's muscular image of war here is bombast. Horses and soldiers were more likely to be lean, hungry, and ragged. *Giorgio Vasari (1511–74) and workshop: The Defeat of the Pisans at the tower of San Vincenzo, from the Salone dei Cinquecento, 1569 (Palazzo della Signoria, Florence, Italy/The Bridgeman Art Library)*

River, leading an army of nineteen thousand men, but picking up another ten thousand along the way. The march began on May 19 and was completed in a month. It counts as one of the more famous logistical feats in the history of modern warfare.

Getting supplies to Marlborough's army had been carefully planned. Owing to the danger posed by superior enemy forces, the march was meant to be as stealthy and as speedy as possible. Hence there was no question of a tail of camp followers. Three- and four-day stretches of hard marching were broken up by a day of cooking and complete rest. Along the way they were met with provisions supplied by allies. The duke led his army, comprised of British, Dutch, and other soldiers beyond the Moselle River, across the Rhine, through Mainz, past Heidelberg, to Eppingen, Geislingen, and then straight east to Donauwörth, on the Danube, to make contact with the supporting troops of the Emperor Leopold I. His final destination, to be reached in tandem with the emperor's field commander, Prince Eugene of Savoy, would be Blenheim (Blindheim) and his victory over a French army.

Bread, drink, and meat all along the way of that march kept spirits up, and Marlborough's men made good time, doing twelve to thirteen miles a day on their marching days, despite an episode of heavy rains and artillery mired in mud. Once they reached the Danube, to be joined there by the forces of Prince Louis of Baden, they fought and won a costly battle against the high fortress of Schellenburg at Donauwörth (July 2).

But now, having arrived and carrying no foodstuffs in their race to elude the enemy, they had to find their own victuals and fodder. The logistics of food supplies had come to an abrupt halt. Or rather, on the spot, the fundamental logistical problem was converted into a murderous, full-scale assault on Bavaria, whose ruler, the Elector Maximilian Emmanuel, was the ally of the king of France. Sources confirm that Marlborough authorized "free plunder." And Mrs. Christian Davies, who was with the army disguised as a soldier, observed that "we miserably plundered the poor inhabitants . . . We spared nothing, killing, burning, or otherwise destroying whatever we could [not] carry off. The bells of the churches we broke to pieces, that we might bring them away with us." She grabbed "men's and women's clothes, some velvets, and about a hundred Dutch caps . . . plundered from a shop; all of which I sold by the lump to a Jew, who followed the army to purchase our pillage." She also "got several pieces of plate, as spoons, cups, mugs, etc, all of which the same conscionable merchant had at his own price."

Moving his troops swiftly over the Bavarian countryside and through some four hundred villages, Marlborough's campaign of plunder, sacking, and burning brought two satisfactions: booty (payment) and food for his soldiers, and the dispersal of Bavarian troops, who had been intended to link up with French forces and to fight the duke's army. In fact, the rape of Bavaria came close to splitting the elector away from his French allies.

Although Marlborough's famous victory at Blenheim was made possible by the logistics of his march from Bedburg to the Danube, it was paid for by the tears and material possessions of Bavarian farmers, peasants, and villagers.

To cast an inquiring eye at a small army, shipped over several hundred miles of the Atlantic Ocean, is to touch on the central question of logistics in early modern Europe.

On June 27, 1627, the Duke of Buckingham set sail from England with a fleet of one hundred boats and in command of just under six thousand foot and one thousand horse. He made for the Bay of Biscay and the Isle of Ré, which faces the harbor of La Rochelle, the last Protestant stronghold in France and at that point under a ruthless siege by the French army. The aim of the expedition was to win glory for the duke, in part to placate Parliament, and to stiffen the Huguenot stand against the French crown. Buckingham, the great splendor-loving favorite of Charles I, king of England, had no military experience. But he was driven by the conviction that he needed none, being a nobleman and hence a natural leader. Besides, he was attended by officers with considerable experience of war on the continent.

The enterprise was to turn into a nightmare, with vanishing food rations at the heart of the disaster.

Reaching Ré on July 12, the English were at once engaged in a brief and bloody skirmish. The French then retreated to their high-walled fortress, the citadel of St. Martin. To storm it would require a determined siege, but the brave duke embraced the challenge, despite the fact that the trained eyes around him considered the fortress impregnable. The only other hitch was that food supplies would have to come from England, moving over four hundred to five hundred miles of open sea. Ré was too small an island to provide the English with a steady stream of victuals.

The commanders of the expedition had set sail with enough food, they believed, for three months. It was an insanely mistaken belief. Rations began to run short within a week of the landing on Ré, in part because of forty-five hundred new mouths, the fleet's sailors. These men were pressed into helping the foot soldiers to blockade the fortress, in order to keep the French mainland army—only four kilometers away—from getting provisions to the besieged.

Now the responsible men in London and around Buckingham suddenly had to confront a few basic questions. How many tons of foodstuffs per month—bread, biscuit, beef, butter, cheese, beer—would it take to feed ten to twelve thousand men? How many boats and of what tonnage must they commandeer to transport these provisions to Ré? How many round-trips to the Bay of Biscay would the food convoys have to make? Would this not depend on the weather? And most important, where were they going to find the money or credit to pay for the needed provisions?

These questions turned into an inscrutable algebra. Army and navy victuallers had different ways of calculating needed food supplies, so that six-month food estimates for any army of ten thousand men varied from 8,200 to 12,000 tons of foodstuffs. The average weight of the boats to be commandeered would be 250 tons. Or was it 300? Tonnage determined the amount of freight that each boat could carry. But cutting through all their tormented considerations, the core question of payment remained. Who would pay? Who would their supply merchants be? That Parliament might offer a few pennies was utterly unthinkable. Members of Parliament, many of them, were already in a fury with the king and his favorite, the prime movers of the Ré adventure, not over the effort to aid La Rochelle but because the two men were seen as wild spendthrifts.

In all this anxious business, stretching from July to November, action and discussion in London morphed into an astonishing drama of dither, false hopes, haste, confusion, rumor, conflicting views, and staggering irresponsibility. On the island itself, most of the besiegers—a "rabble" of pressed men, plus some carried over from a previous armed calamity—must have seen their rations repeatedly slashed. Essential provisions for the leading officers seem to have held. Custom always entitled them to extra rations, intended chiefly for their servants. And the Duke of Buckingham, one of the most hated men in England, was not a fan of the ascetic life. In the words of two historians, this gentleman "lavished £10,000 on his own retinue" and delayed the departure of the expedition to put on "masques and farewell feasts," while "his soldiers, pent up in transport ships anchored in the Thames, were dying at the rate of fifty per day."

Within a day or two of landing on Ré, Buckingham's victualler, Sir Alan Apsley, sent a plea to London for more food, but he did not worry much, because "he expected the [French] citadel to fall within a week." Mad hopes came easily. Back in London, officials proposed to use the leftover provisions from a calamitous raid into Spanish territory, the Cádiz expedition of 1625, although even then officers had bitterly complained "that the supplies were rotten and smelt worse than the leavings of a bear pit."

Aside from what they could scrounge and pillage from the islanders, no other foods reached the besiegers until September 25. And even this shipment sufficed for only another three or four weeks, despite the fact that the men in charge were meant to hold back three weeks' rations for the return voyage to England. In the meantime, with their numbers reduced by combat losses and sickness, the

English blockade of the citadel was a sieve. So that on a moonless night in late September, the French were able to beach a boatload of provisions for the citadel, in addition to several thousand extra troops. The next morning, to taunt the English, they took to waving speared chickens from their high ramparts. Stunned, Buckingham refused to back away, although his striking force was now a mere four thousand troops even after other men had been added. Back in England, critics were baying for his impeachment. He had too much face to lose. And so on October 27, he ordered his men to make a final assault on the citadel. The result was a massacre. In pouring rain, they were easily thrown back by the French, for they had attacked with scaling ladders that were too short for the citadel's walls. Such was their logistical preparation. Many were killed by shot, debris, stones, and chunks of wood. Even in retreat, as they made their way to board boats for England, they had to fight off attacking soldiers. And then it so happened that on the very day of their departure from the island, November 7, a relief fleet sailed out of Plymouth, bearing a small cargo of foodstuffs for them, in addition to more soldiers, most of whom were probably impressed men.

The Ré experiment moved in the shadows of a play of characters in London and took in the worries of Sir William Russell, Filippo Burlamacchi, and Sir Sackville Crow: leading financiers. They had contacts in the food trade; they had helped to bankroll the disastrous Cádiz expedition of 1625; and they were repeatedly approached for loans to buy the emergency food supplies for Ré. But knowing that King Charles could expect no subsidies from an angry Parliament, they were afraid of losses. The king was still in debt to them for their part in the financing of the Cádiz adventure, and his limited resources had already been mortgaged for several years; hence his available income was greatly reduced. Total costs for the Ré expedition would be in the region, conservatively, of £250,000. The king's annual income—drawn from purveyance, wardship, monopolies, and other royal expedients—amounted to something like £500,000, but it had already been spent. And although majesty enabled him to borrow more than one million pounds between 1624 and 1628, he inspired little trust in bankers. Buckingham's lavishing of £10,000 on his Ré entourage was a mark of the way King Charles and his court threw money around.

Of one thing we can be certain, judging by hard English practice of the day: The soldiers who managed to return from Ré would never see the wages owed to them. Unlike Crow, Russell, and Burlamacchi, they would remain creditors of the English crown forevermore. But Buckingham got his comeuppance, an unheard-of happening in these matters: Within a year, he was assassinated by an angry young lieutenant.

THE SOFT CORE OF LOGISTICS: FOOD

Food was the soft core—the most necessary but uncertain substance—in the whole business of moving and supplying armies. For unless it was actually in the baggage train of the army on campaign, it raised constant, urgent questions: Will there be enough food in the next town, the next supply depot, the next stretch of open territory? What are the scouts finding? Will the contractors deliver the promised foods? Geoffrey Parker has shrewdly observed that "no one spoke about the number of *soldiers* on the march, only about the number of 'mouths' (*bouches* or *bocas*) to be fed." And in sieges the besieged, as we have noted, spoke of "useless mouths."

Even if baggage trains had some food, the crucial item, bread, had to be replenished every two days in warm weather, or every four days when the weather was cold. Biscuit was a fallback. Soldiers always preferred bread. And a moving army of ten thousand men, requiring some nine and a half tons of grain for bread every day, easily overwhelmed regional flour mills and baking facilities. An extra five to ten tons of wheat, hauled in daily for immediate milling and baking, was a thing to be achieved only by careful planning—or by means of theft, blows, an abrupt war tax, or a tsunami of money.

But this kind of cash was seldom around for armies. Indeed, cash itself could not summon up in a few days, or even a week or two, new mills, new baking facilities, and many tons of grain brought in from distant points. A Russian study of the nineteenth century found that if an army was to operate without food-supply depots ("magazines"), it had to keep to regions "whose population density is over 35 persons per square kilometre." This meant the most fertile parts of Europe. In 1607, despite the many towns in the Netherlands, "the Dutch army's provisioning train included 3 prefabricated windmills, 3 watermills, 26 hand mills, 25 baker's kits, and tools to build mills and handle grain."

Food shortages led to the undoing of scores of armies in early modern Europe. The royal siege of Protestant La Rochelle, in the spring of 1573, provides one of the models of such a logistical collapse.

Between January and late June of that year, the Duke of Anjou, brother to the king of France, led an army against the fully bastioned port. Starting out with a force of seven thousand men, he would finally have about eighteen thousand under his command, despite having been promised forty thousand and sixty siege guns. The two sides must have prayed for a short siege, with food at the heart of their worries. The *Rochelais* had laid in supplies of foodstuffs, but prices rose at once and stocks began to dwindle. The besiegers, instead, Anjou's men, would eat up the adjacent countryside and be forced to slash rations, while also striving—in vain—to bring in food from afar. Promised a daily supply of 30,000 loaves of bread, 10,800 *pintes* of wine (*pinte*: 0.93 liter), and 20,000 pounds of beef, they may have got some of these provisions in the first weeks of the siege. But the flow quickly thinned out, and by late March the king's soldiers were going hungry. In April hunger was imperiling their lives. May brought degrees of outright starvation. The besiegers had exhausted the foods and fodder of the La Rochelle region, but the most alarming note in May and June turned probably on this question: Was there any food at all available even for sale?

At Metz in 1552, toward the end of the failed Imperial siege of that great urban fortress, it was reported by the famous surgeon, Ambroise Paré, a participant in the events, that there was absolutely no food around to be bought. It had all been consumed, or snatched away to be hoarded.

Bloody skirmishes around La Rochelle were almost an everyday affair. Disease, death, and defection riddled the royal ranks. Ammunition for their big guns ran out even as they were met by "blistering fire from [the city's] 175 cannons of all calibers." When the siege was finally lifted in late June, the besiegers had lost more than half of their numbers, some ten thousand foot and horse. Three fourths of all the officers, noblemen mainly, were either dead or wounded. La Rochelle would burn in many a heart, Protestant and Catholic, for generations.

A few years later, on the other side of Europe, in a war between the Poles and the Russians, the former laid siege to Muscovite Pskov for five months. Neighboring populations and villages were sparse, and food for the army had to be hauled in or looted. But the hunt for edible loot required far-ranging forays, with Polish supply wagons having to be guarded by their famous light cavalry. In September 1581, early on in the siege, the Poles were already riding seventy kilometers in search of food and fodder, with the round-trip taking up to six days of travel. They were eating up the region, and by the following January, their search-and-plunder journeys could last almost a month, because teamsters and cavalry were going nearly 350 kilometers each way.

On the steppes of southern Russia, also sparsely populated, the light cavalry of the Crimean Tatars turned to an additional resource. They took along extra horses on campaign, to be used as food if the need arose. And Muscovy—we are still in the sixteenth century— was already posting granaries for its armies.

In the late sixteenth century, the Spanish army's marching route to Flanders took it from Milan to Savoy, over the Alpine passes, and then through Franche-Comté, Lorraine, Luxembourg, and into the Netherlands. Drawing on a practice begun by the French in the early 1550s, the Spanish used a system of *étapes*: stopping-off points at small towns and villages, where food was distributed to the soldiers. The "Spanish Road" was a known and regular route, not normally subject to the tricky fortunes of war. Now and then, however, soldiers had to pay for the available food, and if they were short of money or had not been paid, they went hungry. Trouble for these troops really began once they reached the Low Countries, where wage money soon ran out and they had to move about in wartime.

Arrangements for supplies along the Spanish Road were handled by officials who communicated needs to merchants at the *étapes*. There was thus a role for private contractors or supply wholesalers (*munitionnaires*). In the seventeenth century, the French often had recourse to them. Supply officials (*commissaires*) would hire private contractors and arrange for them to get foodstuffs to army units, or to set up and stock grain magazines. If harvests had been adequate, the delivery of food in peacetime was not likely to pose difficult problems. Contractors might even be expected to advance food on credit. In Louis XIV's reign, companies of food suppliers spread the risks among associates. But when the crown delayed or failed to make payment—a chronic malaise under Richelieu in the 1630s and early 1640s—disaster could easily follow: no food deliveries. Now responsibility would be disavowed by the contractors, a scenario most likely in wartime, with its unexpected turns.

ARMIES WERE NOT USUALLY DEFEATED by a lack of weapons, courage, or even by loss on the battlefield. They were stopped or destroyed by disease and hunger; and while disease was not a matter for logistics in the science of the day, food always was.

British soldiers, we have seen, feared and hated being sent to Ireland, because soldiering there was very likely to end in death from sickness or starvation. An army might land there with provisions, but these would be rapidly exhausted. In one week of 1643, the Marquis of Ormond's royalist forces in Leinster, numbering four to seven thousand foot and horse, consumed "49,248 pounds of butter, 49,649 pounds of cheese, 447 barrels of wheat and rye, 367 barrels of peas and 356 barrels of oats." The local economy could simply not go on replenishing these quantities, all the less so when military operations ravaged fields and farms. A few years later, in 1648, the Earl of Inchiquin moaned that "divers of my men have dyed of hunger after they lived a while upon catts and dogs."

Hunger and small crop yields were more than chronic in early modern Europe; they were characteristic of the age, of the Continent's subsistence economies. Degrees of hunger, more or less continually, were the lot of 15 to 20 percent of populations, depending upon weather conditions, crop yields, prices, and hoarding. In wartime, however, in the stricken areas, that figure could leap to a figure of 60 percent or more of local populations. Soldiers thus were always concerned about what lay ahead for them in the way of victuals. Bread was crucial: In Geoffrey Parker's words, one and a half pounds "of bread each day was considered the minimum ration without which no soldier could survive." But this ration alone meant slow starvation for a soldier, unless he was also getting other foods. When in the field, walking for six to eight hours daily with a moderate load, a soldier required an intake of 3,400 to 3,600 calories per day. The one and a half pounds of bread provided only about 1,875 calories. Any failure to get the rest made for a gnawing hunger. There were moments in the Thirty Years War when hungry troops, bursting into a village in search of something to eat and finding not a scrap, would seem to go berserk, as they howled with rage and started bonfires, burning some of the houses.

WAGONS AND HORSES

In 1522, the king of England, Henry VIII, allied to the Emperor Charles V, shipped ten thousand soldiers to Calais. Arriving there on August 20, they marched inland, bearing a short-term load of supplies, and reached Doullens, about seventy miles from Calais.

There food supplies ran out. Calais and St. Omer had "a glut of vict-uals," but officials could not get these to the war front because of a desperate shortage of horses and carts. By early October, with deser-tion rife and many soldiers ill, Henry's army began its retreat, return-ing to Calais in ignominy on October 15.

More remarkable still is the fact that an almost identical sequence of events unfolded a year later. Another ten thousand British troops, landing at Calais in late August and sent on to besiege Boulogne, soon found themselves short of food and even ammunition, owing again to transportation and supply-cart failures. The outcome, in mid-November, was another retreat to Calais.

In operations against the Scots, along the northern borders of the kingdom, the English were often plagued by a scarcity of carts, and there too soldiers went hungry. Logistical lessons, it seems, were hard to learn.

The necessity of animals, carts, and wagons keeps us fixed to the core substance of logistics. In providing transport, they provided food. Without wheeled vehicles and pack animals there could be no food, unless it came by water, or unless it was bought or stolen or otherwise grabbed in situ, together with vehicles, if these were lacking.

Food and fodder apart, horses always topped the list of essential plunder for armies; and if there was much hunger, livestock came next. But no needy army would have rejected good carts or wagons: treasure for their baggage train. In 1581–1582, when German troops in Spain, mercenaries of the king, passed through the town of Ante-quera, near Jerez de la Frontera, they rustled 350 oxen and simply stole 150 wagons for their baggage trains. Later they returned eighty-five oxen, but not the wagons.

Flexible rules seem to have called for given numbers of carts or wagons per quotas of men and horses. In the middle of the French Wars of Religion, a Huguenot contract wanted one wagon for every four to six horses. Landsknechts sought to have one wagon for every ten men. In the early seventeenth century, an army might have one wagon for every fifteen men, with two to four horses per wagon. The twenty-four thousand men of Maurice of Nassau's campaign of 1602 marched with a train of three thousand wagons: one wagon for every eight men. Four years later, again in the Netherlands, Ambrogio Spinola's army of fifteen thousand soldiers had 2,000 to 2,500 wagons: an average of 6 to 7.5 men per wagon. In 1629, an army of eleven thousand Spaniards and Italians required 673 pack mules, for an average of one for every sixteen or seventeen men. Cart and animal numbers depended in part on the quantities of supplies to be carried.

From time to time, army officials arranged for carters to deliver wagons to soldiers on the move: for example, along the Spanish Road and in Savoy and Lorraine. But most carriage over the Alpine passes was by pack mules. And occasionally the *étapes* were pressed into lending some of these for use in transport over short distances, only to find, in the end, that as many as two thirds of the beasts came back injured or had perished, owing to their having been misused.

THE NUMBERS OF CARTS AND wagons in the train of an army tell us nothing—here the sources tend to go mute—about how exactly they were used: how many for the officers, for the rank and file, for camp followers, for bread and other foods, for fodder, and for hauling weapons, ammunition, tents, and all the paraphernalia of an army on campaign. A well-equipped field force was likely to carry portable ovens and querns (hand mills for grinding wheat, rye, and other grains). Splendor, too, and the insignia of social class, found their way into the train. The gear of grandee officers—boots, dress, hats, plumes, and other finery—sometimes displaced artillery. In the 1620s and 1630s, although much stronger than the Dutch army, the Army of Flanders often moved with fewer siege and field guns because officers—notes an expert—"used the artillery train to haul their personal baggage." The ground of war, where a nobleman was meant to show his mettle, was also the very place for him to display the trappings of his identity. Vanity made finery more important than guns.

Lest we forget, the looting of towns and villages imposed an additional need. Carts and wagons were de rigueur for booty. Otherwise, how haul the stuff away? In 1512, in their sack of Brescia, one of the great laments of the French soldiers was that they had made such a race for the city that there was simply no time for them, when starting out, to get their hands on the needed carts.

In reflecting on ambulant cities, the most intriguing student of seventeenth-century logistics, Géza Perjés, imagined an army of forty thousand foot soldiers and twenty thousand horsemen. To these he added twenty thousand horses (draft animals) for the baggage train, plus ninety thousand rations of bread, which included the extra rations for the additional needs of the officers and all the auxiliaries connected with the train—teamsters, smiths, craftsmen, pioneers, and so on. His purely rational calculations resulted in a startling impossibility. An army of that magnitude, with more than eleven thousand wagons, supplies intact, and a modicum of space between the wagons, would stretch for 198 kilometers. Even moving at top speed, about twenty-five kilometers per day, the head and the tail of the column would have been separated by eight marching days.

The point of Perjés's exercise was to fix the numerical limits of early modern armies, limits laid down by logistics. He observed that experts of the period—Montecuccoli, Turenne—put the limits at fifty thousand men. Recent studies have shown that an army of this size could only cohere for a few days, unless it was continually supplied by magazines or by the regular delivery of foods and fodder. This, however, was an impossibility for the administrative resources of states in early modern Europe. And any effort on the part of the fifty thousand to live off the surrounding lands would have spread them out widely, over many miles, as they moved about to ward off hunger. An army limit of twenty-five to thirty-five thousand men was more realistic. And even these numbers, campaigning in the most fertile parts of Europe—France, the Po Valley, and the Rhineland—would have been forced to keep roving as they exhausted local reserves and left stripped lands behind.

Large armies, then, when in the field, were bound to have hungry soldiers. The conditions of early modern Europe imposed this. This is why they seem to have averaged, when marching, some twenty kilometers per day, whereas the marching average of modern armies is in the region of thirty-five to forty kilometers.

IN THE LATE FIFTEENTH CENTURY, war horses in Italy were scarce. Good ones sold for not less than thirty gold ducats, and the best went for eighty to ninety ducats, or the wages, over a period of nearly two years, of a master craftsman in the Venetian shipyards. The sale of horses in Milan, or at the spring fairs of Como, Chiasso, and other points in Lombardy, attracted traders from all over northern Italy, as well as from Germany and Switzerland. Yet shortages of the right horses continued, partly at least because hungry soldiers frequently sold or pawned their mounts.

In northern Europe, the seventeenth century saw the price of combat horses reach new peaks. The Army of Flanders, in the 1640s, was importing thousands of horses from as far away as Sardinia, Naples, and especially Poland. Spain itself had few horses to spare because so many were being used up or killed in a hugely popular entertainment, bullfighting. The historian R. A. Stradling informs us that a fine cavalry horse in the Netherlands, in 1646, was worth more than twice the value "of a black galley slave and twelve times that of an Irish infantryman"—which tells us something about the wages of Irish soldiers on the Continent.

We must assume, accordingly, that cavalry officers looked after their horses with the best of care. But even nags required attention. The Veterinary Department of the British Army issued a report in 1908, concluding that "the transport animals of an army shall be regarded as worth their weight in gold," and hence "no care or supervision can be too great or too strict." These claims would have made good sense to Polish, Russian, and Tatar cavalrymen of the sixteenth and seventeenth centuries. And yet the wretched condition of armies in western Europe, particularly in wartime, rendered the proper treatment of horses all but impossible.

In circumstances of near famine, at the height of the Thirty Years War, in a scene that must have had its like countless times, villagers in southwestern Germany looked on as a Croatian soldier, raging over his horse's refusal to move, kept hammering its head. The horse collapsed and died, whereupon the stunned and hungry villagers proceeded to eat it. Had it been overworked, or was it simply starving?

In the course of a day, a horse may safely carry a load of one fifth its weight and only go so far, while also requiring twenty to twenty-four pounds of feed, or even thirty and more pounds, if it is doing hard work. Moreover, as one logistics historian has noted, half of its feed "should be grain and the other half fodder," that is, straw or hay. But once a horse has been "worn out by several days of excessive work and inadequate rations," it becomes "unfit for further use," and in wartime it may as well be killed, for the full recovery of the animal would require good nourishment and four to five months of rest.

Is it any wonder, then, that horses were the first targets of plundering soldiers, once they had stolen food supplies? And that oats, hay, and grass were next? Sold off illegally "by unpaid cavalry soldiers," horses also "died in large numbers during long campaigns and severe winters." Worse still: Since their abuse and undernourishment was common, theft of the animals was the only way to replace the dying ones. But this expedient had an immediate echoing impact on local communities, for it often brought farm work to a halt, such as in delayed plowing or the transport of goods; and in hilly country, carting could turn into a curse. Now peasants as well as soldiers would go hungry.

The 1645 spring campaign of the Swedish general Lennart Torstensson highlighted the importance of keeping horses well nourished. Moving his army of sixteen thousand men against Vienna, the Imperial capital, in late March of that year, he was unable to assault it, in spite of being only a day's march from the city, in part at least because—as the battle expert William Guthrie tells us—"the lack of forage in the late winter had weakened his cavalry," with the result that "the horses sickened and many died."

Armies of twenty-five to thirty thousand men were not unusual in the French Wars of Religion and the Thirty Years War. Their daily access to flour or bread was crucial, but so too was the accessing of fodder for the cavalry regiments, about one third of army numbers. Such a large force often moved—if we include pack animals—with no fewer than twenty thousand horses. John Lynn and others have shown that it was out of the question for that force to carry its own fodder: about five hundred tons per day. Horses had to live off the land, and this required foraging parties that might easily number thousands of men, riding out in widening circles, with a view to laying hands on dry fodder and/or green forage. Necessity drove armies from place to place, and nevertheless many of their horses inevitably died of exhaustion and hunger. In their 1568–1569 campaign against the Huguenots, taking in a swath of France that stretched from Saumur to Limoges and beyond, "the 30,000 men and . . . 15,000 animals" of the royal army moved continually, because they kept eating up local food and fodder within days.

The same logistical limits applied to the large armies of the Thirty Years War. This fact throws light on their apparent rambles, as they sought out river valleys and fertile regions in their hunt for victuals and fodder. The Swedish armies of the 1630s and 1640s, under Banér, Torstensson, and Wrangel, were mammoth search-and-eat engines.

War horses were walked, not ridden, except in combat, in order to preserve them in health. So of all army horses, those of the elite cavalry units were the best cared for, the ones most likely to get their forage rations. Action in battle to one side, work horses, the pullers of guns and wagons, perished first.

WAGON TRAINS AND CAMP FOLLOWERS

In 1615, a German observer noted that "when you recruit a regiment of German soldiers today, you do not only acquire 3,000 soldiers; along with these you will certainly find 4,000 women and children."

The remark singled out a general feature of European armies. Wives, other women, and children, trailing behind columns of soldiers, stood out in wartime landscapes. But varieties of servants, the lackeys of officers, and other helpers also traveled with armies. At the end of the fifteenth century, Charles VIII, the king of France, declared "that he fed 48,000 to 50,000 mouths a day to maintain an army of 20,000 combatants in the field." Female companions of the soldiers were not necessarily their wives. Widows, concubines, and prostitutes were also part of the scene behind the winding columns of soldiers. In 1544, in the wake of King Henry VIII's invasion of France, large numbers of women crossed the Channel to join his forces.

Whether or not the tail of camp followers was longer than the beast itself, no one can say in the absence of sustained studies. In the Low Countries and in Germany, during the Thirty Years War, soldiers were sometimes outnumbered by their camp followers, but this was not generally the case. Geoffrey Parker's study of the Army of Flanders reveals that the tail might number anywhere from 8 to 53 percent of a combat unit. For the Thirty Years War, the best-informed recent view sees a camp-follower ratio that often attained parity: one noncombatant for every soldier.

Apart from women, children, and officers' lackeys, camp followers also included varieties of artisans, such as carpenters, wheelwrights, and smiths, in addition to sutlers (vendors of food and drink), pawnbrokers, medical quacks, old veterans, and all sorts of other hangers-on. Here was the society of the early modern army, a community. But this itinerant city, with all its afflictions, could not have gone on for as long as it did without the solace, comforts, and family ways provided by women. And rulers put up with it because they could not raise large armies, or hold them together, without a tail of camp followers. In this sense, government itself had given rise to that alien society, so wholly divorced from the ways of the everyday world of city, town, and country. Despised and universally feared, the "aliens" were seen as a godless and immoral rabble, and they were feared because they supposedly included thieves, thugs, whores, and killers, and carried infectious diseases.

After 1660, rulers and armies brought in stricter regulations against camp-following wives, as well as harsh laws against prostitutes, including—as the threatened penalties—the branding of the face or the slitting of the nose and ears. But camp following, though waning, passed into the eighteenth century, and garrisons had to make arrangements for the presence of wives and children.

If the women who traveled with officers rode in wagons, this was not true of most female camp followers, whose men were too poor to own a horse, unless plunder in wartime brought one into their hands. Need, however, would soon force the lucky man to sell it, as attested to in the diary of Peter Hagendorf, a soldier who lived through the Thirty Years War. Most women in the train of followers walked, loaded down with clothing, pots, and sacks of other things, while being sometimes accompanied by, or lugging, a child or two. Unless billeted with civilians, they slept in tents, flimsy little huts, or in the open; and so they had to be strong, or too soon they would die of exhaustion, illness, or in childbirth. In the course of Hagendorf's years of rambling with different armies (1624–1649), taking him over the face of Germany and beyond its borders, death claimed his first wife and seven children. When, instead, such a woman lost a husband or a partner to combat or disease, she was instantly cast into destitution, particularly if she had children. Now what? She would have to scheme to pick up extra work around the wagon train and perhaps beg, steal, and whore, or even find herself driven away. But to go where? Back home might be a possibility. Little boys, if she had any, the sons of soldiers, aspired to be taken on as officers' lackeys. Others became petty thieves. Aging widows and old soldiers clung to the wagon train because they knew no better world, or had nowhere else to go.

The sexual partnerships of camp women were dearly paid for by the women. They toiled away at washing, sewing, cooking, hauling, scurrying for food, cutting deals with petty vendors, handling booty, working with forage parties, grinding grain with hand mills, and digging trenches. They did just about everything except fire weapons and wield pikes, though there were cases of this too: soldiers, dead on the battlefield, who turned out to be women. "The bishop of Albi, administering the last rites to the dying at Leucate in 1637, came across several women in uniform who had been cut down."

And here was yet another of their services, one of the most important: The chronic shortage of field surgeons, who were paid little more than skilled craftsmen, put women into the front line of caring for the sick and bandaging the wounds of soldiers.

We can now see why women were at the heart of the wagon-train world. Many others there, such as wheelwrights and smiths, were also necessary; but women and children provided the air, the sights and sounds, that smacked of home. Historians have found, unsurprisingly, that in the course of the Thirty Years War, with its pitiless ways, civilians in the wagon trains more than doubled in numbers. If the dispossessed followed the exterminating soldier, the soldier in return looked for the moral propping up that could only be provided by women and children, as is clearly evident in Peter Hagendorf's wartime diary.

A KEY FIGURE IN THE world of the wagon train must not escape our notice: the sutler, a retailer of food, drink, tobacco, and other things as well, such as clothing, leather goods, and secondhand shoes. Peter Burschel has asserted that an army without sutlers was a poor army, an unpaid army, a hungry army, and—one might add—a wretched and dying army.

No army on campaign could do without the sale of such provisions. The well-off sutlers had their own wagons, but any one of them, poor or prosperous, could choose to leave an army and pass to another wagon train. Occasionally suspected of being spies, most sutlers seem to have been petty vendors of food, beer, and brandy. Women were prominent in the trade and, like the men, criers of their goods for sale in the early morning. Written around 1670, the novel by Grimmelshausen, *Courage, the Adventuress*—Bertolt Brecht's source for *Mother Courage*—is the portrait of such a woman. Although shot through with touches of exaggeration and fancy, the main lineaments of the character—if seen in the context of the Thirty Years War—come through with the morals of the age: abusive, extreme, cynical, and earthy. Forced to live by her wits, defiance, charms, spoils, and sexual availability, Courage—the name of her vagina too—has no choice but to be gutsy and ambitious. Yet she ends, of course, in disease and ugliness, like the war itself.

That most sutlers were petty traders is disclosed by the fact that large armies went into the field with hundreds of them in their coursing columns of wagons. An army of fourteen thousand men, say, in the middle of the Thirty Years War, might include 220 sutlers: an average of one for every sixty-four men, not counting camp followers. Regulations for the Spanish army limited sutlers to three per company. But a company never numbered more than three hundred men, and that number more often fell to about one hundred or less. In her most destitute time as a sutler, Courage was reduced to walking and hawking only brandy and tobacco. These she hauled around in a sack borne on her shoulders. In better times, she had a mule or a donkey, and in her prime she owned at least one wagon, like other well-off sutlers. These were the traders, the richer ones, who must at times have cast anxiety into the poor civilian populations. For they were the vanguard of an approaching army, the ones who rushed into the urban centers to buy up as much food as possible, quickly driving up the prices of meat, cheese, and other foods.

There were some traders who had little or no interest in the petty retailing of food: the merchants, pawnbrokers, and moneylenders who trafficked in almost everything from stolen church bells to costly tapestries, herds of horses and cattle, luxury cloth, and jewelry. The canniest of them were likely to have more than a smattering of two or three languages—French, Spanish, and German chiefly, although a Slavic language would have gone far in parts of Germany. They were certain to have bagged a place in the trains of armies that were about to sack a city or a rich town. The expected booty could then be turned into enormous profits. So there they would be, paying out cash, buying up loot for relative pittances, and then carting it off to other towns to sell at prices closer to real market values. Soldiers wanted cash—cash to buy food and drink, clothing and shoes, and to put up front on the gambling table. They could not lug heavy items around when on the move, unless they had a horse or space in one of the wagons. The rich sutler as pawnbroker was only too happy to serve them.

Soldiers were often in debt to sutlers, a form of bondage that was all but inevitable in view of their poverty and reliance on credit. But one way or another, they would have to pay that debt, because sutlers were well protected both by officers and army regulations. That they were frequently insulted by their debtors is not surprising, particularly if they were Jews. But it was a serious crime for soldiers to assault sutlers. The rich ones were certain to have contacts in army headquarters. After all, in wartime and in their trade, it was their business to know all about the art of bribery. It almost goes without saying, therefore, that pawnbroking sutlers were hated by the common soldier. When caught up in the chaos and violence of battle, they were among the first to be robbed or killed. The rich and clever sutler toiled to be on the winning side.

Over the course of the sixteenth and seventeenth centuries, the moneylending sutler was the key personage in the sale of a cascade of looted wealth, ranging from the carts and livestock of poor peasants to the glitter of crown jewels, libraries, and famous picture collections.

But merchants from neighboring cities usually skimmed off the most valuable lots of booty.

BILLETING

In a letter of 1637 to the Emperor Ferdinand III, the Duke of Bavaria, Maximilian, complained of the Imperialist soldiers in his duchy. When seeking quarters in midwinter, they took over the huts of dirt-poor peasants, pushing them and their families out into "the snow and woods . . . to die and rot of frost and hunger." He wanted the emperor "to call a swift stop to the apportioning of winter quarters" while yet admitting that the soldiers were themselves outright "paupers, stripped bare, exhausted, starved and in such a condition that it is easy to commiserate with them."

In 1594, in the face of unpaid, rebellious, and hungry soldiers, the commander of Spanish forces in Friesland (the far north of the Netherlands), Colonel Francisco Verdugo, could not keep officers from quartering several cavalry companies on people so poor that they had to "go out and beg for their own children and for the soldiers," including even the soldiers' lackeys. The sight, Verdugo added, would have aroused pity in the cruelest of men, and yet the soldiers went on mistreating their wretched victims.

THE PRACTICE OF QUARTERING SOLDIERS on civilians—the most neglected topic in the history of war—was universal in early modern Europe. It normally called for the targeted household to provide a bed or beds, kitchen facilities, firewood, salt, vinegar, candles, and other items. In peacetime, on paper at any rate, this was all regulated, and civilians were meant to be reimbursed for their expenses, or to have these deducted from their taxes. In reality, reimbursement or satisfaction was likely to fall short even in peacetime; and anyway, who could guarantee the honesty, health, or humanity of soldiers?

But there was worse: war, which could easily turn the palpable strains of billeting into brutal episodes. Princes ran out of money; soldiers went unpaid and hungry, and the rules of billeting fell away. Now the unwanted strangers also wanted bread, meat, wine or beer, more beds, more firewood, more of everything. And resistance brought blows, wounds, and even murder.

The drama of the miserable soldier in wartime, joining or pushing poor folk out of their hovels in the winter, was to recur in scenes without end; and the poor went from hunger to starvation. But victims were not always cowed. The quartering of soldiers on civilians, as we shall see, could be so oppressive as to generate revolts and skirmishes.

"Contributions" could be as bad as billeting or worse. Citing the requisitions of the Swedish officer Georg Mittelstedt, in western Pomerania, in 1637, one historian has noted that a group of villages were ordered to provide the following daily rations: five casks of beer, two hundred pounds of bread, sixty bushels of oats, four wagon loads of "good" hay, "a variety of spices for me and my officers," a quart of butter, half a bushel of salt, thirty candles, and also "for the kitchen of the cavalry captain and other officers, 2 sheep, 12 chickens, 6 geese, and 30 eggs." If the villages failed to deliver these items on a daily basis, horsemen, they were told, would go out and collect them.

In November 1494, as noted earlier, the entry of a French army into Florence confronted the Florentine Republic with the fearful problem of having to lodge about ten thousand men. Distributed among hundreds of households, for ten days the soldiers would live and sleep in Europe's most famous Renaissance city. Although Florence and the king of France were allies, Florentines were pitched into a fervor of anxiety, in the fear that at any moment the entire operation could capsize into a bloodbath. They knew that troops could not be trusted in wartime.

Soldiers often came upon households exempted from billeting. In France particularly, entire towns and villages enjoyed this privilege, thanks either to having paid out protection money or because an influential nobleman, or an official with good contacts, had cast his protective mantle over the area. The same was true of individuals with the right connections: They bought or solicited the immunities in question. But in addition, whole classes of individuals were ordinarily exempt from billeting: noblemen, clergy, town councillors, tax collectors, and holders of royal office. Exemptions of this sort were common, running right across the face of Europe.

In October 1678, the French town of Vervien, with a population of about sixty-five hundred souls, had to offer quarters for a short period to as many French soldiers. An average of four persons per family—to take a reasonable figure—meant that the town had about 1,625 households. If the soldiers were equitably distributed, then each of the different households took in four soldiers. However, since some of the leading townspeople would have claimed immunities from billeting, many houses were forced to take in five, six, or more soldiers. The bottom line was that the poor and the modest paid beyond their means, for even if soldiers, as was the custom, slept two and three to a bed, in wartime their bullying demands multiplied.

We need not add that officers got the best accommodations. The social pyramid was, if anything, more entrenched in Europe's armies than in the civilian world. Whenever possible, officers slept in towns, while soldiers—to spare the influential burghers—were lodged in the villages. In upper Italy, around 1500, troops were nearly always quartered in the countryside, rarely in the cities.

In the practice of billeting, civilians carried the armies of Europe on their backs. A Russian saying held that "soldiers were hung around the neck of the peasant." Billeting went on into the eighteenth century, until after the building of barracks began to be more vigorously pursued in France, Germany, Spain, and the Low Countries. Yet in the seventeenth century, whenever possible, villages and market towns more often bared their teeth and resisted the demands of soldiers. In parts of wartime Germany, country people banded together, in cross-village alliances, and sought to kill their oppressors. The consequences could be dire. In the 1620s and 1630s, mass peasant revolts were savagely put down in different parts of Germany and Austria.

France, in the southwest, in the Périgueux and Begerac areas, was the ground of at least forty different revolts against mounted companies of billet-seeking French soldiers. Well organized, the revolts relied on lookout points, warning bells, fortified churches, militias, peasants armed with muskets, occasionally the sound of drums, and even the cooperation of local officials. Revolt, in short, could lead to outright battles, as armed peasants attacked soldiers at town gates or ambushed them in the countryside, on their approach to the host village. In August 1636, the Périgueux town militia (five hundred men) drove a cavalry unit out of a market town that lay within Périgueux's jurisdiction. At Dorat, in the Marche region, in August 1639, the villagers beat back a company of horsemen, "peppering them" with shot from arquebuses. At "Abjat in May 1640, at Grandignan in May 1649 and at Cheronnac in August 1649," villagers rebuffed cavalry units by relying on their fortified churches. Indeed, in the 1640s, for at least five years, the little town of Abjat, in the Grange-sur-Lot area, held out by armed means against arriving companies of the king's cavalry.

The historian of these events, Yves-Marie Bercé, summed up his take on peasant revolts against soldiers by contrasting the work ideals of rural communities with the nomadic, aggressive, idle, and live-for-today life of the soldier.

DYING ARMIES

In 1660, the town of Sancoins, in the Bourbonnais, refused entry to three thousand troops, claiming, it seems, an exemption from billeting. Using "treachery to break into the town," in John Lynn's account, the soldiers then did "as they pleased, raping, pillaging, and robbing." They stole horses and even forced women to pay for the babies that had been snatched away from them. More common by far than this atrocity was the intimate outrage of raping women in public, in the streets of little towns and villages.

And yet for all their flashing of brute muscle, the wartime armies of early modern Europe were fragile. They could be destroyed by disease or famine. Their raw power in the villages was not a specter; it was only too real. But their explosive violence was the mark of their frailty. Soldiers robbed and tormented the innocent because so often they themselves verged on being exterminated not in combat but by their own feeble health. In the middle decades of the seventeenth century, the mortality rate in French armies, even in peacetime, could attain a yearly average of 25 percent, while, for the entire century, European armies in general seem to have been ravaged at the rate of about 20 to 25 percent per year. By contrast, the annual death rates for civilian populations were in the range of 3 to 4 percent, or even very much lower among young men between the ages of seventeen and twenty-six.

The theme of dying armies, yoked to the poor populations whose hard destinies they shared, runs through this book like a refrain. Often trapped in freezing weather and, like their horses, undernourished or teeming with lice in the summer heat, soldiers were a ready target for epidemic diseases. These circumstances suggest that the dying of a large army could be dramatic, especially when it occurred over the space of two or three weeks. We came on such a case in the first chapter, with the army of the French general Lautrec, as it laid siege to Naples in the summer of 1528. Suddenly typhus raced through the ranks of the besiegers, killing them right and left, and in August, in about three weeks, they were transformed into the besieged. The trapped Italian and Spanish soldiers, who were themselves drinking "vile" water and eating "stinking" bread, now came out of Naples to encircle, kill, and scatter the survivors of a once proud army.

There was yet another way in which armies died, more meta-phorical but leading just as surely to their undoing: by desertion. Soldiers might desert quickly, even en masse, or in lesser numbers, their flight eating steadily away at the large body of men until it disintegrated as a fighting unit. The causes of desertion were always the same: lack of pay, hunger, disease, abuse by officers, no hope of a leave, or stubborn resistance to having been grabbed by a press-gang. Briefly, in late August 1632, Gustavus Adolphus brought to-gether at Nuremberg an army of forty-five thousand men. Within three weeks, about eleven thousand deserted.

The history of war reveals that European armies were never more wracked by desertion and mutinies than those of early modern Eu-rope. Spain's Army of Flanders led the way, having the most trou-bled record, with forty-five mutinies between 1570 and 1606. But the large Swedish and Imperial forces of the Thirty Years War came next, and the royal armies of the French Wars of Religion lagged not far behind, as they crumbled, unpaid and miserable, halfway through campaigns.

IN 1552, THE EMPEROR CHARLES V had just over fifty thousand troops at the siege of heavily fortified Metz, an Imperial free city recently seized by the French. In two months, November and December, this army imploded. Half of it was wiped out by "desertion, disease, and disablement." Scurvy, dysentery, and typhus especially were the main killers. The siege was raised in January. All told, disease had eliminated about ten thousand men. Defection and physical impairment—wounds and loss of limbs—took another fifteen thou-sand. At one point, two hundred were dying every day.

King Louis XIII began his long campaign against the remaining colonies of French Protestants in the late summer of 1620. His army started with an attack, in the southwest, on the Protestant city of Montauban, which was under the control of the dukes of Rohan. Before the end of September, after only six weeks, that "army had been reduced by disease and defection to a quarter of its original size." But commanders hung on until the third week of November, when the siege was finally abandoned.

Before we look at the spectrum of diseases that waylaid armies, the larger scene calls for more fixing.

Numbering about sixty thousand men in the early spring of 1576, the Army of Flanders, under Don John of Austria, could muster only eleven thousand men eight months later, "and they were isolated in a few strong points such as Antwerp and Maastricht." Defection and death had eliminated the rest. If conditions ever got much better for Spain's troops in the Low Countries, rounding up the proof would not be easy. The troubles were best seen at the company level, the smallest unit. Thus "the Walloon company of Captain Pierre de Nervèse began life with eight officers and 134 men in August 1629." Ten months later, "only seven officers and thirty-six men appeared at the muster—a loss of 70 per cent."

In July 1586, writing from the Netherlands, the Earl of Leicester confessed to the privy councillor, Sir Francis Walsingham, "that 500 men had deserted in the space of two days, including 'a great many to the enemy.'" Later, two hundred of the deserters were captured on the Dutch coast, trying apparently to get back to Britain, "and 'diverse' were hanged as an example." The undermining of Leicester's army was not the work of disease but of desertion, of impressed men running away, and of hunger, the best explanation for defection to the enemy ranks.

Spain's Army of Flanders always included large numbers of Italian soldiers, and their misfortunes were likely to match those in the Spanish regiments. "In 1587 some 9,000 Italian infantry marched to Flanders, but a year later there were only 3,600 left, the others having died or deserted." If disease constituted the biggest mortal threat, acute discontent also had its part in the collapse of armies, as in the mutinies of six Italian companies in 1584 and 1596. Garrisoned in Aerschot, they had not been paid for six or seven years.

Ireland in 1600 was the ground of a collapse connected strictly with disease. In that year, four thousand recruits arrived from England to man the Derry garrisons. A year later, only fifteen hundred remained, the rest having succumbed to dysentery and typhus.

The crowded garrisons of early modern Europe, sleeping two or three soldiers to a bed, were nurseries of disease, no less so than armies on campaign. In the Thirty Years War, many more of Sweden's conscripted youth would be killed by bacilli in garrisons than by weapons in combat. But out in the field, a diseased army could implode in wholesale disaster.

Gearing up for action in and around Nuremberg in June and July 1632, Gustavus Adolphus and Wallenstein maneuvered for a decisive engagement, while also seeking the advantage in numbers and position. Disease and desertion, however, spiked by the August heat, were undoing their armies. Commenting on Wallenstein's forces, one of the leading historians of the Thirty Years War, Peter Wilson, notes that "the concentration of 55,000 troops and around 50,000 camp followers produced at least four tonnes of human excrement daily . . . [in addition to] the waste from the 45,000 cavalry and baggage horses. The camp was swarming with rats and flies, spreading disease." But the regiments of the king of Sweden were no better off. His army of many thousands was holed up in Nuremberg, along with the city's forty thousand inhabitants and one hundred thousand refugees, all of them prey to disease and hunger. If we reflect for a moment on their access to clean drinking water, the imagination quails at any attempt to grasp at the unsanitary conditions of that mass of humanity. A minor battle nearby, at Alte Veste, on September 3–4, was won by Wallenstein, but had no marked importance, apart from exposing the myth of the king's invincibility. By the time Gustavus broke out of Nuremberg on September 15, he had lost "at least 29,000 people" to disease and famine, and meanwhile, in the space of two weeks, another eleven thousand deserted.

The two armies now drew away: Wallenstein's too sick to give chase, the king's beating a woozy retreat, despite having been newly supplied with reinforcements. Two months later, at the great battle of Lützen (November 16), which ended in a draw, Gustavus Adolphus met his death and Wallenstein would never be quite right again, in going on to all but court his own assassination. But the numbers of men who fought on that cold November day were vastly diminished: Wallenstein, at the start of the battle, had just over twelve thousand men, and Gustavus about eighteen thousand.

Some three decades later, in the space of five months (by early August 1664), the Emperor Leopold's army, raised to fight the Ottomans and originally numbering fifty-one thousand troops, was found to have lost more than half that number to disease, desertion, and the need "to garrison border fortresses." That army went on disintegrating.

THE GREAT CONTAGIOUS MALADIES OF the day were plague, typhus, and varieties of typhoid and dysenteric fevers. Contemporaries were of course inexact about their ways of referring to disease. When there was widespread pestilence, they frequently used the blanket word "plague." But other terms, such as for typhus, were "war-plague," "soldier's disease," "camp fever," "head disease," and "Hungarian fever."

By tracking the movement of armies and infectious diseases, study has shown that soldiers were the foremost transmitters of deadly bacteria: of plague first of all, and then of the different mortal fevers. In Germany, the plague epidemic of 1632–1637 "began in the south with Bavaria, Württemberg, the Rhine Palatinate, and the lower Rhineland . . . along with areas of Saxony and Silesia bordering on Bohemia." Later, the disease moved northeastward, down "the Elbe into Brandenburg," and then east again to the Oder River and Pomerania. The path of the disease was "broadly similar to the main military movements of those years."

Plague—bubonic plague, a rodent-borne disease—required the presence of the rat that carried the infected flea, and rats moved slowly. But men carried the flea—in their clothing, bedding, and baggage—over long distances, so the causes of the moving path of the disease can be readily pinned down.

Soldiers on campaign were bound to be riddled with lice and fleas, owing to their cramped and filthy living conditions, particularly as they bedded down for the night. When Simplicius, the soldier-hero of Grimmelshausen's novel about the Thirty Years War, says that being infested with lice was "like sitting in an ant heap," the exaggeration seems to carry a hard core of truth and experience. The louse and flea were the raw carriers of the plague and typhus bacteria. Typhoid and the varieties of dysenteric fevers were caused, instead, by the ingestion of food or water contaminated by the feces of human carriers of the disease. In the stinking encampments, with their entourages of camp followers, the regulations that prescribed degrees of cleanliness fell on deaf ears. Fecal matter slipped easily into the drinking water and food chain.

Typhoid fever had mortality rates of up to 25 percent. Plague was more than twice as deadly, particularly when its bacillus entered the lungs or bloodstream. Death rates now shot up to between 50 and 70 percent of all those infected. Many soldiers seem to have developed immunities to the whole range of infectious maladies. The diarist Peter Hagendorf, who lived right through the Thirty Years War, was one of these. And Hans Heberle, the shoemaker, must rank as a classic example of the civilian who survives waves of contagion, while all around him people die of plague, typhus, and relapsing fever.

IN THE CALCULATIONS OF CONTEMPORARIES, the numbers of conscripted and mercenary soldiers who were killed in battle or by disease were habitually a matter of guesswork or politics. Once the death of leading noblemen and officers had been noted, the task of getting at the true numbers of casualties turned into a matter of hit and miss, the natural result of princely and elite attitudes toward the common soldier. But conflicting reports of casualties, with their

great disparities, could also be motivated by politics, as in their concealing of losses in defeat or even in victory.

One of the most detailed studies of combat losses, focused on
three major battles of the Italian Wars (1494–1559), concludes that
politics, lies, and wishful thinking were responsible for the sharp
differences in casualty estimates. Figures for the dead at the battle of
Agnadello (1509) varied from six thousand to twenty thousand men;
at Ravenna (1512) from ten thousand to thirty thousand; and at Marignano (1515) from eighteen thousand to thirty thousand.

PLUNDER

WE MET THE taking of plunder full-blown in the sacking of cities. But the subject also had a unique dimension with compelling details. Pawnbrokers, art collections, books, ransoming, and other interests break into the picture—even the plundering of states. The subject deserves separate consideration.

The biggest haul of the seventeenth century came out of the Imperial palace at Prague, and more specifically from its *Kunstkammer.* Here the Emperor Rudolf II of Austria (d. 1612) had assembled the finest art and curio collection in Europe, with pictures by Leonardo, Michelangelo, Raphael, Titian, Tintoretto, Dürer, Breughel, Bosch, and other masters. More than another fifteen hundred rare items and objets d'art went to complete the collection, including bronze and amber figures, agate and earthenware vessels, clocks, medals and coins, mathematical instruments, and Indian curios. But this "museum" would not remain in the possession of the Habsburgs. At the end of the Thirty Years War, just as the Peace of Westphalia was about to be signed, and with Prague in the hands of the Swedish army, Gustavus Adolphus's daughter, Queen Christina of Sweden, had the collection seized, including the books, and shipped to Sweden. As soldiers hurried to complete the packing, this brazen act of wholesale theft may even have delayed negotiations in Westphalia. Items were pilfered on their way to Sweden, but on April 14, 1649, the haul finally reached Stockholm. There indeed, for some years, residents had already been witness to the construction of palaces paid for by war booty, the property of Swedish officers, noblemen chiefly. When the Scottish soldier Sir James Turner made a short visit there in 1640, he entered a city, he said, greatly "beautified with those sumptuous and magnificent palaces which the Swedish generalls have built, as monuments of these riches they acquired in the long German warre."

Historians frequently refer to plundering soldiers. They seldom highlight the crooked doings of princes.

JEWELRY, BAGS OF SILVER AND gold coins, plate, candelabra, and silks: These were the prized objects of looting soldiers. Larger items, such as ornate furniture, were typically pawned—converted into cash for food, gambling, or even for desertion from the army. Men with more educated tastes might also be on the lookout for pictures, sculptures, books, tapestries, or even imported rugs and carpets from the Middle East. Of all these, in fact, Europe's cities had considerable quantities. Herds of horses, too, if sold at true market values, fetched high prices. Another form of plunder was one of the most lucrative and widespread of all activities in war zones: the capture and "possessing" of people, especially the rich or titled, with an eye to ransoming them. And we shall see that even houses and whole palaces could be ransomed. Here, as in the case of all valuable booty, army officers were the leading predators.

But before proceeding with marketable plunder, we must cast a glance at loot of a quite different order, far less obvious but far more fateful. I mean the theft of states, of lordships and principalities. This was all-encompassing booty which also, in a sense, cast a veil of validation over the ordinary forms of plunder. For according to a rule in logic and Roman law, if, in the affairs of the world, the greater right over something be granted, then all the more so must the lesser one be allowed, because it is covered by the more inclusive right.

In this connection, then, we must ask: What about the outright expropriation of states, such as when a ruler seized a free city or a territorial state by the force of arms? Was this not a form of theft, even though it would be masked by self-righteous argument, claims regarding "the laws of war," rhetorical flourishes, and legal sophistries? Florence's conquest of Pisa in 1406 was plunder. In the fifteenth century, Venice's armed seizures on the Italian mainland—Vicenza, Verona, Padua, and then Brescia and Bergamo—were plunder, if also, more grandly, acquisitions in the process of "state building." They extended the Serene Republic deep into Lombardy.

In the sixteenth century, the Valois-Habsburg struggles for the kingdom of Naples and the duchy of Milan were combat for spoils, as well as for prestige and alleged matters of hereditary right. When German princes imposed the Lutheran or the Reformed (Calvinist) Church on their subjects, they confiscated lordships and vast landed estates belonging to the bishoprics and religious orders of the Roman Catholic Church. Many contemporaries saw this as outright plunder. The Edict of Restitution (1629), Ferdinand II's formal attempt to reclaim the old episcopal lordships and estates of the Catholic Church reaching back to 1552, was certainly regarded by Protestant princes as an outrageous act of thuggery. In the 1630s, Cardinal Richelieu and King Louis XIII were ready to see the duchy of Lorraine razed, rather than let its ruler and subjects have an autonomy which kept them outside the kingdom of France. Here was a contested sovereignty, to be sure, but the matter was being decided by steel and fire.

Armies in the Thirty Years War took the looting of states out to new frontiers. In his campaign to hold on to the kingdom of Bohemia, Ferdinand II crushed its rebellious Protestant nobility (1620), sequestered their estates, and ended by putting half of all Bohemian territory into the hands of new owners, chiefly by means of sales to favorites. By 1625, Ferdinand's ambitious general Wallenstein was the owner of lands there that amounted to about one quarter of the country's total. Later, like the stateless Bernhard of Saxe-Weimar and by the force of arms, he would seek a whole state for himself, the duchy of Mecklenburg, with the approval of Ferdinand.

But the most enterprising of all land and state grabbers was Gustavus Adolphus. In his fleet march through German lands, as his army swelled to more than ninety thousand soldiers, he became increasingly imperial in his outlook, proposing in effect to lay down a political and religious destiny for all the German princes and people. He even imagined raising an army of 225,000 men, his visions beckoning him into France and Spain. After his death (1632), Axel Oxenstierna, his great minister, fought to keep the Swedish conquests intact by handing out conquered lands and lordships to Swedish generals. These attempted alienations, with no basis in law, were intended to be their payment as army officers. In turn, they were to use their new lands and incomes to pay their officers and soldiers. Plunder in early modern Europe had never known such scope and brass.

It would be too much to say that the seizure of petty or partial sovereignties served to validate the wartime plunder of soldiers in town and country. There was nothing in the air so precise and clear as this. In the lawless disorder of war, the acquisitive activity of princes could look "natural" or acceptable. Priests and pastors easily pointed to God's wrath and condign punishments. In this climate, well-informed plundering officers and soldiers had little trouble finding moral comfort in the conduct of their political superiors. When two officers, as we shall see, told a German parish priest that their starving soldiers had an unconditional right to a share in the property of local villagers, they were suggesting that the force of necessity pushed conventional legal boundaries to one side and brought in a different way of seeing and being. The fact that rulers continually flouted the moral law with impunity by breaking all promises to soldiers, and that they thus engaged in theft by giving soldiers no choice but to be thieves: This—in the talk of plundering officers—was bound to diminish or alter their sense of what robbery was, as they moved like locusts over lands in war zones.

Princes such as Philip II of Spain, the Emperor Ferdinand II, and Maximilian of Bavaria would have been horrified to be told by a friendly party that they were responsible, in a very real sense, for the wild looting, arson, and murdering that went on at the hands of their soldiers. But no priest or government minister was ever likely to say this to them; and if one had—conscience ever striving to put a good face on things—they would have found ways to reject the accusation.

FRITZ REDLICH, THE MAIN AUTHORITY on war booty in early modern Europe, traces the origins of unfettered plunder back to the idea of the medieval feud, to major grievances that had no redress except in war. Once a dispute had been pushed to the status of a feud, everything was permissible. Custom allowed adversaries to carry the fight out to the utmost extremes, to do as much harm as possible not only to the enemy but also to all those from whom he might receive any kind of assistance: servants, subjects, tenants, and allies. In other words, the winning side could take all, regardless of any peacetime notions of justice, whether lodged in Christian doctrine or in "natural law." Redlich does not say so, but there is much in this form of take-all victory that goes back to the warrior ethos of the "barbarian" Goths and, before them, to the imperial legions of the Roman army. The process turned into the praxis of might makes right.

In the late middle ages, a line of canonist (legal) commentators sought to exclude priests, nuns, women, and children from the designs of plundering soldiers. But their voices fell on deaf ears. In the sixteenth century, efforts were made to check looting in friendly territory; and new rules aimed to control the distribution, sharing, or dividing up of booty. But it soon became clear, for example, that captured cannon and gunpowder belonged to the *plena potestas*, or full powers, of sovereignty—hence to rulers. For the rest, the primary right to the major share of any plunder in question belonged to the officers, above all to captains, colonels, and their superiors.

The premier land pirates of the age were the commanders of the Swedish armies in the Thirty Years War. Although coming from one of Europe's poorest countries, they captained some of the largest and most effective fighting units of the second quarter of the seventeenth century. And yet, although being professionals who needed regular payment, neither they nor their armies could count on receiving their salaries and wages from the small tax or domain moneys that went into the royal coffers of the Vasa family. Swedish officers and armies had to live mainly off the wealth of the foreign lands that they traversed or occupied. Their need of "contributions" easily lost all sense of measure. In danger, and with the ordinary soldier frequently in tatters, Swedish officers and their men often grabbed everything of value that they could get their hands on.

In effect, then, the military wages and stipends that should have been paid out of Swedish taxes or foreign subsidies, in order to avoid robbery in the field, were extracted instead in the field from the peoples of occupied lands. War was turned into a self-funding activity.

MAXIMILIAN I OF BAVARIA HAD an outstanding art collection, rich particularly in German work, with pictures by Dürer, Holbein, and the Cranachs. When Gustavus Adolphus took Munich in May 1632, he cleaned out Maximilian's palace, as well as the houses of the local nobility, and had much of the booty wheeled away. An assortment of items was put up for sale, and Golo Mann reports that "art dealers from Ulm, Nürnberg, and Frankfurt hurried to the capital to obtain the stolen goods at auctions." After Gustavus's death at Lützen, in November of the same year, what remained of the collection was dispersed, to be divided up apparently among some of his leading officers. Later, when Duke Maximilian tried desperately to have his treasures returned, his efforts came to nothing. And we must wonder if he was ever nagged by the fact that he himself did not have clean hands, as we are about to see.

Special collections at Stuttgart and Tübingen were looted by Imperial and Bavarian troops in 1634 and 1635. But the cardinal act of Catholic thievery involved the celebrated Palatine Library in the Castle of Heidelberg, the property of the Elector Palatine, Frederick V, the so-called "Winter King" of Bohemia. When Heidelberg was stormed in 1622, the library was claimed by the plundering Duke of Bavaria, Maximilian, and donated to Pope Gregory XV. The consequent convoy of mules, bearing 196 cases of books and accompanied by the papal librarian himself, left Heidelberg in February 1623, went up the Rhine, passed through Munich, and worked its way over the Alpine passes to Rome, to be received by the next pope, Urban VIII. All was fair in war at least, if not in love.

Many thousands of pictures and other art objects were stolen from private houses and churches in the war-torn parts of Germany, to be borne away and sold or cherished, when they were not lost or ruined. Art and books, however, were "elitist stuff." Most officers and men, in a plundering frenzy, had eyes first of all for cash and the quick-sale objects in precious metal or studded with gems. For these, two cities in the path of war—centers of production and sale—topped the list: Nuremberg and Augsburg. The Swedish army occupied the first in 1632 and the second in 1634. Both then passed to the control of Imperial armies.

Nuremberg and Augsburg were at the heart of the goldsmith's trade, especially the latter, which had 185 goldsmiths in 1615 and, by comparison, only 137 bakers. The variety of plate, gold, and silver objects that could be pillaged was remarkable; and all were frequently in use by town councils, by the families of patricians, and in churches. Suffice it to list platters, flagons, drinking cups, ceremonial vessels, pitchers, boxes, bowls, ewers, basins, beakers, chalices, candelabra, table fountains, and still more. Later, after the Thirty Years War ended and goldsmiths streamed back to Augsburg, orders for their work came down from Sweden—commissioning objects that would go into the new palaces of the Swedish officers who had found fortune and spoils in Germany.

IF WE SEEK AN EXAMPLE of plunder on a gigantic scale, the Sack of Rome (1527) must be the first on our list. For in a few days, a city replete with the magnificent wealth of many clerics and laymen was stripped of its caches of gold and silver coins, jewelery, plate, hangings, precious objects, church valuables, and resplendent dress.

Shortly after dawn, on May 6, 1527, the Emperor Charles V's army in Italy, numbering upward of twenty thousand men and under the command of the Duke of Bourbon, breached the walls of the Trastevere part of Rome. Unpaid, ragged, hungry, living off the land, and desperate, here was a swarm that had started out from near Milan three months before, at the outset of February. They were ten thousand Germans, five thousand Spaniards, about three thousand Italians, plus lesser units of others, all of them hardened professionals. Some of the Landsknechts had strong Lutheran sympathies. And as those angry mercenaries made their way south, several mutinies had ended with the shouts, "Pay! Pay!" En route, bread was chronically scant; and when on occasion they could have had more, they found themselves short of the horses and wagons to get it to them. Logistics again. Wine they had, coming on it as they trekked through Emilia, the Romagna, and Tuscany, but it only served to make them more demanding. When their officers learned that Pope Clement was negotiating with Imperial officials, hoping to secure a peace or a long truce, they passed this information on to their men, and a mutiny erupted.

What, turn back—they evidently thought—and be denied the opportunity to sack either Florence or Rome? Florence too had been dangled as a target, and the fury of the soldiers mounted. Many of them were without shoes, their feet bundled in rags. The mutiny became so serious that Bourbon himself had to hide. His tent was plundered and one of his gentlemen killed, the work of Spanish soldiers. But the Germans too were up in arms. They threatened their captains with a show of pikes; and when their charismatic commander, the old George Frundsberg, famous for the discipline and bravery of his troops, addressed them in powerful and moving terms, they spurned his plea. He crashed down on a drum, the victim of a stroke. Taken to be treated in Ferrara, he would never soldier again.

Bourbon next realized that an attack on pro-papal Florence would be out of the question. His army was in no shape for a sustained siege. The terrified Florentines had been graced with just enough time to prepare their defenses and to bring a contingent of troops into the city. So the Imperial army now bypassed the road to Florence and made for Rome.

The assault on May 6 began at about four A.M., in thick fog. Before seven A.M., Rome's walls were being scaled at two different points, straightaway exposing the city's feeble defenses. The Duke of Bourbon himself moved in the front line of action, leading the attack. Attired in white, in keeping with the flashy officers' fashion of the day and hence a perfect target for the defenders, he was holding a scaling ladder when killed by an arquebus shot, just as his men had broken through the walls. The command passed to the Prince of Orange and to Ferrante Gonzaga of Mantua. After an hour or two of fierce fighting in Trastevere, resistance collapsed. But Rome would not belong to the invaders until that evening. They were followed into the city by their camp followers, as well as by a tatty throng of ex-soldiers, deserters, thieves, vagrants, and other recent pickups: men who would seek the crumbs of booty. But soon, too, merchants and pawnbrokers would arrive on the scene, intent on buying up the best of the loot.

Although their killing of civilians commenced at once, the soldiers were so sure of themselves that they seem to have refrained from their hurricane of robbery until the army was in control. But once the storm broke, with officers leading the way, there was no checking them as they heaved themselves into the work of collecting their pay with a princely interest. The ransoming of prisoners passed into a frenzy. No ransom paid exempted the victim from the next wave of determined predators, and no rich man escaped their thuggery, not even neutral or friendly foreign ambassadors. If ransoming was usually governed by customary rules, all were broken. Soldiers strained for everything they could possibly extract, in the likely belief that here was the opportunity of a lifetime to become rich. They demanded ransoms from captive noblemen and wealthy clerics that far exceeded the yearly incomes of their victims: a standard scale in the business of war ransoming. Every house and almost every church and palace was ransacked, with the exception of the few *palazzi* that had been occupied by commanding officers for their own lodging; and even these had to be closely guarded to fend off plundering bands of soldiers.

Many of the noble and rich folk in the city had sought safety in the palaces of dignitaries, two of the most important being those of the Portuguese ambassador and the Marchioness of Mantua, Ferrante Gonzaga's mother. But a ransom was put on these very palaces and on many others. Three or four palaces went, so to speak, for sums that varied from 35,000 to 45,000 gold ducats. Each of the refugees within had to pay his or her share of the total sum. Portugal's ambassador, however, also had a stash in his palace of 500,000 ducats in coin, goods, and valuables, deposited with him by rich merchants, bankers, and noblemen. The lot, all of it, was seized and hauled away. Other palaces lost goods valued at 150,000 and 200,000 ducats. And cardinals themselves went for the price of 10,000 to 20,000 ducats, or they were dragged around, humiliated, and killed.

The staggering magnitude of these sums may be gauged by the fact that in the early sixteenth century the richest Italian state, the Venetian Republic, counted on total yearly revenues of little more than one million ducats (1,150,000).

But aside from the looting of churches and convents, no act of plunder was more revelatory than the one suffered by refugees in the grand palace of the *Santissimi Apostoli*. The mother of one of the two Imperial commanders, Isabella d'Este, the Marchioness of Mantua, was lodged there. Yet even she was regarded as a prisoner. In a sack, the rules of war admitted no exceptions. She had taken twenty-two hundred well-connected people into the palace, including twelve hundred women, intending to offer them protection from the assaulting horde. Not a bit of it, at least not in the business of ransoming. Anxious negotiations and bargaining took place over the course of two days, with troops carefully guarding the palace.

The final agreement required the prisoners to pay a total ransom of 52,000 ducats: 20,000 for the Spanish grandee officer, Don Alonso de Cordova; 20,000 for Alessandro Gonzaga; 2,000 for Landsknechts; and, it appears, 10,000 for none other than the marchioness's son, General Ferrante Gonzaga. When the marchioness finally left the palace on May 18, it was almost immediately sacked.

One of the historians of the Sack claims that the Imperial commanders made nothing from the rape of Rome, because they were too busy lending money to ransomed friends and relatives. In her view, most of the loot went "to the common soldiers." There can be no clinching evidence on this point. But judging by the military mores of the age, we may assume that the whole array of officers, if not the field commanders, got away with much of the loot. Quick money famously ran like water through the hands of Landsknechts and the men who fought in the Spanish *tercios*. Unpaid, they were all certainly in debt. In one hour, a year later, Sebastian Schertlin, a German officer and petty nobleman, gambled away 5,000 ducats. Nevertheless, in 1532 he bought the castle of Burtenbach in Germany, together with cattle and furnishings.

The end of the third day of plundering brought an order to halt the looting, but the command was ignored and the violence went on for another five days. In booty and ransom money, estimates of the spoils range from four to twelve million gold ducats—more than four times Venice's annual public income. Modest parts of the loot would soon go up for sale in Rome's Campo di Fiore: "gold-embroidered garments of silk and satin, woollen and linen cloths, rings, pearls, and other costly articles."

I have not brought the Sack's carnage into focus, because the subject here is plunder. Historians of the event hold that thousands of people were slain. Schertlin, the Landsknecht captain, said that six thousand people had been slaughtered. On the day of the assault, rushing through the streets just after their escalade, troops killed anyone they encountered. An Imperial commander, Prospero Colonna, arrived in Rome on May 10, to find his palace sacked and bodies

strewn in the streets. As so often happened in the sack of cities, inhabitants now faced the ugly task of the collecting and disposing of
bodies. Few men wanted the job, even if the smells and horrors
called for the payment of a good wage.

ITALY SERVES AS OUR CENTER POINT for the large question of booty,
and more exactly for booty of the sort that would have ransomed
kings, as realized in the assaults on Brescia, Genoa, Rome, and lesser
cities such as Prato and Como. For it was in the Italian Wars (1494–
1559), with Italy's rich northern cities constantly in view, that Europe's
armies learned not to loot—this was rife in medieval warfare—but
rather to go into battle, when in view of large cities, with the hope or
even the expectation that the treasure of kings lay in wait for them.
The same hope was taken back to Germany by Landsknechts, and
to France by officers of the royal army. Many of the French return-
ees, including common soldiers, would be drawn into France's Wars
of Religion (1562–1598), and the lesson of Italian loot would pass
from there directly into the Thirty Years War, borne by the many
Landsknechts who fought as well for Catholics as for Protestants in
France.

Speaking of the assault on Brescia in 1512, an informed contemporary estimated the value of the French haul at three million *écus*.
He alleged that most of the plundering soldiers went home with so
much booty that they gave up soldiering. Even if the smack of exaggeration weakens this claim, we can easily imagine that some of the
returning soldiers used their spoils to buy land, to invest in family
châteaux, or to set up somewhere as tradesmen.

Genoa was the next big city, before Rome, to be pillaged. The
assault on the great seaport followed directly from the victory of an
Imperial army at the Battle of Bicocca, near Milan, over the main
body of French forces in Italy. On April 27, 1522, employing arquebus and cannon, Imperial troops tore apart two packed squares of
fifteen thousand Swiss pikemen, newly hired by the king of France.
Next, after a short delay, the triumphant army went on to attack

French-controlled Genoa and its garrison of sixty-two hundred defenders.

But something extraordinary was now about to happen. The Genoese ruling class was split into two noble factions. One revolved around the Fregoso clan, and they held power in the city with the support of the French. The other faction—its leaders in exile—was captained by another noble house, the Adorno, and they, along with many of their followers, were now serving in the ranks of the approaching Imperial army. Moreover, as they reached the outskirts of Genoa, they were joined by hundreds of armed country folk, local tenants and supporters of the Adorno clan.

Made up of twenty thousand German, Spanish, and Italian soldiers, commanded by the Marquis of Pescara and by the Roman nobleman Prospero Colonna, the Imperial army smashed its way into Genoa on the evening of May 30, 1522, entering through the shattered Gate of San Michele. All resistance had been broken. The battle had started even as the Genoese doge, Ottaviano Fregoso, was seeking to negotiate a surrender. When Pescara's Spaniards burst into the city, Colonna, who had been dealing separately with Fregoso's emissaries, was driven to add his German troops to the attack.

Now for the unexampled event. Thanks to the critical influence of the Adorno exiles in the ranks of the invading army, a strict command had gone out to the Imperial soldiers, ordering them to confine their passions to the looting proper. There was to be no killing, no raping; and the sources report none. Pescara and Colonna were somehow able to rein in their mercenaries. The booty alone sufficed. One of Genoa's chief chroniclers, Uberto Foglietta, described the booty: "a great quantity of silver and gold jewellery, precious stones, and apart from furnishings of surpassing value—bettered by no other Italian city—the looters took immense sums of money from citizens for ransoming them, their houses, and their children."

The sack lasted two or three days, from the night of May 30 to June 2. All citizens were quarry. The army made no allowance for party or faction, meaning that the pro-Adorno houses in the city were also rifled and ransomed. Foglietta added a startling detail. He noted "with shame" that the Genoese citizens in the Imperial ranks "put on the same garment of the soul as the foreign enemy, like a plague picked up from contact with them. They concealed their faces with masks and broke into the houses of their fellow citizens to rob them, just as if they were searching for booty in a strange city, one given over to plunder by reason of war." One timely song of the sack of Genoa said that even the "laundry cauldrons" had been stolen from the houses. With all the more reason did much of the city's "art and movable wealth disappear." An extraordinary arrangement, however, rescued a few major sites from the orgy of theft, most notably the customhouse and the palace of the great bank of San Giorgio.

Under the looming threat of a new French army, which had just crossed the Alps, the Imperial commanders led their booty-laden men out of Genoa on June 4, but with the Adorno now occupying city hall. They moved north into Piedmont to keep an eye on the French and to live off the countryside. Too much of Lombardy had been devastated for the easy scrounging of food and fodder.

IN NORTHERN EUROPE, THE STORMING of Magdeburg (1631) issued in a great fire, with the loss therefore of much of the coveted booty, as reported in Chapter 3. But the sack of Antwerp (1576), a city of international bankers, merchants, and shippers, offered wealth on a scale that approached the Roman plunder of 1527. An official estimate put a price tag of five million gold florins on the spoils.

The sack of Mantua (1630) comes into view here next, not only because of the nature of the plunder but also because the event, coming in the middle of the Thirty Years War, brought two horrors together: plague and a plundering army. The story begins in 1629, with a clash between two different branches of the Gonzaga dukes of Mantua, Nevers and Guastalla. Charles of Nevers, head of the French branch of the house, had seized control of the city. Title to the duchy required the approval and seal of the Emperor Ferdinand II,

and Nevers did not have this. He had, however, the support of King
Louis XIII of France.

Imperial troops—thirty thousand foot and six thousand horse—
entered Lombardy in the autumn of 1629, and in late October about
ten thousand of them, mostly infantry, began to put a noose around
Mantua. During the previous year, the entire region had suffered an
agricultural collapse. The Po Valley lay in the shadow of famine.
Little grain had been harvested; heavy rains had flooded and retarded
the working of mills; and the large presence of German soldiers
had put an intolerable strain on food supplies. Imperial assaults on
Mantua in December were bloodily thrown back. The siege was
raised at Christmas, and the besiegers settled into the surrounding
countryside during the winter and spring, exacting heavy contributions from the landed nobility and living mainly off the land.

In late May, 1630, the attack on Mantua was resumed. Now the
emperor's soldiers easily defeated a half-hearted Venetian army, allies of the upstart duke, and rapidly imposed a tight blockade around
the ancient city. They finally stormed and took it on July 18. But it
has to be emphasized that the entire operation was carried out in the
midst of plague, the bacillus of which was very probably carried into
the region in October 1629 by the soldiers themselves. By the spring
of 1630, the disease was everywhere in town and country. In the
city itself, during the four months between March and mid-July,
about twenty-five thousand defending soldiers and inhabitants (refugees included) were killed by the malady. In the weeks leading up
to the capture of the city, 250 to 300 people were dying every day,
and bodies lay in the streets for days. Light winds carried the stench
of the dead through windows. Yet so eager were the invaders to
make good the emperor's claims on the duchy, an Imperial fief, that
they pursued the siege and seizure of the city right through the
plague's carnage. Or was it the case, rather, that they were steered
and driven by the prospect of a sack? When at last entering Mantua,
they found six to seven thousand sickly-looking survivors where

once there had been thirty thousand souls. The appetite for booty seems to have been as ravenous among the officers, and especially the generals, as among the common soldiers, many of whom had died or deserted. Only twelve thousand of the original thirty thousand foot soldiers went into the city, but they were followed in by many hundreds of camp followers and scavenging hangers-on.

No sooner was the city taken than General Johann von Aldringen posted three thousand soldiers around the ducal palace to prevent all unwarranted entry or the exit of goods. Once the seat of the supreme European art collection, assembled over more than two hundred years, the palace had been despoiled of its most important pictures and statues by Duke Vincenzo II in 1627 and 1628. Working through a secret agent, he had sold them to the king of England to the disgust and anger of his subjects. But in July 1630, the palace was still replete with statuary and hundreds of important pictures, not to speak of carpets, tapestries, collections of arms, medals and cameos, or a golden dinner service, crystal and silver tableware, jewelry, stately furniture, and of course the great ducal library.

Everything was wheeled away, ostensibly for the emperor, in truth for the principal officers. The top general, the Italian Rambaldo Collalto, but particularly his man in the field, Aldringen, got the most valuable objects. Two other generals, the drunkard Mattia Galasso (aka Gallas) and Ottavio Piccolomini, also took possession of large shares of the loot. The remaining objects, in an orgy of dispersal, passed into the hands of the officers just under them, while some of the pictures and books were apparently dispensed in an offhanded fashion.

In the meantime, throughout the city, every palace and every house, however humble, was emptied of valuables. We can only guess at the fortunes that were carted away from the great houses. The ghetto and its five pawnbroking banks were totally looted; and Mantua's eighteen hundred Jews—although allowed to return in October—were expelled from the city, each permitted to take along no more than three ducats. The five banks are thought to have lost about "800,000 *scudi* [ducats]."

Although the looting was meant to be limited to three days, the looters and buyers sold or removed booty from the city for the next fourteen months, the duration of the military occupation. Much of the plunder came from churches and convents. The Imperial army was acting for a fervent Catholic, the Emperor Ferdinand II; the generals were Catholic officers; and most of the men in the rank and file were supposed Catholics. Yet none of this modified the so-called "laws of war." A city taken by storm was prey, all of it, for three days, unless, exceptionally, as in the case of Genoa, the victorious commanders agreed to exempt specific places.

The loot from the Gonzaga palace alone has been valued at eighteen million ducats, "equivalent to three times the tax revenue of the kingdom of Naples," or "several times the value" of Spain's royal share of the silver annually mined in Mexico.

Throughout the plague-stricken city, meanwhile, there was a frenetic rushing about. In certain cases this gave rise to unusual sights, such as soldiers' wives or partners "shamelessly" flinging off their filthy garments in the streets and breaking into great houses to wrestle dresses away from resisting women; then, putting on their swag, racing back out to dance in the streets and mimic the bowing of grand folk. It was a show of triumph over death from plague. More important, for markets at all events, the buying up of booty was soon in full swing, pawnbrokers and merchants, especially from around Milan, having followed the soldiers into Mantua. Later, some of the loot would turn up in Milan, Cremona, Rome, Como, and other cities: furniture and tapestries, for example, in Brescia, and in 1635, ten pictures in Bergamo. Articles were even pilfered from General Aldringen's booty wagons. A German colonel ended up with silver plate and portraits of Gonzaga princes. One of Aldringen's relatives, a bishop, got the main part of the ducal library. But in the face of plague, in the summer heat, and in the scurry to complete the plundering in three days, it was impossible to keep track of the thousands of looted items. Excluding the most valuable objects, the big looters would have had only a rough idea of what exactly was being hauled away for them. Many pictures were thrown about or destroyed by soldiers, and some books—from one of the finest and oldest libraries in Europe—were sold by the sack in the marketplace.

Ferdinand II imposed tough conditions on Charles of Nevers, the French Gonzaga, before finally investing him with the duchy of Mantua. The new duke was forced to give up lands to the Italian branch of the family and to surrender various towns in Piedmont to the Duke of Savoy. But all he got in Mantua's ducal palace was the barren *palazzo* itself and Mantegna's frescoes, which no one, apparently, dared to hack away. The problem of carting all that off, including parts of walls, was perhaps too daunting.

ECONOMISTS AND HISTORIANS HAVE SOMETIMES looked upon war as an economic stimulus. Reflecting on the sack of cities, and more specifically on Antwerp, Rome, and Mantua, can we say that their plunder put large amounts of "surplus" capital into circulation, thereby stimulating business and work, such as in the building trades or in new enterprise? William H. McNeill held that war "intensified market exchange," while the economic historian Richard Goldthwaite "emphasized the recycling of soldiers' pay back into the economy." To pursue the devious implication here, we may ask, Is the explosive dispersal of capital a positive material stimulus? Does it move wealth around, create work, and reconstruct capital, while also adding to it? If so, should we set about "constructively" destroying farms, villages, and cities in order to stimulate economies? Before 1628, the province of Mantua held a population of about three hundred thousand people. By its devastation, the result of plague and war, that province paid an incalculable material and moral price for the rape of Mantua. Should the survivors have thanked the Imperial army for giving them a chance to rebuild farms, houses, barns, and stables?

A chapter on the plundering ways of early modern armies should perhaps close with a statement about "silent" plunder: the sort that could not speak with an upper-class tongue, insinuating a sense of the "taste" that went into collecting objets d'art, or the presence of market values in stolen tapestries and jewelry. I mean the plunder of the foods, animal feed, horses, and livestock of villagers and country people. This was not booty of the sort whose worth rose high above subsistence levels; it held no great store of surplus value. It was existential plunder, swiftly consumed by the hungry soldiers themselves and by their horses. Yet here, too, all the same, there was true value. I almost want to say incalculable or "infinite" value, because the stolen foods gave life or, by their absence, death.

Human life itself must in some sense be the common denominator of all value. In their pursuit of a phantom objectivity, historians need not back away from the moral questions raised by the analysis of politics and diplomacy.

Hell in the Villages

T HE SINGLE STORY of a rape or murder, committed in a village, may trouble us and be fixed in memory. Thousands of such crimes, spread over hundreds of villages, turn instead into numbers, and these are likely to leave us cold. The imagination is not able to grasp the shape of terror in such quantities. For this reason, the history of war in rural Europe is destined to remain sociology, a tale of numbers and abstractions, and in this sense to remain untold. Yet the front claws of war were always to be found at two points: around the walls of cities in the thick of sieges, and out in the country, moving with armies along a snaking line, bringing terror to villages and market towns.

In the 1620s, the favorite tactic in the Low Countries, in the war between Spain and the Dutch Republic, was to raise money for troops by sweeping deep into enemy territory and wresting it from the people there. If the local inhabitants refused to pay, their villages were reduced to ashes. In May 1622, Prince Fredrik Hendrik of Nassau "embarked on such an expedition, pillaging the southern Netherlands with 3000 horsemen, 2300 musketeers and six guns." Pushing south as far as the walls of Brussels, that small army set fire to seventy villages, and the prince's troops "returned to the Republic with booty, money and some hostages." We see no faces.

And neither do we see any when a Florentine army conquered Pisa in 1406. The operation was a matter of all-out war against civilians. Florence's mercenaries ravaged and plundered Pisa's country-side at will, with much of the loot, such as grains and livestock, then finding its way to Florence for sale. Almost exactly 150 years later, in combat for the control of Siena (1554–1555), Florentine and Imperial forces bloodied and looted the farms and villages of the Sienese countryside in swaths of destruction that went on under the political eye of the much-admired patron of the arts, Cosimo I, the Medici Duke of Tuscany. He followed the events with keen interest, watching the costs of his mercenaries, and was well-informed about the tactics of his field commander, the Marquis of Marignano.

Since more than 60 percent of soldiers came from humble rural and market-town stock, peasants in wartime were likely to be the victims, for the most part, of men who were much like themselves. The policies behind the orgies of destruction in agrarian Europe issued from commanding officers and leaders who sprang from the territorial and urban nobilities; and they tended to regard peasants as slow-witted or basely cunning, brutish, and born to work in the fields so as to produce the food for their social betters. The Florentines had a saying: "The country makes good beasts and bad men." In northern Europe, on the contrary, the nobility loved the woods, the open country, and hunting. But in competition with the tax-gathering state, they also sought to get their hands on as much as possible of what the peasantry produced in the way of surpluses.

SAINT-NICOLAS-DE-PORT WAS A LITTLE TOWN in the duchy of Lorraine. In the 1630s, the duchy was turned into a battleground in a war between France and Sweden on the one side and, on the other, the Duke of Lorraine and the Emperor Ferdinand II. On the morning of November 4, 1635, about three hundred horsemen rode into Saint-Nicolas-de-Port. Speaking "different tongues, some were dressed in the German manner, others like Croats." They broke into houses and churches, using axes, and then attacked the inhabitants, stealing their clothing, stripping garments from their backs, and beating them with sword blows or "billy clubs" (*nerfs de boeuf*) to extract the whereabouts of their hiding places for valuables. They were just as brutal with nuns and priests. Three days later—the horsemen having departed—into the town rode the German Protestant and Swedish troops of Bernhard of Saxe-Weimar. They burst into the church, where they "raped women and killed the celebrant priests by battering them with candle holders and chalices." Not finding enough loot, they set fire to the roof of the church, having first wiped lard onto its supporting wooden beams to increase the intensity of the fire. The roof burned so fiercely that the lead melted, "pouring down like rain in a storm." The bells, it seems, also melted, and the entire church was destroyed. Not yet content, and evidently in a raging fury, the soldiers set fire to the whole town, running down streets, igniting one house after another and killing anyone who got in their way.

In 1624, Saint-Nicolas-de-Port had 1,659 households. By 1639, the number had plunged to a mere 45.

If on occasion cities met the savagery of war face-to-face, as in sackings and sieges, villages in the lanes of war met it time and time again. Combing through episodes in the diary of the priest Alexandre Dubois, in the first chapter, we touched on soldierly hell in the village of Rumegies. Without food stocks, without a scrap of political clout, and too often without protective walls, villages and little market towns in war zones lay open not only to the passage of armies, but also to the "war rides" of armed horsemen: the scouts of an army nearby, or simply freebooting soldiers.

When in April 1634 Stephan Mayer, the parish priest of Unteregg, dived under the rushes and excrement of an outhouse, managing to conceal himself, he avoided the clutches of eight Swedish horsemen. The past few years had taught him that he would have found his death at their hands. Belonging to the estates of Ottobeuren, a monastery in southern Germany, near Memmigen, the village of Unteregg had been in the path of war for several years, as had most of that part of Upper Swabia. But the intolerable woes had arrived with the barbarities of Swedish troops in 1632. Soon

Imperial armies, too, would arrive, equally given to atrocity, as in their bloody massacre of 1633 in the neighboring town of Kempten.

Stephan Mayer, however, was more fearful of the violence of the Swedes. He recalled—the historian of these events relates—that they had "bored through the leg" of the local miller and "roasted" the man's wife "in her own oven." They had also "whipped five- and six-year-old children with sticks and dragged them around on ropes like dogs." At about the same time (1634–1635), large quantities of money, livestock, and food were extorted or pillaged from the Ottobeuren estates. "A single raid ended with sixty wagon-loads of booty hauled off from Günz and Rummeltshausen." G. P. Sreenivisan goes on to observe that the lands of the monastery, including Unteregg and other villages, lost more than 95 percent of their horses and cattle. By September 1634, peasants and even some of the rich farmers were starving to death, on top of which came plague. (But what would it feed on?) As "peasants gave up tilling the fields and many took flight," the "economy collapsed." Meanwhile, villagers were already eating dogs, cats, mice, "horsehide, twigs, and rats," no less than "the moss from old trees, nettles, and grass like beasts." Reporting what one woman had said to her own father, Stephan Mayer quoted: "'Father, you would not believe what good soup can be made from mice.'" Not surprisingly, Sreenivisan came on reports of cannibalism.

Ottobeuren's peasants were winding through the same hell that enveloped thousands of other German villages during the Thirty Years War.

THE LITTLE ALSATIAN CITY OF Colmar was flanked by a countryside given to vines for the production of wine and brandy. Here, in the 1630s, the raids and assaults of soldiers brought ruin to farms and vineyards; they plundered grain and livestock; and peasants fled for their lives. Colmar itself lost 40 percent or more of its population.

War came to Hesse-Kassel, to villages near the Werra River, in 1623, and returned almost yearly in the form of passing or occupying

armies. Billeting was an immediate and nasty burden for the peasantry. But once local authority had made an agreement with army
officers, it was against the law for villagers to resist, however abusive
the soldiers might be. Official complaints were usually ignored. By
1626, the strains of war had led to violence. Village inhabitants were
killed; soldiers trooped in with plague and dysentery; nobles abandoned their lands; peasants fled. In the 1630s, according to the historian of these events, J. C. Theibault, "being caught by soldiers in the
open was tantamount to a death sentence." Villagers could suddenly
disappear. In those years, the Hessian countryside was made desolate.
Meat became a rarity, while "meager handfuls of grain" were about
as much of this substance as villagers were likely to see. Hordes of
mice saw a good deal more, and while they multiplied, the population of Hesse-Kassel plummeted by 40 to 50 percent.

Hesse-Kassel's "dark night of the soul" was to be the experience,
again and again, in other parts of Germany. In the southwest, in the
county of Hohenlohe, halfway between Frankfurt-am-Main and
Augsburg, war taxes drove Langenburg into a fiscal nightmare. Poor
harvests counted for nothing in pleas to lighten tax loads. From about
1627 to 1636, military commanders pitilessly forced the district to
make payments on a monthly or even a weekly basis. And the orders
might come from either side of the clashing war makers, depending
upon the army in control: The "ruthless agents of the imperial and
Swedish armies bore down savagely on peasant householders." Now,
as the historian Thomas Robisheaux tells the story, many villagers—
rich tenant farmers amongst them—had to sell off capital assets to
fuel the unforgiving motor of war taxation. They sold land parcels,
"the last reserve stocks of grain," herds of cattle, and later on nearly
all of their livestock. By 1630, without "oxen, horses, or even cattle
to pull the ploughs, the tenant farmers could no longer work their
fields." Even "supplies of seed grain vanished." Soon "vineyards
went untended" and many fields "returned to waste or pasture."

In 1631, the widowed Countess Anna Maria of Hohenlohe
addressed the Empire's war agents with fervor, pleading for patience

toward her subjects. But when were war and the unpaid hungry soldier ever the stuff of patience? And so no stop was put on the clawing away at Hohenlohe's last resources. Bread began to disappear from public sale in 1632. When flour for bakery shops came to an end, the retailing of bread became a thing of the past. By July 1634, at least in some villages, there seems to have been no food at all, and people starved to death in the fields. The scenes that we have seen before were now replayed. "Those who survived," as in the village of Bächlingen, "did so by eating cats, dogs, the bark of trees and stubble off the field." But famine also had the company of plague, which had struck in 1633 and peaked in 1634–1635, with the result that the drop in the local population was catastrophic and "fields, pastures, and vineyards turned back into forests and swamps."

The Thirty Years War called forth a run of fascinating diaries, one of the most remarkable being from the hand of a German Benedictine and covering the years from 1627 to 1648.

Born the son of a baker, Maurus Friesenegger (1590–1655) took holy vows in the mid-1620s. He was parish vicar of the Bavarian village of Erling, near Munich, from 1627 to 1638, and at the same time a monk in the Benedictine abbey of Andechs, a pilgrimage site on the hill above Erling. In 1640, he was elected abbot of Andechs— understandably, perhaps, since he seems to have been a brilliant speaker.

Friesenegger's interest in the ravages of war took in Bavaria and eastern Swabia, stretching from Straubing to Augsburg and Memmingen. His diary is a chronicle of violence, of life lived in the path of traversing soldiers in a time of famine. Some of his more telling moments turn into narratives.

The region was afflicted by plague in 1627 and 1628. July of 1630 brought the outbreak of a "horrible cow and horse disease." Large numbers of deer, "wild swine," and other animals also died in the neighboring forests. The war, he noted, came ever closer. In October 1631, after defeating the Imperialists at Breitenfeld, the Swedish army moved south from Saxony, plundering castles, churches, and convents. Such a sweep of soldiers always involved assaults on the adjacent villages as well. In a warning of November 1631, the ducal government in Munich urged the convent of Andechs to deposit its treasures and valuables in certain strongholds, and demanded a loan of 6,000 florins for the support of soldiers.

In April and May of 1632, the plundering Swedish army began to close in on Freisenegger's world, as it ate its way through the villages around Regensburg, Freising, Augsburg, and other points, leaving a spoor of death and destruction. On the eighteenth of May, a vanguard of eighteen horsemen reached Erling, broke into the convent, and for two hours heisted whatever pleased them. More soldiers arrived in the succeeding days, also in search of food, drink, and loot. They helped themselves to food stocks, cows, poultry, and fifty head of cattle, as well as to kitchen utensils, tableware, and all the bed linen, including pillows and cushions. Moved perhaps by anti-Catholic fury, they smashed doors and windows, chests, cabinets, and cupboards. After their departure, the dormitory, the refectory, and the corridors were littered with straw and excrement, horse and human. The stench and "horrors" were so awful that it took five men about ten days to clean up the worst of the filth. "But I can't really say," adds Friesenegger, "whether more was stolen by foreigners or by natives," for there were so many mercenaries coming and going that the cloister "was always full of men and women, each stealing whatever they liked."

Moving back and forth between "the Holy Mountain" (*der heilige Berg*), as Andechs was known, and his parish down below, the diarist also recorded the track of terror in Erling. Here, as in the neighboring castle of Mühlfeld, soldiers set fire to most of the houses and went off with wagons, plows, sheep, pigs, all the poultry, 137 of 140 horses, and 396 of 400 head of cattle.

From this time on, the region as a whole became a gateway for looting armies; and frequently, in their thieving, "Catholic" Imperialists turned out to be no less brutal than the "Protestant" Swedes and their German allies. Hunger, anger, and strident poverty in the armies on both sides made them equally rapacious. In July 1632, Erling still lay mostly in ashes. With the return of the Swedes in November, the Erlingers fled into the woods, preferring the ice of the forests to the hands of their tormenters. In late December it was the pillaging turn of the Croats, who ransacked every standing house in Erling and even carted off sheaves of grain. Days later, only a guarantee of protection from Munich enabled the village and convent to escape the looting of two hundred Imperial horsemen.

Erling went into that winter still half burned down, the standing houses without roofs and without much of the woodwork because soldiers had ripped it out for their cooking fires and heating needs. Strong winds in the new year tore away at trees and houses, and then in February the Croats returned, breaking into the local mill, where they grabbed all the grain and flour, despite Erling's guarantee of protection.

The year 1633 brought more waves of freebooters and hungry companies of cavalry. In March the Erlingers had to take up arms to fight off a gang of mounted marauders. In early April, with their few horses, they began the springtime planting, while always keeping spotters on the vigil for horsemen. But by the middle of the month, the approach of Swedish soldiers drove them into the mountains; they no longer trusted the local woods because the enemy had taken to prowling there, too, in search of the Erlingers. Yet once more, the Swedes smashed all the woodwork in the Holy Mountain, while again stealing the tableware, clothing, wheat, oats, "and any of the villagers' goods in the convent." When the Swedes fled at the approach of Croat cavalry, two of them hid in empty chests of grain. Finding them later, the peasants killed one and buried the other alive with his dead partner.

Since Europe was experiencing a Little Ice Age, May came in with frost and killing cold. Grain and bread prices rocketed. Individuals or convoys, bearing loads of grain on the roads, were always in danger of being assaulted and seeing their guards killed. And the brigands might be Imperial soldiers or troops under Sweden's banners.

Throughout the summer and autumn, the theft of horses was rife, inexorable. Often poorly nourished, as we have previously observed, or forcibly overworked by cavalrymen and teamsters, the animals were dying on a massive scale. September ended in a wretched harvest, with peasants tying themselves to carts, pulling and hauling and doing the work of horses. On the thirtieth, a regiment of Imperial Spanish cavalry (one thousand horsemen) arrived in Erling, and again the villagers fled. November and December became a logbook of passing or fleeing troops, looters, and the persistent theft of yet more horses and cattle, frequently the work of rambling Swedish cavalry. Based in nearby Augsburg and backed by the city's Protestants, the Swedes made raids into the surrounding lands, seeking out foods, fodder, and booty. Then, on the twenty-first of December, a whole army passed through Erling, taking up the whole day and part of the night.

As he looks into the faces of soldiers, Friesenegger is by turns inquiring, outraged, shocked, horrified, moved to pity, and fleetingly meditative. One thing he knew, and this was that "continuous war turns men into beasts." Keeping an eye unflinchingly on the shifting path of the war in Bavaria and eastern Swabia, he strained to understand the returning tides of military cruelty; and when he saw as much misery in soldiers as in his peasants, detecting there one of the causes of their brutality, he achieved that understanding. Yet he could not but condemn them. They were the invaders, the strangers. His first concern had to be the safety of his parishioners, the people of Erling. He concentrated therefore on the wreckage of war, the collapse of farming, the effects of hunger and disease, the spectacle of immiseration, and hence on half-naked peasants, hungry and ragged soldiers, the theft of seed corn, and deserted villages in the path of war.

One late-December scene would perhaps long live with him: the arrival of a troop of soldiers in Erling. When they found "nothing but empty houses and no people [nor any food], something terrifying took place. The whole village seemed to go up in flames. They took the stools and benches out of the houses, tore down the roofs, built terrifying fires in the streets, and filled the village with screams and shouts, which could only have been caused by hunger and despair."

Now and then Friesenegger's diary expresses his own haunting fears, and brings in fleetingly the names of generals, lesser officers, and many others; but it never offers a sustained, individual portrait. His interests took in events, the classic stuff of local chronicles, not the gossipy portraits of individuals. And who could blame him if, in the endless stream of plundering strangers, one face blurred or faded into another?

Made in the midst of famine, an extraordinary claim troubled him, particularly because it was voiced by Imperial colonels. One had flatly declared that "the goods of the peasants belong to the soldiers as much to the peasants themselves." And an Italian colonel, a Milanese count, had later repeated the asseveration: "What belongs to the peasants belongs to the soldiers, and they are extremely hungry." Friesenegger could not accept the implication—how otherwise to explain it?—that the soldiers were in some sense fighting for the peasants, and that they thus had a natural right to local food supplies, however scant. Two soldiers had just starved to death.

It was January 1634, and our diarist was now seeing the juggernaut of the Thirty Years War. Andechs had more than one thousand soldiers crammed into its outer buildings. That winter, like the last, had turned into an icy nightmare. Soldiers tore away at all visible wood in the cloister, as in the houses of the village, to use for their warming fires. They had been promised food supplies from headquarters in Munich, but none arrived. Maddened with hunger, they pounced on the remaining food of the local peasants, and not just the food—in some cases on their shoes and stockings as well. When they finally departed, later in the month, peasants as well as monks were faced, says Friesenegger, with "a horror" of filth and waste and stench both in the cloister and in Erling. In the village itself, beds, benches, chests, and the wood stripped from wagons, carts, and plows had all been burned. But now, with the soldiers gone, "the evil only changed," as disease made its assault: "dysentery, Hungarian fever, strange pustules, pains in the limbs, and swellings." Many villagers died, but "how could it be otherwise! There were no medicines, no tranquillity, no bread, no beds, no straw, no ovens, no wood, and all this in the middle of the greatest cold that lasted from November to February, with all the houses standing open to the winds and winter."

Yet soldiers continued to troop into Erling. In July plague struck. One household was wiped out; others lost four or five members, and the dead often lay unburied. The living were afraid to go near them. In the nearby village of Kerschlach, "eight or more people lay dead in one house for six weeks, some half-eaten by dogs." By the end of the year, Erling's five hundred souls had fallen to 190, "and out of 87 married couples, only 20 remained."

It is hard to know where to cut off the flow of Friesenegger's diary, the woes of which went on, with ups and downs, to the end of the war. In the early 1640s, Erling was beginning to piece life together again, when the last years of the war again produced a deadly harvest of the old evils. Along the way, new ones had appeared. Packs of wolves, long vanished, returned to race through the countryside, preying on livestock, and the peasants were unable to check their onslaughts. More surprisingly, the entire region had to live for some years with hordes of tenacious "mice of different kinds and colours," particularly rampant at harvest time. Other sources speak of mice "as big as cats." But Friesenegger, making no distinctions, must have been referring to voles and wood mice, too, which also helped to swell the periodic explosions of rodent populations. The creatures survived the icy winters by overrunning fields of wheat and other grains and stowing away their pickings beneath the ground, so that peasants even took to digging up the buried spoils.

The fate of a village like Erling, small and of absolutely no strategic value, rarely troubles historians. In this sense, Friesenegger's record of events has very little significance in *historical* terms. Yet most of Europe lived in such villages, and many suffered Erling's fate. The diocese of Augsburg alone had four hundred different parishes, and when armies streamed over the countryside, the soldiers spread out widely, working their way through hamlets, searching out food, fodder, horses, livestock, and loot.

Inadvertently, then, our diarist was speaking for hundreds of other villages in Bavaria and Swabia, and for that matter in Württemberg, in the Rhenish Palatinate, Hesse, Brandenburg, southern Saxony, and many other places. All fell prey to the violence and atrocities of passing armies, Imperial and Swedish, or French in the later stages of the war.

FRIESENEGGER'S DESCRIPTIONS OF WARTIME VILLAGE life are fully echoed in other writings, one of the most memorable being the chronicle-like diary (1618–1672) of the shoemaker Hans Heberle.

A confirmed Protestant and member of the district militia, conservative, married, and a family man, Heberle came from the Swabian village of Neenstetten, in territory ruled by the city of Ulm. His wake-up call to the realities of war was sounded in 1625, when Imperial troops invaded territorial Ulm and tore through various villages. They were back in 1628, together with their "whores and boys" and other camp followers, at one point seeking billets in almost every village. Army discipline was still rather strict then, and the violence of soldiers was punished, now and then, by the death penalty. But billeted cavalry were already demanding more than the straw, hay, wood, salt, and candles of their official rations.

Heberle's sobering education in the homicidal character of hungry soldiers really came in the 1630s, after Imperial troops returned to the Ulm district in 1631 and swept through villages, pillaging, burning, extorting ransom moneys, and causing Ulm to levy special war taxes. The next two years also brought plagues of Imperial troops. But the surprising poison came in August 1634, with the arrival of a Protestant army under the command of Duke Bernhard of

Saxe-Weimar. Being a Protestant village, Weidenstetten—Heberle was now living there—took no precautions when informed that Bernhard and his troops were on their way. He was certainly not regarded as an enemy, even if, as a soldier in wartime, he could not truly be called a friend. But what the villagers did not know was that Bernhard was a hugely ambitious warlord who depended on the plunder of war to hold on to his troops; and he could not do without these, because he was intent on using armed force to carve a state out for himself.

There they were, then, the people of Weidenstetten, having failed to hide their goods or to move their livestock away. Hungry and unpaid, Bernhard's troops fell on them, stealing horses and other animals, "bread, flour, salt, lard, clothing, [stocks of] cloth, and all our wretched things. They beat and shot and stabbed people, killing a few of them," and carted off whatever they could carry. Since Bernhard's army had spread out in order to pillage as much as possible, the same scenes of violence were unfolding in other villages, where armed resistance was met with arson and destruction. In Weidenstetten, five houses and five barns went up in flames.

Territorial Ulm now became a wide avenue for retreating or advancing armies, especially after the defeat of the Swedes at Nördlingen in early September 1634. From this time on, the Weidenstetten villagers no longer waited for the arrival of terror on horse and foot. The moment they got news of the approach of troops, they would pack their carts and wagons and flee over the twelve miles to Ulm, where thousands of peasants from other villages also collected, they too having abandoned their houses and few possessions. During the long course of the war, Heberle and his neighbors were to make thirty different escapes to that city, where they might remain for a week or two, or for months at a time, with their families crammed into wagons: filthy, hungry, too poor for the risen price of many foods, freezing in the winter, and exposed to disease. The duration of their stay depended entirely on the danger posed by armies. In 1634–1635, an attack of the plague ate away at Ulm. Heberle lost two sons, a stepmother, three sisters, and a brother. Yet soldiers continued to come and go in the villages, and each time the locals paid with their poor goods, with beatings, with flight, with their lives.

A picture of the shaky foundations of peasant life comes from a study of the county of Hohenlohe. Here, in remarkably fertile land, one measure of seed grain could produce seven or eight measures of harvested grain. With eight acres of this land, a family of three could produce enough grain to feed itself for a year—no surplus envisaged. A family of eight to ten people required about twenty-five acres of that land for their subsistence. Thomas Robisheaux found that in his Hohenlohe sample region, 52 percent of households "never produced enough grain on their small plots of land to feed themselves," while another 20 percent or more lived on the margins of self-sufficiency. Hence in bad years, with prices soaring, these families had to buy grain in order to survive. Clearly, then, only a minority of families ever produced sizable surpluses for the market.

If we transfer these findings to areas where the land, more commonly, was not nearly as fertile as in Hohenlohe, and where in fact the yield ratio might be four or even three to one, we realize at once that the German countryside was a world of poverty for most people. But this was generally true of the whole of agrarian Europe. A tenacious German peasantry held on to life by doing paid farm labor, keeping a kitchen garden, raising a pig or two for the market, or growing and spinning flax into thread for sale. Yet overnight that poor life could be put on the edge of a precipice, even for an enterprising peasantry. For the moment soldiers began to touch it, hunger and then famine spread in the wake of their plundering, arson, and calamitous impact on farming. Often, indeed, in their hunger, they even stole the seed grain. No wonder, then, that both soldiers and peasants starved.

In campaigns against civilian populations—and this was the ordinary business of war for armies—fighting around the walls of cities, in the midst of a siege, constituted one of war's bloodiest edges:

echoes of *The Iliad*. And if that edge elicited the utmost cruelty from soldiers, it had the same effect on the besieged civilians, who felt that they were fighting for their lives.

Between besiegers and besieged, every kind of foul exchange was bound to take place at the city walls, with soldiers on the outside declaring that they would rape mothers, wives, and daughters once they stormed the city, and defenders firing back vows to castrate and skin or decapitate any would-be invaders. In religious conflict, the abuse settled on saints and popes, or on the alleged special God of the evangelicals. Two fleeting scenes give point to the extremes.

At the siege of La Rochelle in the spring of 1573, many of the city's women distinguished themselves by their bravery at the walls. Some of them slipped out of the city occasionally "to strip dead enemies of arms and equipment." But in their most blistering role, they also helped to front defense right at the walls, particularly by "casting cauldrons of boiling pitch and tar into the midst of storming royal troops."

A more dramatic—and vengeful—feature of defense was put into play around Turin's walls in late August, 1706, in a war provoked by the Duke of Savoy's personal problems with King Louis XIV. Following a siege of several months, French forces finally moved to scale or burst through the city's walls. The most spirited assault was repelled on August 27, when the French lost thirteen hundred men and the *Savoyards* about four hundred. At the end of that day, hundreds of wounded French soldiers lay wailing and pleading for help in the ditches around the walls. Turin's defenders proceeded to throw tons of firewood, pitch, and oil down into the trenches, on top of the wounded men. They then set fire to that mix of man and matter, and from the walls and ramparts snipers targeted the wounded who tried to squirm away. We can be sure that neither Louis XIV nor the Duke of Savoy would carry that scene around in his conscience.

The incandescence of feeling at the walls of cities under attack, with fire or boiling pitch crowning the most painful deaths, had its match in the hell of villages, in peasant hatred for soldiers. On August 20 and 23, 1617, some twenty kilometers to the northwest of Turin, the Leipzig colonel, Caspar von Widmarckter (1566–1621), left hundreds of sick soldiers in two tiny towns, evidently abandoning them while affecting to believe that they would be looked after. When his regiment departed, the townsfolk, villagers really, chased the sick men away, and in one case put some of them onto hay carts and set fire to them.

Killing for God

BEGINNINGS

It was the spring of 1562, marking the outbreak of the Wars of Religion in France. The air for many townsmen crackled with anxiety. Talk about murder and violence over questions of worship punctured daily conversation. People would soon flee from anxious Rouen, the country's largest city after Paris. Some of its inhabitants tried to hide at home, while others would beg relatives or friends to protect them. Fear and hatred over religious differences were all but palpable.

Rouen's ominous moral climate also enveloped Toulouse, Lyon, La Rochelle, Tours, Blois, Troyes, and other French cities. In the late 1550s, the Reformed (Calvinist) Church had found legions of converts with such speed—critically so in the ranks of certain of the country's elites—that many Huguenots, the new devotees, believed that they would soon snatch the entire kingdom away from the old Roman Catholic Church. Their violence was launched in 1560, with the smashing and defacing of religious images at La Rochelle and elsewhere.

Religious tempers had first flared years before, in 1534, when people in Paris and at least five other cities woke up on a Sunday morning, October 18, to espy printed placards on their way to Mass, posted in the most visible places. In Amboise, one had been tacked to the door of the king's bedchamber. Such was the bold new

Word of God. It was headed, "True Articles concerning the horrible, gross, and intolerable abuses of the papal mass, concocted directly against the Holy Supper of our Lord." In their contemptuous
dismissal of priests, the four paragraphs of the communication highlighted four hard-hitting points, adding up to a scorching indict-
ment of the Mass. The violence of the placards was a dagger in the
bosom of traditional religious beliefs.

Huguenots were never to number more than about 10 percent of
the French population. But in March 1562, horrified by a massacre
of Huguenots in Champagne, near the town of Vassy, the more militant of them opted to seize power. They did so at Rouen, Lyon, Blois,
Tours, Orléans, Bourges, Poitiers, and lesser places. At Bordeaux,
however, and at Dijon, Aix-en-Provence, and Toulouse, they were
defeated in bloody skirmishes, in the last of these after five days of
fierce fighting in the streets. The incandescent passions made it clear
that religion and politics could not be split apart, not in the ordinary
beliefs of the age. Already in December 1559, a leading Paris magis-
trate, the Calvinist-minded Anne du Bourg, had been burned at the
stake for heresy. More than a whisper of sedition had passed through
his actions. He had published a pamphlet claiming, essentially, that
no French subject was bound to accept the legitimacy of a king who
contravened the will of God: in effect, a king who did not share
Anne du Bourg's religious views.

Early in 1560, Rouen's Protestants began to abandon their covert
meetings and to go public. By July, several thousand of them, it
seems, were assembling regularly to listen to preachers in front of
the magnificent cathedral. Then, on April 15, 1562, about six weeks
after the killings at Vassy and days after a massacre of Protestants in
nearby Sens, the Huguenots suddenly and surprisingly seized control of the city, with its population of about seventy thousand inhabitants. A major center of international trade on the Seine River,
Rouen lay within reach of oceangoing vessels. Moments of frenzied
change would follow. On May 3 and 4, armed Huguenots went
about, aiming to convert the entire city by force. They passed from

one church to another, smashing baptismal fonts and altars, pilfering the objects in precious metal, shattering statuary, defacing images, and building bonfires in the streets, into which they threw music books, tapestries, pews, lecterns, and other wooden items. Catholic services came to a halt. Priests, Catholic merchants, and local officials got out of the city. In June, Rouen's doctrinal violence was replicated by Catholics in Paris: All Huguenots were expelled from the city.

Catholic and Protestant armies took the field, captained by and consisting of professional soldiers, veterans of the Italian Wars—which had ended in 1559, leaving them unemployed. These servants of the "warriors of God" wasted no time in revealing their credentials as masters in the art of wholesale plunder and ransoming. When given the chance to loot, they often ignored distinctions between Catholic and Protestant.

In the summer of 1562, as Catholic armies began to close in on the new Huguenot strongholds—Lyon, Blois, Tours, and the others—the besieged sent out pleas for help from other Protestant cities. By early October, Rouen's Huguenots were praying for the arrival of a promised six thousand soldiers from England (they never came), for the very good reason that they were confronting a royal army of thirty thousand men. On October 21, the besiegers broke through the walls and stormed the city, as Calvinist leaders and pastors fled for their lives. Although officers tried, allegedly, to restrain them, the king's soldiers threw themselves into a three-day sack. They looted the houses of Huguenots, ransomed the houses of Catholics, and even plundered Catholic churches. About a thousand people lost their lives in the assault, more than at the sack of Antwerp, "the Spanish fury" of 1576. The quantities of loot were such that merchants from Paris swooped in to the city to buy it up at prices that would be turned into handsome profits.

That was Rouen. But during the summer of 1562, similar events unfolded in the other cities won back by royal armies.

★   ★   ★

THE FRENCH HAD TURNED IN a wild fury against the iconoclasm of the new believers, converts who despised the Catholic Mass and the old pantheon of saints. Here, Catholics felt, was a doctrinal arrogance which had also spurred that enemy on to seize power in the principal cities. When the men on each side fought because they saw themselves responding to a summons from God, they were engaged in a holy war, driven by "a promise of divine aid that would lead to victory even in the face of great odds." Yet it was war of a sort which, in its searing intensity, made every atrocity possible, including the murder of children, the disemboweling of pregnant women, and the bizarre configuring of massacred body parts. Strangely, God did not seem to intervene against the inflicting of gruesome mutilations.

Europe had seen the spilling of blood in the name of religious causes long before. Late in the eleventh century, the clash between popes and emperors, fighting over the appointment of bishops, put armies into the field; and piercing voices were raised against a corrupt "cardinal" clergy. In France, the thirteenth century began with a merciless crusade against the communities of Christian dualists, Albigensians or Cathars, in the southern part of the kingdom. Seen as dangerous heretics, they were wiped out. In the third decade of the fifteenth century, pope and princes unleashed a sequence of vicious onslaughts against "Hussites" in Bohemia, the Czech-speaking lands, targeting their views of communion, of an acceptable clergy, and of sin-remitting indulgences. The "heretics" rose to the challenge. Again and again, between 1420 and 1432, the Hussite Czechs inflicted startling defeats on their invaders, Germans chiefly, by cunningly deploying famous "war carts" and new gunpowder weapons. In the end, however, they were driven to make an accommodation with orthodoxy, but only after having split into radical (Taborite) and more moderate sects. The moderates defeated the Taborites in sanguinary battles and were then able to make peace with their neighbors.

COMBATIVE HOLINESS

The votaries of militant Calvinism and the outbreak of holy war in France, with its flights of refugees, carried the Protestant cause into the Low Countries. Here, too, the decade of the 1560s became pivotal in the fortunes of war. Geneva, the school of complete Calvinism, was sending out scores of ardent pastors and preachers, trained to spread the Reformed word of God and determined to overturn all the structures of the old Church. The supposed summons from God, in clashing Protestant and Catholic intonations, was heard by men from across the social spectrum, from mean Flanders cobblers and tailors to the Habsburg King of Spain Philip II (1556–1598), and the Emperor Ferdinand II (1619–1637). The latter "swore a solemn vow at Loreto to uproot Protestantism in his realms."

King Philip II had been warned about heretics by his father, Charles V, who saw them as rebels engaged in treason. Deeply religious and something of a true ascetic, Philip was never to acknowledge anything but strict orthodoxy in matters of religion. When "heresy" began to infect his subjects in the Netherlands, he became inconsolable and swore that he would never rule over heretics. Rather than do that, he said, he would prefer to be stripped of his crown. He must carry out God's will, and hence saw himself as the instrument of God.

IN A TIME OF NEAR famine (1565–1566), with bread prices beyond the reach of the poor, the stern claims of Calvinism were taken up by people in western Flanders. The opulent laxity of the old Church became an easy target of criticism, particularly because its lucrative posts were held mostly by men from well-heeled or well-connected families. Orthodoxy and all its trappings took on the appearance of outrageous comfort. In June and July of 1566, many towns in the Netherlands witnessed assemblies of people outside their walls, gathered to listen to Calvinist preachers. In mid-August tensions snapped, and bursts of iconoclasm ripped through "more than 400 churches and chapels." By the twenty-second, the big cities of the southern Netherlands buckled, giving way to similar scenes, and the iconoclastic hurricane then swept north into Holland. Antwerp's churches, all forty-two of them, were pillaged, and great piles of objects were "hauled out into the streets to be smashed."

The assault on churches and their paraphernalia was the work of organized gangs, each numbering anywhere from twenty to fifty rioters. In some cases, the poor artisans among them were paid to do the defacing and smashing of images and statuary. Their attacks were usually followed by a gorging on the food and drink found in the premises. But interestingly, unlike iconoclasts in France, they refrained from the murder of priests and from attacks on the symbols of political authority. No matter. Spanish governors saw the mutineers in a political light, and the iconoclastic orgies became the triggers of the so-called Eighty Years War. A year later, over the Alps, came one of the best generals of the age, the Duke of Alba, leading an army of ten thousand Spanish and Italian soldiers with a long tail of camp followers. They reached the southern Netherlands in August 1567, to be billeted in Brussels, Ghent, Antwerp, and lesser places.

The story of Spain's military occupation of the Low Countries has been brilliantly told by Geoffrey Parker and others. Suffice it here to stress the fact that a war with clamorous religious beginnings was turned into a struggle for independence from Spain. But the religious underpinnings were to be there always, and they should be borne in mind, because they added a cruel twist to the struggle. In Holland and other northern provinces, the Catholic Church was uprooted and outlawed. And in the southern provinces, under Spanish rule, governors worked to hound Calvinism out of existence. Roughly half of Antwerp's population, about thirty-eight thousand Protestants, emigrated to the north in the late 1580s, having first been forced to sell "their homes and immoveable possessions."

The war had passed instantly into the hands of professional soldiers, many of whom—time would reveal—had no real interest in the "correct" forms of worship. They were soldiers first and foremost, seeking to survive and profit. This meant that in their plundering and violence, the armies on both sides, when unpaid, when hungry, when in dire need, were likely to show little regard for religious differences. Some of the English and Scottish mercenaries who fought on the Dutch side did so, it is true, for confessional reasons more than for the lousy pay. But they were not typical fighters. The remorseless violence that often marked the capture of garrison towns, such as Haarlem, Zutphen, Naarden, and Maastricht, conformed with the so-called "laws of war" and was not the mere result of religious animosity. If a town failed to surrender when called upon to do so, it lost all hope of mercy if the attacking army then stormed it. Cruelties in the wars between Spain and the United Provinces were always bound to include a religious ingredient, but that ingredient could not be easily picked out of the stew of other motives.

In the "bloodlands" of the French civil wars and the Thirty Years War, on the contrary, the unyielding claims of religion and even of holy war stood out nakedly. This was never more clearly visible than in the sieges of La Rochelle, Sancerre, Paris, Magdeburg, and Augsburg. Here, as we have seen, war was taken to such extremes that it appeared, at moments, as though the people under siege were prepared to commit collective suicide in the name of God and correct worship. They conceived of holy war as a struggle that might require a fight to the last man, woman, and child. In the five sieges, an urban oligarchy, backed by army officers, set the agenda and saw it as right, as godly, for people to starve to death in the defense of "true" religion. Paris aside, those in command of the other beleaguered cities had the support of Protestant pastors who readily took up the task of preaching holy war. And any resistance to this call—looked upon as treason—was made subject to the penalty of death.

In the summer of 1590, Paris offered a different visage of war *à l'outrance*—war to the last degree. Here starving men were spied upon, searched, arrested, jailed, and even hanged for expressly wanting peace and a reconciliation with the man whose army was besieging the city, Henry of Navarre, the aspiring king of France. He had not yet renounced his Protestant faith. Paris had long been fanatically Catholic, and preachers were encouraged to argue that death was better than the rule of a heretic. But few people in Paris were ready for martyrdom. When the murderous siege broke the resisting will of the Parisian populace, the will to survive surfaced and began to clamor for a peace agreement. The city, however, was under the despotic control of the Council of Sixteen, and behind them loomed the chieftains of the powerful Catholic League, an aristocratic union whose members had sworn to keep Henry of Navarre away from the throne even if he should convert to Catholicism. They used processions, threats, food handouts, and fiery sermons to keep the people of Paris in line with the wishes of the League. Theatrical color was also added. In the great procession of May 14, early on in the siege, the bishop of Senlis and the prior of the Carthusians moved at the head of a column of "monks and friars armed with arquebuses, halberds, and daggers." They were saying, in effect, that they themselves were ready to draw blood. To hammer the point home, "they marched in ranks, four deep," their cassocks pulled up, their cowls "lowered down to their shoulders," and "some wore a breastplate or a helmet."

In the effort to keep the starving people of Paris from rebelling, the promises of men in holy orders knew no bounds. Preachers argued that it would "endear them to God" if they died of hunger. According to a leading, if hostile, witness, Pierre de l'Estoile, they even said "that it is better to kill one's own children than to receive a heretic king." He threw light on these words by claiming that he had heard a well-known Catholic argue that it was less dangerous in the hereafter to have eaten a child, if driven to do so by starvation, than to have recognized a heretic as king.

Holy war was the type of war, perhaps the only type, about which men could seriously say, with a good conscience, that it should be fought to the last degree.

THE TRIGGERS OF THE THIRTY Years War lay in religious belief, and first of all in the combative Catholicism of two princes: the Emperor Ferdinand II and Maximilian, Duke of Bavaria. They cooperated in the events (1618–1620) that led to a victory over Bohemia's Protestant aristocracy at the Battle of White Mountain (1620). The losers, grandees, were treated as rebels, because they had sought to take the kingdom of Bohemia away from Ferdinand by offering it to a Calvinist, Frederick V, head of the Palatine Electorate. Ferdinand's men and the Order of Jesuits now moved into the Czech-speaking kingdom, intent on bringing it back to the Roman fold. Twenty-six of the rebellious noblemen were executed, but all the others were also divested of their landed estates. Half of Bohemia's lands passed to the possession of new owners: leading officers in Ferdinand's army and aristocrats who had remained loyal to him and to the Roman church.

In 1625, Ferdinand and Maximilian drew two militant Jesuits into their immediate orbit. William Lamormaini, a Belgian, became the confessor to Ferdinand in Vienna; and the German Adam Contzen entered Maximilian's intimate circle as his confessor in Munich. They were chosen in part because their religious attitudes conformed with those of their penitents, the two princes. Maximilian, as it happened, was also the founder of Germany's Catholic League. Meanwhile, the re-Catholicizing of Bohemia added fuel to the ongoing war, turning several of the Empire's Protestant princes against Ferdinand and Maximilian. The war entered an even sharper phase in June 1625, when Christian IV, king of Denmark, seeing himself as the defender of the Protestant cause, invaded Germany with an army of mercenaries, only to be defeated in several battles.

Catholic victories in northern Germany fired Ferdinand's ardent Catholicism, in the wake of which he issued the Edict of Restitution (March 1629), calling for the Protestant restitution, within the Empire, of all properties seized "illegally" from the Catholic Church since the Peace of Augsburg (1555). In effect, the document challenged the ownership of vast stretches of landed wealth, confiscated from bishoprics, monasteries, churches, and women's convents. The duchy of Württemberg alone stood to lose the lands of fourteen large monasteries and thirty-six convents.

The edict was profoundly divisive, and Ferdinand lost the support of the Protestant electors of Brandenburg and Saxony. But the aims of the edict also split Catholics, including the Jesuits themselves. Militants favored it, while moderates feared that it would intensify the war's burning hatreds. In Rome the pope himself, Urban VIII, was dubious about the edict, fearing that it would pose a challenge to the diplomacy of realpolitik statesmen like the powerful Cardinal Richelieu. Nor could the king of Spain be happy with it, because it would cause grave troubles in Germany and thus undermine Habsburg alliances in Spain's fight for the Low Countries.

As it turned out, the edict opened the way for the entry of the king of Sweden, Gustavus Adolphus, into Germany in 1630. Although the war had already been widened by Christian IV and by France's string-pulling, only now did it really become an all-European storm. And while its beginnings had holy-war roots, opponents of the edict now also saw it in the light of power politics, of new territorial ambitions, and of a domineering Habsburg emperor who aimed to tear up the traditional liberties of Germany's princes and free cities. Cardinal Richelieu himself, fearful of having France surrounded by Habsburg might, had no qualms about putting his Catholicism to one side and throwing his weight behind Germany's Protestant princes. In the cockpit of politics, politics came first, not religion.

Encouraged and then partly bankrolled by France and Richelieu, Gustavus now stepped into the fray both as the upholder of German liberties and champion of the Protestant faith. He had his army pastors preach holy war to his soldiers. They heard prayers twice daily, sermons once a week, and sang hymns as they marched into battle. The king aimed to lend force to the religious motors of the war: There could be no doubt of this. Important sectors of the

German Protestant population regarded Gustavus as an "anti-papist" warrior sent to them by God. The city of Magdeburg passed quickly to his side. But it was some time before he was able to secure the allegiance of any major German prince. Wherever he met resistance, his armies turned into battering rams. Rulers, he declared, must be for or against him, for God or for the Devil—that is, for or against the Protestant cause. There was no third way. As for neutrality, said he to the ambassadors from Brandenburg, that "is nothing but rubbish which the wind raises and carries away."

At the sound of Gustavus's drums, we cannot help remembering that the power of the kings of Sweden was based, to a large extent, on their dismantling of the Roman church in Sweden in the sixteenth century. This achievement was completed, like its parallel in England, by the royal sequestration of all ecclesiastical property, a vast patrimony that had been built up over centuries.

Holy war, like all major wars, was fought on two fronts: at the level of leadership and policy, and out in the villages and cities under siege, where religious differences could mutate into wild furies.

Heartened by their militant Jesuit confessors, Ferdinand II and Maximilian of Bavaria dreamed of seeing a re-Catholicized Holy Roman Empire of the German Nation. When Lamormaini and Contzen, the two confessors, came under fire both from leading Catholic clerics and statesmen, the general of the Order of Jesuits, the Italian nobleman Muzio Vitelleschi, tried to protect them. Personally, he approved of the Edict of Restitution and could envisage a Europe of restored Catholicism. In prudence, however, he concealed his views and made no attempt to turn the edict into official Jesuit policy, which would have released a storm of political criticism in Spain and France as well. The Order, after all, had more than sixteen thousand Jesuits, most of them in Catholic Europe.

The edict generated a blaze of diplomatic activity at the princely courts: a war of words, outrage, legal sparring, recrimination, and varieties of blackmail. But out in the world of field armies, in the different theaters of operation, holy war meant panicky flight, plunder, murder, arson, rape, and strange atrocities. There, too, adversaries used and suffered a hail of words, such as in the cascades of broadsheets and pamphlets that spewed forth a toxic propaganda, and in the sermons of priests and pastors. Calvinists in particular argued that Habsburg imperialist policy posed a threat to all Protestant Europe.

On rare occasions, the two front lines of holy war—parish violence and the making of high policy—met, remarkably so in Paris, in the massacre of St. Bartholomew's Day, August 24, 1572. With the likely connivance of the king himself, Charles IX, several of France's top noblemen had the great Huguenot leader, Gaspard de Coligny, brutally assassinated in conditions that fell just short of being public. The murder took on the appearance of a license to kill and instantly set off a spree of killings. In the succeeding days, about two thousand Huguenots were massacred in Paris, many of them in their own houses. The virus then raced through the provinces. In the weeks that followed, provincial France saw the slaughter of hundreds of other Huguenots; and streams of refugees from beleaguered towns wound their way into Huguenot strongholds to find safety. The sieges of La Rochelle and Sancerre came directly out of that cutthroat climate, a frenzy stirred up by the court nobility itself. Searing, self-righteous passion had no measure. When news of the massacre of St. Bartholomew's Day reached Rome, there was rejoicing, and Pope Gregory XIII celebrated with a hymn of praise, the *Te Deum*.

Holy war in Germany seldom reached the emotional pitch of the French Wars of Religion. The fact that these were out-and-out civil wars, with the bitterness that often attends such conflict, may explain the difference. The battles of the Thirty Years War involved too many foreign armies for this epochal conflict to be seen as a civil war. And seventeenth-century Germany was not, in any case, a nation-state. It was a loose confederation of states and quasi-states, many of them tiny political entities.

I HAVE SUGGESTED THAT WAR at its most bloody-minded was in the sieges and blockades driven by religious passion. Here, in stark hunger and under a rainstorm of missiles, is where men were most likely to stop counting the dead, while wanting to believe that God was on their side. The sieges of Augsburg, Magdeburg, La Rochelle, Sancerre, and Paris attest to this, particularly in the anguished testimony of survivors. Day and night, working as a stimulus, the infernal workings of famine opened the way for priests and parsons to argue that it was better to die, better for the sake of one's immortal soul, than to comply with heresy. Or, as a Protestant, better to die than to make peace with papists and fall under the heel of the Whore of Rome.

The experience of Magdeburg underlines the extremes of holy war in Germany. It was the first city to side with Gustavus Adolphus in his opening campaign against Ferdinand II and Roman Catholicism, and he was delighted by this alliance, although it was one that would all but cost the city its life. Yet less than a year later, he expressed no gratitude and little pity over its having been stormed and burned. On the contrary, he blamed others for the tragedy, and he charged the people of Magdeburg with "incompetence, carelessness, lack of energy, [and] even treachery." In the weeks leading up to the storming, he was in a position to move and deploy his army in its defense. But in addition to juggling other priorities, he was checked by the feeling that the Imperial army was superior; and he had no wish to risk a defeat so soon after his invasion of Germany.

Proud Magdeburg was regarded as the citadel of the evangelical stance in Germany. Passing to Luther's side in 1531—one of the first large cities to do so—it came to be known as "the chancellery of God and Christ." Two acts of collective heroism enhanced the city's reputation: successful resistance to a siege laid by the forces of the Duke of Saxony, Moritz, back in 1550–1551, and then very recently, in 1629, the city had again foiled a siege, this one imposed by Wallenstein. Songs and the makings of an urban myth had thus collected around the city, turning it, in the public mind, into the quintessential Protestant stronghold. And something of all this had been filtered into the self-image that drove and inspired Magdeburg to resist Tilly,

Pappenheim, and their Imperialist troops in the winter and spring of 1631.

The storming of the city was therefore all the more shocking when the news broke, casting an immediate penumbra of fear over all the centers of German Protestantism. In the first seven months alone, no fewer than 205 pamphlets and 41 flyers turned the news into a kind of "media event." Yet the catastrophe had been brought on by an unbending minority of evangelicals in the city: by their repeated rejection of Tilly's offer of peaceful terms, by their hard but vain belief that God would send Gustavus Adolphus to them, and by the most die-hard of all the Protestants in Magdeburg, the garrison commander, Dietrich von Falkenberg, who kept assuring the town council that the king was on his way. Right to his final hour, this soldier proved that he was ready to sacrifice his life for godly religion. His readiness to be a martyr, however, also entailed the possible sacrifice of all others in Magdeburg. In the event, about twenty thousand people perished.

IT SEEMS A HARD AND unwelcome thing to say in a democratic ethos, but the bald truth is that terror can wipe out religious differences and impose orthodoxy, or at least this was the case in sixteenth- and seventeenth-century Europe. Terror put an end to the spread of the Calvinist "heresy" in France. In the early 1560s, it was moving out and winning converts so fast and easily, in the towns above all, that many Huguenots looked forward to engulfing the whole of France. The civil war, however, halted their advance, and the massacres of 1572 began to reverse the process. Shaped by compliance and accommodation, forced conversions back to Catholicism—conversions made out of fear—were likely to become the real thing in the next generation. Of course many Huguenots emigrated, abandoning France for the Low Countries, for Germany, and for England; but the many who stayed, and who clung to their Calvinism, were gradually worn away in the seventeenth century, and then put outside the law by Louis XIV's Revocation of the Edict of Nantes in 1685.

In Germany and the Empire, the Religious Peace of Augsburg (1555) laid it down that princes had the right to determine the religious faith of their lands, Catholic or Lutheran. The arrangement entertained no toleration for Calvinism or other Protestant sects. In law, in the give-and-take of international relations, the will of one prince could now impose religious practice and doctrine on millions of people. This bond between ruler and the accepted form of worship jibed fully with the desires of the Habsburg emperors, but also with those of the kings of Spain, France, Sweden, and England. In their realms, the wrong religious view was treason.

The State: Emerging Leviathan

America's military adventures are paid for with borrowed money.
John Gray, black mass

BANKERS AND PUBLIC DEBT

War on a large scale was impossible without bankers, and early modern banking, with its daring operations, would have been impossible without war.

In our day, the state may step in to save a country's banks from insolvency. In early modern Europe, on the contrary, bankers stepped in on occasion to keep the state from defaulting.

To raise an army called for cash and a line of credit. This is what paid for mercenaries, as well as for food, artillery, pack animals, fodder, wagons, and the web of services required to deliver them. But taxes (the "sinews of power") could not be collected in a day. In affairs of this kind, even efficient administrations require time, and the early modern state was far from being efficient, especially since war could easily devour, in a few months, two or three years of public revenue. How lay hands on the like?

Enter bankers and moneylenders.

Indeed, they had appeared on the scene long before, and, like prosperous merchants, were almost a natural feature of the European urban landscape. The explosive rise of cities in the late middle ages, together with the long-distance trade in luxury cloth, spices, grain, and precious raw materials, had given birth to banking. It was already a complex activity, as was the financing of war, by the beginning of the fourteenth century, when double-entry bookkeeping made its first appearance. Early bankers often became billionaires, in our terms, on the profits of lending to princes and to cities. Thus the Medici, Strozzi, Fuggers, Welsers, Doria, and many others, whose loans were usually secured by their proprietary hold over runs of taxes and other rights. Long before 1500, princes and urban oligarchs were drawing on a sophisticated system of moneylending and on international financial networks. A king could borrow money in Antwerp or Lyon, to be paid out in Milan or Naples; or, having borrowed it in Madrid, he could arrange to have it disbursed in Brussels and Vienna. Bankers sat, so to speak, at the key points of these operations, taking in deposits from noblemen, bishops, merchants, high-ranking officials, nuns, widows, monasteries, cities, princes, and even small-time moneylenders such as pawnbrokers. Often, indeed, syndicates of bankers pooled their resources to make mammoth loans to kings.

Generally speaking, bankers' account books reveal that their depositors were likely to earn a yearly interest of about 5 percent. The deposits were lent out by the bankers at rates of from 12 to 35 percent, and they could leap to 67 percent. But high interest rates—let it be emphasized—met with strong disapproval everywhere in Europe; they smacked of greed ("usury") and almost of robbery, and could be seen as illegal. Bankers, therefore, were not forthcoming about profits or inflated rates of interest; and information about these matters is among the most difficult to nail down in research. The profits of sixteenth-century papal bankers are still mostly shrouded in mystery.

On top of interest costs, exchange transactions of the sort that moved capital across the face of Europe long commanded fees in the range of at least 12 percent of the sums to be moved. The armies of Spain, France, and the Empire frequently called for the dispatch of funds in this fashion. At one point in the 1540s, Mary of Hungary, sister to the Emperor Charles V and regent in the Habsburg Netherlands, had money sent from there to her troops in Germany. The sum was repaid in Flanders with funds from Spain, but the entire transaction involved a double transfer, and 40 percent of the original money lent was lost in the two currency exchanges.

When in 1575, in debt to Genoese bankers, the king of Spain suspended interest payments on loans, the archbishop of Genoa lodged a bitter complaint, claiming that the action would ruin convents, hospitals, poor folk, and other small-time depositors in his diocese. If there was exaggeration in his claim, there was also some truth in it.

Wallenstein, one of the generals of the Thirty Years War, managed to put one hundred thousand soldiers into the field because he was able to borrow huge sums of money from a remarkable banker, Hans de Witte. The Fuggers of Augsburg were the chief bankers of the Habsburg Emperor Charles V, the biggest borrower, debtor, and warlord of the first half of the sixteenth century. Second in this line of distinction was the king of France, Henry II (1547–1559), most of whose funds for war were loans from Italian and French bankers. Charles V left a staggering debt of nearly 30 million ducats, about five or six years of royal revenue. But he was greatly surpassed as a spender by his son, Philip II, king of Spain, whose voracious military needs tethered him to the leading Genoese bankers of the day—the Centurione, Grimaldi, de Negro, and Spinola—and to a debt, when he died in 1598, of 100 million ducats: some nine or ten times his augmented yearly receipts.

THE BANKRUPTCIES OF THE HABSBURG kings of Spain reveal the ways in which leading states paid for war. Nothing in ordinary government spending, such as administration or the household expenses of princes, ever approached the costs of war. In managing war costs, the key measure turned out to be a revolutionary stratagem: the consolidating and funding of public debt, hence deficit financing.

The roots of this procedure were in the thirteenth and early fourteenth centuries, in the fiscal demands of the chronic warfare that nagged at the great merchant republics of Venice, Florence, and

Genoa. Germany's free cities also had recourse to similar measures in the fourteenth century.

Italian city-states were among the first to draw all government debt together, with a view to paying it by converting the debt into bonds. Purchased by citizens and subjects, shares in government debt earned a yearly interest of about 5 percent; and in the early years the principal was often paid back, unless war came along to knock expenses out of control. Now debt soared, and repayment of the capital became more difficult. Taxes, meanwhile, being tied to the debt, went to pay the interest on it, so that even when restitution of the invested capital became more infrequent, the yearly interest on it was paid. Government bonds could thus be turned into annuities, and people with the capital to invest were able to live on the returns. Long-term public debt had thus, at this point, become little more than the sum of government bonds.

Between 1557 and 1662, in the middle of dire fiscal crises, the kings of Spain were driven to acknowledge bankruptcy ten times. The default of 1647 throws light on the key operation that marked these events, while also revealing solutions that were astonishingly modern.

War had driven the royal government to the brink of a financial collapse. Even in the late sixteenth century, the enterprising Philip II, steeped in debt, had been unable at times to pay his servants. In 1647, Philip IV and his council of finance found themselves forced to suspend payment on loans from thirty-three contracting bankers (*asentistas*). The debt amounted to more than 14 million ducats. Now all the revenue which had been streaming out to them as interest on the loans was halted, in spite of the fact that binding contracts linked specific sources of revenue, such as particular taxes, to the loans. The contracts also called for repayment of the principal.

Panic ensued. There was next a general audit, and then negotiations stretching out for nearly eighteen months. The monarchy was "too big to fail," too important to be allowed to go into an uncontrolled unilateral default, a financial collapse euphemistically known nowadays as "a credit event." The bankers had too much wealth invested in Spain's sovereign debt to stand by and do nothing, for in addition to the immense losses for them and the wrecking of their reputations, the failure would have caused a financial meltdown in the great seaport of Genoa, if they had all been Genoese. But as it turned out, only three of the bankers were from Genoa. One was English, one Flemish, and one a Florentine. All the others, twenty-seven of them, were Portuguese New Christians: that is, Portuguese Jews whose families had converted to Christianity in recent times.

Making distinctions, the king's financial counselors worked to cut deals. The Genoese and two of the Portuguese bankers were exempted from the suspension of payments. Special arrangements with others were also made. But the general solution lay in the crown's decision to convert the short-term ("floating") debt to the bankers into a class of select government bonds (*juros*). Over the next fourteen years, payment on these special *juros* would go to redeem part of the principal. Thereafter, the payment of interest on the remaining bonds would begin. In effect, the short-term loans were converted into long-term debt. That conversion, however, eliminated the heavy payments on the high-interest loans, thereby freeing the mortgaged taxes that had been pinned to those loans. The freed taxes could now be used as collateral for the raising of new short-term loans.

Meanwhile, the special bonds issued to the bankers were meant to earn a yearly interest of 7.15 percent, rather than the flat 5 percent of the ordinary government bonds. The bankers were also given the right to sell their *juros* on the open market. But in this, apparently, they were not very successful. The interest of 7.15 percent was seldom paid. And James Boyajian, the historian of these proceedings, sees wholesale fraud in the affair. Toward the end of the seventeenth century, the heirs of the bankers were still creditors of the crown for princely sums.

Was it the case that the proceedings added up to little more than fraud? Possibly. Yet the solution had a completely modern spin. We speak of "managing" or "restructuring" sovereign debt. Spain's bankers and ministers did just that: They managed a default. In our day, to manage a default is to convert the original debt into new debt with the same value. The new debt, however, now carries a lower rate of interest, and its maturity is extended over a longer period of time.

AUGSBURG'S TOP BANKERS, THE FUGGERS, lost money in their relations with Charles V, but it must have been a fraction of the profits garnered, over more than thirty years, from the rights that had been made over to them—rights over the silver and copper mines of the Tyrol, and over runs of taxes even in faraway Naples. The banker Hans de Witte committed suicide over his impending losses when his chief debtor, Wallenstein, was dismissed as the supreme commander of the Imperial army. The risk of loss was built into the nature and ventures of big banking, above all in dealings with powerful princes. But it was also the case that the resulting profits were fit for the ransom of kings, and no one knew this better than the bankers themselves.

From the time of his first bankruptcy, in 1557, Philip II of Spain made it clear that financial relations with him could be dodgy. His Genoese bankers saw the revenue that was meant for them—taxes linked to the repayment of their loans—exchanged for the government bonds known as *juros*. The revenue thus released, such as taxes on wine and salt, would then be used to raise new short-term loans of the kind that provided immediate cash and supplies for the Spanish army. Yet this high-handed procedure did not frighten bankers away, nor did the financial crunches of 1560, 1575, and 1596, even when it was claimed that their loans were mired in usury. In canon law they no doubt were. The Genoese clung to the king because they knew that over the longer term the profits to be realized from their ties with him would richly exceed any money lost along the way, or any that might be made from shipping and long-distance trade. More than two hundred years of banking know-how guided their handling of Spain's royal debt: an expertise gleaned from the

Venetians, the Florentines, and their own forbears. They knew about disaster in banking. It had a history. As early as the 1340s, the great Florentine banking houses of the Bardi and Peruzzi had crashed, owing to a run on their deposits: a run set off by rumors connected with the knowledge that they had made a loan of some 1.3 million florins of gold to the king of England, Edward III.

In the late sixteenth century, the reputation of Genoa's bankers was unrivaled. They ran the international financial fairs at Besançon and then Piacenza. Held four times yearly, and peaking at Piacenza in the period from 1579 to 1627, these eight-day affairs served as clearinghouses for Europe's biggest bankers and international merchants. Here they raised "baskets" of money, settled accounts, rolled debt over, and discounted foreign bills of exchange. Typically, in a deal, the main lending house—Centurione, Lomellini, or another— would give its name to the loan transaction and fork out the largest share of the sum to be lent. But other bankers and their capital were also brought into the investment, in order to spread the risk. When the kings of Spain defaulted, the bankers would then be forced to deal with depositors back home. But we need not weep for Genoa's bankers: They flourished on the profits to be made from war. Their arrangements carried privileges not passed on to their depositors, one of the most lucrative being the right to export (and traffic in) specified amounts of bullion, notably silver from the New World. This specie was then profitably exchanged for gold, because silver was much sought after in the Near East. Next, the moneymen from Genoa could also count on the hefty profits from the fees imposed on exchange transactions, such as when they paid out their loans in Antwerp, Brussels, or Vienna. Here, if it was wage money for soldiers, their contacts frequently paid the loans out in kind, in food especially, but also in weapons and other supplies. Such payment also resulted in profit, and this was partly passed on, in the form of lower fees, to the bankers in Madrid.

The heyday of the New Christian Portuguese bankers at the court of Spain spanned the years from 1627 to 1650. Most of the Genoese banking firms, in 1626–1627, were pushed to one side, more or less suddenly. King Philip IV was straining to cut expenses on loans, and the new breed of men from Portugal made this possible. Relying on far-flung networks of relatives and acquaintances, these men could reach out for more favorable terms to distant Hamburg, Rouen, Amsterdam, Constantinople, Venice, and even Brazil, where Portuguese Jews and other new converts dominated the sugar and slave trades. With these informed contacts, Madrid's New Christians were able to offer the crown better loan terms and lower fees for distant exchange transactions—reason enough to move the king's banking business from the old Genoese houses into new hands.

But if the kings of Spain survived more than a century of war-inflicted debt, the like could also bring regime change, particularly in smaller states.

One of the most famous of all Renaissance dynasties, the Medici, owed its origins to war and debt. In the early 1430s, the Republic of Florence, already in grave financial troubles, edged into a war of conquest with the neighboring city-republic of Lucca, plunging Florentines more grievously into debt. The war put a terrifying strain on the collection of income and property taxes, and cast the urban oligarchy into a political crisis. Florence's richest banker, Cosimo de' Medici, now came to be seen as a mainstay for the city. A strong faction gathered around him. Knowing how to deploy his money among leading citizens and supporters, he maneuvered untiringly to increase his personal political power. By working hand and glove with cronies in the city's political councils, he and his followers manipulated elections to government office over the course of a generation (1434–1464), always drawing more and more power around the banker and his family.

Cosimo's direct male descendants then used their inherited wealth and authority to devote themselves to politics full-time, to buy (with cash) princely position in the Church, to abandon banking, to control Florence's chief offices, and to turn the Florentine Republic into a princely despotism. The most famous of them, Lorenzo the Magnificent (1448–1492), even pilfered large sums from the public till. The ascent of the Medici house and the snuffing out of Florentine republican liberty went back to an insane war with Lucca, to a credit crunch, and to a banker who also turned out to be a ruthless politician.

THE PUBLIC FINANCE MACHINE

The heart of Europe's most effective public-finance machines was the consolidated or unified funded debt: a brilliant invention because it facilitated borrowing for war, while also drawing subjects or citizens into supporting the state by investing in it. Henceforth the state would be in debt to the more prosperous parts of its population, individuals as well as corporate groups. In practice, this involved the payment of periodic interest, not the doling out of large sums to redeem or buy back shares in the debt. Now, too, the state could raise short-term loans, issue high-interest bonds for these, and even pay back the principal by pledging particular taxes or rights to the short-term lenders. Specific streams of revenue, such as the excises on meat, salt, grains, or wine, were mortgaged for a year or two. This utilizing of the integrated public debt gave remarkable mobility to the state, as it rushed to employ the newfound cash (or credit) in the fighting of its wars.

There could be no funded debt without taxes and rights of the sort that generated income, for these alone produced the cash to pay interest on, or redeem, government bonds. Here, in tax revenue, was the other half of the public-finance machine.

Up to about the mid-thirteenth century, rulers had only the income from their domains: their own lands, feudal dues, and the sums reaped from the local administration of justice. Receipts from local tolls also entered this picture, and some princes, like many free cities, claimed a monopoly over the ancient salt tax. In Spain, a religious frontier, the crown was entitled to a large share of church income, intended for use in warfare against Muslims.

In the fourteenth and fifteenth centuries, the armed extension of territorial boundaries, animated by richer economies and swelling ambitions, raised expenses and demanded a thickening stream of revenue. But nobilities and urban elites used their political weight to avoid taxes on land and income, or to have these treated as levies of last resort. The galloping rises in public revenue thus came chiefly from the so-called indirect taxes: customs duties and levies on every kind of foodstuff, especially on beer and wine, meat and grains, as well as on manufactured goods, notably cloth. These were levies that always weighed heaviest on the poorer classes. A tax on flour, meat, salt, or wool more easily emptied the pockets of the farm worker or the urban craftsman and day laborer.

In generalizing about taxes, we must bear in mind that they varied considerably from one region or country to another. Denmark, Hungary, Bohemia, and parts of Austria and Germany, such as Brandenburg and Saxony, made a point of privileging noblemen and exempted them from direct taxation. The French and Spanish nobilities also enjoyed major tax immunities, and the tenure of office exempted many thousands of rich bourgeois from direct taxes. The French *taille* of the sixteenth and seventeenth centuries, a direct tax on property and income, was levied principally on rural landholders of non-noble status, and in Burgundy no nobleman was ever touched by it. Moreover, much *taille* income in France's frontier provinces (the *pays d'états*) remained there, and did not begin to reach the king's coffers in substantial sums until the 1630s and 1640s. One Castilian tax, the *servicio*, was paid solely by commoners (*pecheros*), marking a clean distinction between them and noblemen.

Moving hand in hand with the incidence and changing face of war, the rise of regular taxation began in the fourteenth century, with sales taxes that were meant to be temporary, such as the *aides* in France, the *alcabala* in Spain, the excise in parts of Germany, and their equivalents in the Italian city-states. All these raised the prices of food, drink, and goods. Here and there a hearth or poll tax also saw the light. The costs of war gradually turned the sales taxes into permanent levies, which came to be seen as constituting "ordinary" taxation. Parenthetically, since the ports on the Baltic Sea took in very profitable customs duties, they would be fiercely fought for by the Swedes, Danes, and Poles.

The wars of the sixteenth and seventeenth centuries led to an incessant quest for more revenue, as we have noted, so that at certain moments in wartime Spain, France, and Germany, even noblemen felt the fiscal pinch, such as in emergency "contributions" or the freezing of interest payments on their shares in the public debt. In Germany, the Thirty Years War had such an impact on princes, minor though they might be, that they began to hound their reluctant *Reichsstände* (territorial assemblies) for the funds to have their own standing armies: the most costly of all government undertakings. From this time on, in military matters, this would be the main fiscal direction for Europe, and Brandenburg-Prussia soon moved to the forefront of the quest for armed force. More than ever, taxes too came to hold the center point of concerns for the life of politics.

Here, in short, was the birth of the modern state: a tax-hungry polity. And it might be an absolute monarchy, best profiled in eighteenth-century Prussia, or a constitutional and limited monarchy, notably England after 1660, where Parliament was crucially involved in the business of levying taxes. Venice to one side, the new Dutch Republic was the outstanding example of a republican tax-seeking state.

Armies and taxes, then, were the cardinal concerns of the early modern state, and this of course would also include navies where called for. Tax money was the first and most urgent business of the state. With taxes it paid for war, and with its armies the state sought territory, security, influence, commercial interests, and new sources of taxation. Yet it farmed taxes out to financiers, thus putting one of the chief functions of the modern state, the collecting of taxes, into private hands. Here a crucial aspect of administration was alienated, and the state lost both income and degrees of control. To be sure, tax farming put cash up front for the debtor state, enabling it to get on with its war-making for a while longer. But the farming out of taxes was always an expedient, something of a short-term solution, a remedy—though not necessarily seen as thus—for administrative failure; and it was costly, because much of the revenue was drained away in private profit. In the late seventeenth century, England snatched taxes away from the tax farmers and made the collecting of taxes an integral part of the state's expanding bureaucracy.

SPENDING

France's Italian Wars (1494–1559) carried the crown's expenses to unprecedented heights, even though its armies in Italy were meant to live largely off the occupied lands. The gap between revenue and spending widened inexorably, and from the early 1520s, agents of King Francis I began to seek cash from foreign bankers at the fairs of Lyon. Some of the sources of royal revenue were offered as collateral. At one point the king was in debt to eighty-seven different Italian bankers, among whom were forty-five from Florence and seventeen from Lucca. The government also started to finance long-term debt by selling *rentes*, bonds in the royal debt, promising a steady return of annual income for buyers. But neither these nor bankers' loans nor the unencumbered taxes brought in the income to meet war costs. Now, with far-reaching consequences for the French state, ministers began to sell government offices, gradually turning this recourse into an important source of cash. Officials had already hit on this stratagem in the fifteenth century, but it became big business only after 1520 and went on to the eighteenth century.

Yet all the ready cash and credit raised by the different means fell far short of enabling kings to pay their way. In 1559, France's public debt amounted to 43 million *livres*: three times its annual income, with interest eating up 8 million *livres* per year, or over half of yearly revenue. Just the year before, King Henry II had managed to field an army of nearly fifty thousand men, of whom more than twenty thousand were expensive German and Swiss mercenaries. Large numbers in that army, however, would go unpaid. No wonder, then, that in 1559 the crown was squeezed into halting the payment of interest to its creditor bankers and possessors of *rentes*. It was a declaration of bankruptcy. From this time on, periodically, the government would have trouble selling *rentes* or securing loans from bankers, unless it agreed to pay exorbitant interest charges.

And then the outbreak of France's Wars of Religion (1562–1598) all but tore the country apart fiscally, as commanders in the field, Huguenots as well as royalists, simply grabbed and spent any tax money that could be diverted their way. By 1576 the royal debt had climbed to 100 million *livres*. Cramped without remission by the wars, the kings of France could not beg enough money or credit, however strident their pleas, to send out armies strong enough to defeat the Huguenots and to bring the wars to an end. Verging repeatedly on bankruptcy, their ministers occasionally halted interest payments on *rentes*, such as in 1585 and nearly so again in 1598. Later there would be outright bankruptcies in 1602–1604, 1648, and 1661, with moments of disabling fiscal strains in the 1630s and 1650s.

Meanwhile, the sale of offices went on, the numbers of proprietary officeholders climbing from 4,041 in 1515 to 11,000 by 1600, then leaping to 46,047 by 1665, with another jump to about 60,000 before the end of the century. Many of these men, such as in the courts, were trained in law and sprang from moneyed, socially ambitious families. But there were also venal *officiers* in the treasury, in the tax network, in administration, and even at lower levels socially, including some who held office as fishmongers.

Venal officeholders cross the middle of the fiscal scene here, not only because the money to buy office put substantial sums into the royal coffers—in the first half of the seventeenth century, about 28 percent or more of ordinary revenue—but also because they were sometimes forced to make loans to the crown in return for *rentes*, especially during the middle and later years of the century. They thus became cogs in the country's public-finance machine. They received an annual income (*gages*) on the investment made in the purchase of their offices. But fiscal emergencies often suspended the payment of *gages*, or, if not this, the officeholders might be obligated to accept *rentes* as payment. In a further twist, they could buy the right to will their offices to heirs by paying an annual fee. Obviously, then, they had a vital interest both in the liquidity of the state and in milking it. The contradiction here pitted war and sovereign debt against the private income, honor, and tax exemptions that came with the holding of office.

Officeholders in Spain, too, would nurse the shadowy contradiction between their seeking to maximize the profits of office while also needing a truly solvent state. In Castile alone, by 1665, the holders of venal offices, especially in the municipalities, numbered about thirty thousand men. This made for a ratio of "one officeholder for every 166 inhabitants." In France, by contrast, with its 46,047 *officiers* in 1665, the ratio was "one for every 380 inhabitants." So that if French owners of office constituted a state within a state, we have to say that the Spanish ratio was far more alarming and pointed all the sooner to an unhealthy body politic.

In the fifteenth century, the great Florentine humanist Leon Batista Alberti accused the members of Florence's merchant oligarchy of treating the state as though it were their shop: a source of business and profit. He declared—and it was true—that they speculated on the republic's consolidated debt, intent on using the profits to dower their daughters. Proprietary officeholders in France engaged in a similar, if more complicated, operation. Their privatizing of office ate away at the centralizing potential of the state, but their corporate interests, swinging in a contradictory direction, also made them want a solvent state. In this extraordinary dialectic, the dangers cut two ways. In one direction, the holders of venal office went after as much profit from the state as they could get their hands on; but in the other, they themselves ran risks, such as in being obligated to lend money to the state, or in seeing their income from *rentes* and from office suspended for the sake of the state.

Taxes, meanwhile—the ultimate font of public income—were skewed to favor the officeholders and to disfavor the many who could least afford to pay the sales taxes, the special war levies, and the ad hoc charges for the billeting of soldiers. Nevertheless, in the seventeenth century, the country's fiscal pincers would be sharply felt, now and again, by the officeholders too. For the France of Cardinal Richelieu (1624–1642) and Louis XIV (1661–1715) was a chronicle of bigger armies, longer wars, ballooning taxes, awesome public debt, and bristling discontent. In the 1630s and 1640s, the government had to turn its troops against rebellious peasants, and then face a revolt of the nobility, including episodes of civil war from 1648 to 1653 (the Fronde). The causes of these uprisings lay in official corruption, in the violent billeting of soldiers, and in oppressive taxes.

The story of war finance in France, particularly under Louis XIV, has far too many intricacies to present here. Summaries must suffice. The Nine Years War (1689–1698) and the War of the Spanish Succession (1702–1714) saw French armies of 320,000 and 255,000 soldiers take the field. These colossi required sums of money that no degree of ramped-up taxation could find, even with soldiers camped on the backs, so to speak, of their own civilians or of those in occupied foreign territory.

To meet the unforgiving need for money, Louis's finance ministers looked beyond taxes and turned to stratagems that brought in hundreds of millions of additional *livres*. They marketed streams of new *rentes* and life annuities; they debased the coinage; and they employed syndicates of financiers to sell patents of nobility, to invent and sell numerous new offices, and to extract "forced loans . . . from existing officeholders." In addition, they halted payments on *rentes*, lowered interest rates, and even slashed the capital sums involved in runs of old *rentes*. Officeholders now saw themselves truly hounded, and in the eighteenth century their obstructionism would often hobble the crown's ability to finance wars.

At the beginning of the seventeenth century, annual revenue amounted to about 98 million *livres*. By midcentury this tally had risen to more than 500 million *livres*. The frontier provinces—e.g., Provence, Languedoc, Dauphiné—had been hammered into line and were now paying much of the take from their *taille* into the royal coffers. With the help of a new poll tax, the rise in revenue continued, but there was no increase in the net usable income. By 1714, Louis XIV's wars had cut this revenue to 27 percent of what actually came in. The rest vanished in "servicing" the debt, in alienated revenue, and in special administrative costs, such as salaries for venal officeholders. On Louis's death in 1715, France saw itself saddled with a debt variously estimated at between 1.7 and 2.5 billion *livres*.

Russia—to take a sidelong comparative glance—had a variety of direct and indirect taxes, including taxes on land and capital. In the 1670s and 1680s, more than 60 percent of the tsar's income went to the army. Heavy billeting and forced peasant labor for military purposes were not included in that figure. If paid for, those services would no doubt have claimed more than the whole sum of tsarist income. The bottom line was that the tsar's army "lived to a large extent 'off the land' at home and abroad." Rather along similar lines, earlier in the century, Gustavus Adolphus, in knocking together a military empire, burdened Sweden with very little debt relative to costs. His armies in Germany had no choice but to live mainly from plunder, above all from "contributions" in cash and in kind, and from the subsidies offered by allies. It was a predatory solution imposed by Sweden's sparse population and rivulet of revenue. In the 1630s, the Swedish treasury could seriously fantasize a "war budget of 4,377,732 riksdaler," when the real figure was likely "to be anywhere between twenty and thirty millions."

In view of Sweden's agrarian economy and material poverty, Swedish victories in the Thirty Years War have something freakish about them. The country's armies, however, were led by brilliant generals: Gustavus Adolphus, Johan Banér, Gustav Horn, Hermann Wrangle, and Lennart Torstensson. Even their major victories were the work of German and other foreign mercenaries, not of their relatively small numbers of Swedish soldiers, who served for the most part in garrisons. Nothing like this would be seen again.

IF SERIOUSLY TOUCHED BY THE Thirty Years War, no German prince or city emerged from it without a crippling overload of debt. In many cases, the debtor simply defaulted and suspended or repudiated interest payments on it. In other cases, repayment was carried over into the eighteenth century, with some payments to heirs still being made in the nineteenth century! In the war's financial crunch, towns and local assemblies had been coerced into paying huge sums of protection and ransom money to Imperial or Swedish forces, and they were forced to borrow the sums to be paid out. Cities usually issued interest-bearing bonds, thereby weakening themselves for the coming struggles with their own princes. They were soon to feel the tightening noose of princely absolutism and the rise of standing armies under the control of princes.

After the war, many princes also found themselves steeped in debt; but their estates or *Reichsstände* (representative assemblies) were frequently bullied into paying it. One of the foremost magnates, for example, the elector of Saxony, Johann Georg, had been driven to default on 10 million florins of due interest, and he was still in debt for the sum of 25.2 million florins on his death in 1656. The astounding size of this debt—about 16.8 million talers—may be appreciated by noting that in 1649, just after the war's end, the costs of the Swedish army in Germany (63,700 soldiers) ran to 500,000 talers per month, giving rise eventually to a bill for 15 million talers.

★ ★ ★

IN MATTERS OF PUBLIC FINANCE and the storms of war, the Dutch Republic also faced an internal enemy that was always the same: debt.

For much of the seventeenth century, according to an expert on the matter, "almost 90 per cent of the [Dutch] Union's budget was devoted to warfare," first in the struggle for independence from Spain, and then, from the 1670s, in fighting off the French and the acquisitive designs of Louis XIV.

Up to about 1648, the armies of the Dutch Republic ranged in size from forty thousand to seventy-five thousand men, most of them foreign mercenaries. Average yearly war costs, in the final decades of the war with Spain (1621–1648), totaled about 24 million guilders. But the mountain of debt rose, and Holland alone, the richest of the seven United Provinces, saw its share of the expenses climb to the yearly sum of 16,527,948 guilders, in spite of the fact that its annual revenues brought in far less: only 10,847,690 guilders.

Although the many details varied from one Dutch province to another, the bulk of tax receipts came from sales taxes on salt, beer, soap, bread, meat, fruit, fish, vinegar, grain, coal, beans, milling, wool, and even building materials, dice, playing cards, and firewood. If the Dutch had a reputation for paying their mercenaries on time, it was also the case that, like others, they paid wages that amounted to about half or even less of what unskilled workers might earn. Moreover, contrary to many a claim, they could be very late in paying, particularly, as often happened, when some of the United Provinces failed to pay their share of the agreed sums for the maintenance of soldiers. Units of Scottish and English soldiers issued a bitter stream of complaint against their Dutch paymasters.

In 1648, at the end of the war with Spain, Holland alone carried a debt in excess of 125 million guilders, and interest on this sum claimed more than 53 percent of revenue. But luckily for the Dutch, generally speaking, interest did not rise above 6 percent, because investors in the debt had confidence in the collective financial decisions of the United Provinces and their Council of State.

THE STATE

The European "sovereign" state came out of a dense scatter of medieval microstates and half-states: mini-kingdoms, lordships (feudal fiefs), tiny principalities, and cities. The larger and more enterprising of these—Venice, say, or Capetian France—absorbed neighboring "statelets" by the force of arms, by means of defensive treaties, or by political claims, heredity, and the rites of marriage. It was a process of seizure and acquisition, leading to the ascent of the modern state in the period from the fourteenth to the sixteenth centuries.

But the process left a trail, a spoor. For the state can be a monster, above all in war, and it often struck contemporaries this way: Maurus Friesenegger, Alexandre Dubois, and a host of Huguenots. In this embodiment, supreme political authority has a history with a multitude of visages. Our own day is not a stranger to the spectacle of monstrous states.

The monstrosities of the early modern state were most visible in Europe's great powers. They put huge armies into the field, as we have seen, but could not afford to keep them there, save by means of theft and violence against their own people, not to speak of what their armies did to other peoples. They tended to treat their ordinary soldiers like the scum of the earth, broke every contract with them, and yet demanded their loyalty or were ready to see them flogged, mutilated, branded, shipped out as galley slaves, or hanged when they deserted. Using the poor, the unemployed, and the marginal, including common criminals, as cannon fodder, they can be said to have pursued a politics of social cleansing. They depended upon entrepreneur officers for the raising of their armies, thereby abandoning critical elements of control over numbers, quality, and costs. The besieging of cities, the most sustained and shrill of all acts of war against civilians, was the norm of warfare for them. When their armies went unpaid or hungry, the plunder and ravaging of rural communities was also a norm for the great powers. And they often proved to be largely worthless in their efforts to handle the mortal questions of wartime logistics.

The early modern state strained to find more revenue for war, but put the collection of taxes into private hands, thus opening the doors to profiteering, corruption, and thuggery. It made tacit contracts with its own people, promising the periodic payment of interest on their investments in the public debt, but then proceeded, time and again, to break those contracts by the abrupt withholding of payments. It was driven to seek out short-term loans from bankers, then maneuvered to conceal the alarming interest rates from the responsible diets and assemblies. In Spain, the Empire, France, Poland, and England, acting in a frantic quest to pay its debts, the early modern state was capable of debasing its coinage by melding base metal into its silver coins, thereby wreaking inflationary havoc in the marketplace. And it sold government offices, converting into private property that which more properly belonged to the order of public administration and politics.

The question of accountability comes up.

Was it the case that the kings of France and Spain, or that German and other princes, were absolute rulers, answerable only to their consciences? Not in the least. In every case, their authority was checked by one or more bars: custom, representative bodies, councillors, the law, or even the threat of rebellion.

The power of taxation was the one most ringed in by restraints. Representative bodies of one kind or another nearly always claimed the right to levy taxes, and in these matters the prince had to negotiate with them. This was the case in Spain, France, England, Sweden, Denmark, Poland, most of Italy, and in the world of German princes. But at the end of the middle ages, and more pressingly so in the sixteenth and seventeenth centuries, relying on the turmoil of war, princes were able, more and more often, to intimidate and manipulate representative assemblies into providing some of the revenue needed for armies. Never all of it. The strongest arguments in favor of military funds hinged on security concerns and dynastic claims.

For Germany, public finance in the electorate of Brandenburg provided a pattern of things to come. Here the epidemics and barbarities of the Thirty Years War eliminated half of the population, and many farms remained wasteland for years after the war's end. Brandenburg's elector was able to use force majeure to levy taxes and to raise a little army without the approval of the provincial diet. Then, after 1648, Brandenburg returned briefly to traditional fiscal procedure. But in 1653, with the Northern Wars (1655–1660) on the horizon, and after much haggling, Frederick William, the Great Elector, got the estates to fund a small army for six years, in exchange for which he extended aristocratic privileges. These included the tax-exempt status of nobles and the freedom to impose the worst kind of serfdom (*Leibeigenschaft*) on the Brandenburg peasantry. Later, in his campaign to take Pomerania and Prussia, he ignored his provincial assembly, imposed taxes unilaterally, increased the size of his standing army, and even used his soldiers to force the payment of taxes. In twelve years (1660–1672), his army went from seven thousand to twelve thousand men. But by the time he died, in 1688, Brandenburg-Prussia had a standing army with a European reputation. Running to between twenty and thirty thousand men, its size was strikingly out of "sync" with the principality's modest economy and small population. Annual tax revenue had trebled to about 3.4 million talers. The period's most ambitious state was here in the making, but it was also one of the most heavily taxed in Europe.

That the early modern state retained its bellicose features for so long was a fact connected with the surrounding material world. Leading princes had emerged from the late middle ages as warlords, as the foremost official thugs; and the whiff of this armed background long persisted. Menace and swagger were a part of the political landscape, imparting an air that clung to certain princes—to Henry VIII of England, Henry of Navarre, Gustavus Adolphus, and to many northern noblemen. But more important, the alleged rights of dynasties, fiercely defended by princes, were turned into the engine that powered European foreign relations. And meanwhile, princely nagging for more revenue, more soldiers, more rights never ceased.

FOR ALL ITS CLERKS, AGENTS, secretaries, and field officials, the administrative apparatus of the early modern state was porous. Ties of patronage, special interests, inexperience, privilege, and the ownership of office foiled the better execution of tasks in the stickiest areas: war and public finance. Tax collecting and the recruiting of soldiers, each at the parish level, too often lay beyond the resources of government. By contrast, courts of law, or the job of legislating, presented no comparable challenges. The emerging state thus shied away from collecting its own taxes, and was unable to discipline its swelling armies. We have seen this ad nauseam. Ministers were aware of their failures. The French crown introduced a web of "fiscal intendants" (*intendants des finances*) whose job was to monitor the provincial administration of taxes. But in the seventeenth century, they were frequently alleged to be notoriously corrupt, and it has been suggested that the whole of France's "central financial administration was involved on a permanent basis in a conspiracy to commit fraud." Two of the most powerful first ministers of the age, cardinals Richelieu and Mazarin, ended with private fortunes that beggared belief: the first with 22 million *livres*, and Mazarin, a greedier courtier, with 37 million. Their way of life was unlikely to inspire honesty in their subordinates.

The aristocratic republics of Venice and Genoa, little states, were the first to link and coordinate war and taxes. But they were small fry on the changing chart of European power politics. Far more successful in the linking of war and taxes was the Dutch Republic, with its vast reserves—Holland especially—of commercial and maritime capital. Next in the successful juxtaposition of armies and revenue came the princes of Brandenburg-Prussia. Shortly after 1650, they began to take firm control of public finance by binding it strictly to military needs. In working to build a "power state," they developed a system of roving agents ("commissaries") who supervised the administration of taxes and affairs connected with the army. In the eighteenth century, these officials, often trained in law, became key figures in the organization of the Prussian state.

CHURCH LANDS WERE NOT MARGINAL to the fortunes of the fiscal-military state. England, Sweden, the Dutch Republic, the Rhenish Palatinate, Brandenburg, Hesse-Kassel, and other Protestant states paid their armies in part with wealth that had been looted from the Catholic Church. According to the historian R. L. Frost, the Swedish military state would have been impossible "without the Reformation . . . [and all the church land that then passed] into Crown possession. In 1523, it possessed 3,754 farms, the Church 14,340, the nobility 13,922, and the tax-[paying] peasants 35,239; by 1560, the Crown owned 18,936, the Church none, the nobility 14,175, and the peasants 33,130."

There was more. Having subjected the Lutheran and Calvinist churches to their control, princes quickly turned to enlist their support in the pursuit of blunt political aims. But Catholic princes were not novices in the art of using the Church for political ends. Priests and prelates had lent themselves to such purposes since time immemorial. Now and again, in the sixteenth and seventeenth centuries, about 18 to 25 percent of all royal revenue in Spain came from a tax on the clergy (the *subsidio*), from so-called "crusade" money (a papal grant for the fight against Muslims), and from the wealth of the country's great military-religious orders of Santiago, Alcántara, and Calatrava.

Jesuits attracted the venomous hatred of contemporaries precisely because they were seen to be meddling in politics. As confessors to kings and emperors, it was assumed that they worked to insinuate a special agenda into the earthly aims of their mighty penitents. And when they seemed to get in the way of high policy, as in the clash between Bourbons and Habsburgs in the 1630s and 1640s, to take one example, Cardinal Richelieu himself stepped in to clip the wings of King Louis XIII's Jesuit confessors. Meanwhile, back in Rome, the nobleman Muzio Vitelleschi, general of the Order's sixteen thousand priests, had to walk a fine line between moderate and more aggressive worldly policies, especially as the rank-and-file Jesuits were themselves likely to be divided in their political views.

The emerging new state, in short, in Protestant as in Catholic lands, now occupied the temporal space once held by a church whose popes and wide web of prelates had once sought to compete with kings.

SOVEREIGNTY AND THE POLITICS OF WAR

By the fourteenth century, the study of Roman law and a rich line of legal commentary on the powers of the pope had come together to issue in a full-blown conception of sovereignty and political absolutism. No European state, however, was strong enough—or ambitious enough—to exercise the envisaged "plenitude of power" until the sixteenth century.

In the matter of sovereignty, the Holy Roman Empire of the German Nation had a strange appearance. It was a kind of state, but it was not sovereign, because it consisted of states that verged on being sovereign. The emperors Charles V and Ferdinand II tried to expand its powers—in vain. It had virtually no army as such; its princes had armies, although they contributed on occasion to an Imperial force. It had no significant rights of taxation; these were claimed by the different princes and Imperial cities. And it could not make treaties that obligated its princes and cities, unless these agreed. In fact, German princes were free to conduct their own foreign policies and to make treaties, provided only that they did not enter alliances against the emperor. Militarily, then, the Empire turned into a big power only when the emperor was joined, say, by the electors of Bavaria and Saxony. But after 1650, such banding together went into a decline.

By the late sixteenth century, the major European states were well on their way to being sovereign. French and Spanish kings stood up to the papacy, and not seldom bent it to their will. Protestant states spurned the authority of the pope and used the power of the Reformed Churches to advance their political designs. In Catholic lands again, the new state, moving gradually against the claims of regional assemblies and mighty local lords, pursued a monopoly over the powers of taxation and official violence within its borders. The rights to legislate and to dispense justice were already a part of its sovereignty.

THE QUESTION NATURALLY PRESENTS ITSELF: Did political theory gain entry somehow, as an active force, to the claims of the state's evolving sovereignty? Yes, but only when resistance to the state generated intellectual challenges. Arguments now had to be aired by government ministers and lawyers, and these claims migrated out into the forums of ideas, to give or to take in themes and inspiration.

In the spring of 1420, in a tart exchange between two Florentine ambassadors and the privy councillors of their mighty northern neighbor, the Duke of Milan, the Florentines felt a slap on the face when they were suddenly told by one of them (a canon lawyer, no less), *Ius in armis est*, "Right is in the force of arms": that is, might makes right. They were shocked by this outburst. And yet they knew—they must have known—that behind the punctilio of diplomacy this was what politics often came down to in relations between states. It had been so in conflict among Italian city-states for two hundred years. Evidently, then, the Florentines were reacting out of an entrenched feeling of decorum, the feeling that although brute power was the ultimate enforcer in an international dispute, you did not admit it in so many words, not in diplomacy. Instead, you employed masks and artful words.

Shortly after 1500, dynastic claims began to vie for the proscenium of international politics with another principle: that of the "balance of power" in relations among states. The notion rested on a conception of regional security, and the argument behind it simply held that the leading European powers could not allow any one of them to become strong enough to pose a potential threat to the others. There was nothing in law, as in the case of dynastic rights, to give this political stance any legal validity, but none was required. Armed might sufficed to give it presence and force. Learned contemporaries found the stance in the politics of the ancient world. But fifteenth-century Italy, they observed, provided a recent and more instructive field of comparison. Here, for a time, the leading states—Naples, the papacy, Milan, and the republics of Florence and Venice—hit on a solution for their quarrels. In their quest for equilibrium, each was to have its proper weight. However, their achieved balance was soon wrecked by the clash between Valois and Habsburg princes in the Italian Wars (1494–1459), a fight over rival dynastic claims to the kingdom of Naples and the duchy of Milan. Their claims were farfetched, but their armies provided the necessary teeth.

Dynastic and "balance of power" arguments thus collided. In 1589, toward the end of France's Wars of Religion, the supporters of King Henry IV, still a Protestant, lashed out at the aspirations of the Habsburg King of Spain Philip II, with a plea to the effect that France was being dangerously encircled by Habsburg power. Philip's army occupied the southern Netherlands; one of his Habsburg cousins held the Imperial crown in Germany; and Philip, with money and troops, had thrown his support behind the intransigents of the French Catholic League, the very men who were fighting tooth and nail against Henry IV, against his claim to be the rightful king of France. His Calvinism, a supposed heresy, was being invoked to override his dynastic right.

A few decades later, Cardinal Richelieu, France's chief minister (1624–1642), made the struggle against Habsburg power the key to his foreign policy as he worked to get a continental political balance. He pursued this objective with armies, money, propaganda, spies, ambassadors, and streams of letters. Tormented by the weight of his increased taxes and its bigger army, France hovered in a state of near rebellion against the cardinal, and leading magistrates saw his butting into the Thirty Years War as *his* war. In 1636, peasants "hacked a tax collector to pieces and dismembered a surgeon whom they mistook for a revenue official." Yet Richelieu was not deflected from his course. He subsidized the Dutch Republic in its struggle against Spain and, with a view to blunting Habsburg power in Germany, was a central figure in negotiating the entry of Swedish armies into the Thirty Years War. In pursuit of this policy, he also hounded the Order of Jesuits and was ready for a clash with the pope himself.

Richelieu was a practitioner of a recent doctrine and ancient praxis: "reason of state." The meaning of this expression, concisely put, was that all action in the interests of the state, however seemingly immoral, was justified by the higher a priori good of the state. Thus, for example, if a king ordered guardsmen to slay a group of high court judges for "reasons of state," they would do well to carry out the deed. By the later sixteenth century, the reasoning behind this view was being taken back to the great Florentine political thinker, Machiavelli, as if he had been the architect of a new code of conduct.

In a short work, *The Prince*, composed in 1513, Machiavelli had torn away the flummery and masks of formal political discourse and idealized advice in handbooks of conduct for princes. War and the maintenance of power, he argued, were the prime business of the prince. This was best seen in the ways of any successful "new" prince, who, more than hereditary princes or rulers, had to fight with every means at his disposal, fair or foul, to seize and hold power. Along the way, however, it was always better to have subjects and citizens on your side.

Historians have underlined the importance of inherited dynastic rights in the politics of early modern Europe, and noted that these were viewed as "ideologically sacrosanct." But in his reflections on political power, Machiavelli implicitly cast the claims of dynasty aside by suggesting that in a time of uncertainty and flux, a prince's birthrights could not possibly suffice in a struggle for the survival of the state. This, instead, required armed might and exceptional political prowess. And if the principle of dynasty ruled much of European diplomacy for more than four centuries, this was also because strong lines of princes—Valois, Habsburg, Bourbon, Hohenzollern, Vasa, Romanov—were able to back up their dynastic claims with menacing armies. Without these battering rams and the support of allies, their arguments concerning the ties between territory and blood lineages would have been blown away like so much codswallop; and other claims regarding "natural" frontiers, security concerns, or economic necessities would have been thrust forward to govern diplomacy and foreign affairs.

Machiavelli had been schooled in the committee rooms, at once brutal and subtle, of Florentine politics. He had seen Italy overrun by foreign armies, princes in the act of grabbing states, governments pushed aside rudely, the reign of one of the most corrupt priests ever to deck the papal throne (Alexander VI), and shameless exhibitions of political cynicism in the conduct of Italian and other rulers. Cast out of office and banished from Florence when the Medici overthrew the republic in 1512, Machiavelli took hold of himself by turning to reflect on the nature of political power, a man now haunted by its ghosts and living in a humble country house.

Although a republican himself, when composing *The Prince*, in his disenchantment, he let his imagination take flight as he constructed a portrait of what it meant and what it took to possess or to make a princely state: that is, to exercise absolute political power. In sketching the portrait, he seemed to bring up to date the everyday realities of reason of state. Here, at all events, was an echo of the Milanese declaration to the Florentine ambassadors: "Might makes right." And here too we pass over to ground that generated a cascade of questions and a vast literature.

What was the state, and what its powers? How had it come into being? For whose good? Or rather, what was the good of the state? How did it relate to "natural law," to "divine law," to the church, to kings, to "the people"? Was it possible, for the sake of the state, to transmogrify criminal activity into something acceptable and right? Was the realm of politics a world with its own values, detached from all Christian morality? Was the prince, or supreme political council, somehow an embodiment of the state? What was tyranny? Could a tyrannical prince be justly assassinated? Were people, communities, and subjects meant to be consulted by those who stood at the head of states? What was treason?

The stream of questions went on, and so did the answers in treatises, histories, primers, and pamphlets. If we had nothing else as evidence, the literature on those questions alone would be rich testimony to the overarching ambitions of the new state, as it threw its shadow over the life of Europeans in the form of more taxes, more armies, billeting, officials, political emergencies, and calls to invest in its bonds.

Serious reflection collected around the supposed origins and power of the state, while also stressing the benefits of absolutism. But some political thinkers pointed to the dangers of absolute power, particularly when lodged in the person of a prince. They called for a check and "bridles" on the supreme executive authority: a job best done, as they saw it, by assemblies of noblemen, clergy, and town councils. It was a call, in short, for forms of limited monarchy. Writing amidst the tumult of the French Wars of Religion, Jean Bodin (d. 1596), the most distinguished advocate of absolutism before Thomas Hobbes, could see no other solution to the horrors of civil conflict than the powerful hand of absolutism. Yet even he held that new taxes required the consent of the governed. He based this claim on the idea of private property as enshrined in the a priori dictates of "natural law." From where could the substance in tax yields come, if not from private property?

Conflict between Protestants and Catholics brought to light another cluster of questions. Could a king be denounced as a heretic, or be held to account for governing against "the laws" of God? Did kings hold power directly from God, from "the people," or in some tricky fashion from both? And if indeed their reign was "ungodly" or "heretical," could they be deposed? Deposed by whom? Could they be legally killed? Killed by individuals, or did regicide have to be the work of an official body of some kind?

Religious diehards topped the lists of those who took the more extreme views in answers to these questions: men such as François Hotman, Theodore Beza, Philippe du Plessis-Mornay, Guillaume Rose, and Juan de Mariana. But this particular stretch of the debate peaked in the late sixteenth century and quickly subsided. It could not hold a persuasive plea for very long. The arguments in favor of deposing ungodly kings, or of killing heretical "tyrants," disturbed moderates on both sides of the confessional divide and won little approval. In a world ruled by "anointed" kings, powerful noblemen, oligarchies, and churches that bent to authority, the educated classes were too tightly held by the habits of deference and obedience to hearken to any but those voices that supported princes and dominant elites.

Yet one departure into extremes calls for a comment here: the formal execution of the king of England, Charles I, in 1649. Unless this event can in some fashion be counted as an assassination, it stands alone in the chronicles of the period. And yet it may be readily fitted into its larger political world, for in the anatomy of the state as a limited monarchy, king and representative council (diet or Parliament) were meant to come together as one in the leading affairs of state. Civil war, however, denoted a profound schism in the state; and this indeed was the pressing background to the beheading of Charles I. In the bloody clash between king and Parliament during the 1640s, Charles lost, was brought to trial, and sentenced to death. If he had triumphed in the civil war, heads would certainly have rolled on the other side, although less dramatically so. Compared to that of a king, the beheading of a clique of parliamentarians would not have been seen as such a pointed challenge to the authority of "the state."

Some fifty years earlier, France was the ground of a scene with affinities to the English event. In August 1589, with the assassination of King Henry III by a Dominican friar, the next man in line to the throne was the Protestant prince, Henry IV of Navarre. France's civil war now took a bloodier turn, and the new king—hard though the event is to imagine—might conceivably have ended on the scaffold if he had been defeated, like Charles I, and captured on the field of battle. He was opposed by a formidable alignment, including Paris, the Paris *Parlement*, the powerful Catholic League, the University of Paris, and an array of Catholic grandees, all with the external support of the pope and the king of Spain. The French state, in short, was divided against itself: the working relationship between king and representative elites had broken down. The divisions would not be healed until Henry IV made a public conversion to Catholicism.

IF PRINCES EXPOSED THE LIMITS of their authority by turning to the necessary assemblies or diets for more taxes, as warlords they were able to assert themselves more menacingly. For even with their limited means, they managed to provoke or start wars, then faced their people with the fait accompli. Once a war started or an invasion threatened, the all too convenient "facts on the ground" argument tended to constrain assemblies into voting for more revenue. Again and again in the Italian Wars, in the French Wars of Religion, in the Netherlands, in the Thirty Years War, and in the Northern Wars around the Baltic Sea, princes sent armies into the field, knowing perfectly well that they, the rulers, would quickly run out of what it took to keep them there: cash and credit. Now more tax money was likely to dribble in, but too slowly, never enough, and nor would any short-term loans suffice to keep their armies from mutating into swarms of desperate men. The inevitable came next: Their soldiers ended by finding the wherewithal for war in the houses of enemy civilians, by scraping it from the backs of their own peasantry and modest townsfolk, or, in dire circumstances, by taking it from the pockets of their elites.

AFTERWORD

Many years ago, as a novice historian at Harvard University, I believed that the most demanding kind of history lay in tracking the ties that link high culture, social structure, and politics. Here, it seemed to me, was history of the sort that stretched the intellect and the historical imagination out to their limits. Other young historians at Harvard shared my views. We regarded "military history" as the realm of simplicity, and therefore not worth pursuing. Needless to say, I have lived to recognize the silliness of such an assumption.

I went on to spend my working life on historical problems far removed from the history of war and armies. But when at last I turned to war, that very distance or estrangement, I hoped, would enable me to see it freshly: from a vantage point that had not been fixed by grooming as a military historian.

Social structure, ideas, politics, literature, and art had dominated my interests for years. Yet it was these problematic concerns that led me, as in a search for substance or solidities, to approach war at the points where the armed violence was actually taking place. The venture turned into a study of soldiers and their victims. I had soon realized that the victims of war in early modern Europe were more likely to be civilians than soldiers. And the more I pursued my researches, the more clearly I saw that to analyze the dynamics of war in terms of the cartography of high politics, as is still done in textbooks and political histories, is to present it from the standpoint of those who ruled. In this view of war, the story is taken over by dynastic rights, diplomacy, personalities, balance-of-power considerations, the strategies of generals, and major battles. War in these trappings *is* the business of princes and prime ministers; it is turned into rational and practical activity; and this hands a kind of carte blanche to the parties responsible for conflict. The gore and ugliness are pushed aside, despite the fact, as we have seen, that war was bound to issue in astounding impracticalities, mutating into a wholly irrational enterprise.

Fortunately, however, among its other tasks, the new military history has attempted to throw light on the life of people who were overrun by plagues of soldiers in villages, small towns, and the infernal points of combat around the walls of cities and fortresses. Yet war is always two wars: the bloody war on the ground and the paper war in the lofty business of strategies and high politics—that is, the war of the rulers and statesmen.

Looking back at the end of his life, Louis XIV confessed that he had "loved glory too much." He meant—for this was how he saw his *gloire*—that he had been too much in love with war and its victories. Can we believe that such a man had any true sense of the horrendous doings of his armies out in the small market towns and country parishes, even in 1688–1689, after he and his minister Louvois ordered their army to torch all the cities and towns of the Palatinate, including Heidelberg, Tübingen, Speyer, Worms, Mannheim, Esslingen, and other places, with scores of thousands of people being driven from their homes? The event was extreme, but Louis's attitude suggests a great deal about the ways of European rulers. In their representations, they sought to avoid the imagery of suffering and carnage. They went to war, they claimed, to uphold supposed rights or justice, or in the name of European political stability. The announced causes seldom had anything to do with the well-being, safety, or industry of their people. And when, in the middle and later sixteenth century, they waged war for religious reasons or "freedom" of conscience, they were ready to impose their own beliefs on countless numbers of subjects by armed force. This right was theirs—the reasoning dictated—by law and divine right, or as authorized by the religious Peace of Augsburg (1555).

The paper war, as I call it, removed the bloody ground war from probing moral questions. If these were raised, despite the political and military chessboard, ministers were there to belittle, contest, deny, excuse, or reason away alleged atrocities. We are thus back to reason of state, where the aims of politics and the "good" of sovereign authority ride above everything else, because sovereignty is the mark and legal condition of the large, self-determined community. As a form of the state, how can this be anything but good? Are not "failed states" places where civil horror is the order of the day? But successful states can also be the ground of horror.

Reducing a village to cinders was small beer in the grand design of a war fought to impose a dynastic right or to help restore the balance of power. If these reported aims—dynasty and the equipoise of military muscle—then turned out to be brazen lies, they nonetheless sufficed. They supplied in spades the arguments that justified military action. Meanwhile, nowhere did ministers of state see any grounds in wartime for relating armies to moral questions, despite the common assumption that princely authority was divinely ordained. God, after all, moved in mysterious ways.

A school of thinkers, beginning with the Jesuit Giovanni Botero in the late 1580s, sought to argue that Christian morality and hard-nosed political realism could be reconciled. In one form or another, this line of reasoning, which holds that war and moral goodness may be joined together, ghosts its way down to our own day, such as in the view that the ideals of freedom and self-determination, or the quest for "human rights" and security against terrorism, may justify war. In these claims, the implied moral agenda is obvious. But from the moment a war is launched on such grounds, the touted ideals are overwhelmed or infested by contentious political matter. Moral questions are elbowed to the sidelines, or they are simply infused with power politics.

Since the paper war put the desperate armies of early modern Europe outside the boundaries of all customary morality, when we approach that history as though we were foreign-office experts, we collaborate with the designs of *raison d'état*. We allow high politics to govern our view of war, and we take hold of armed violence in a world beyond good and evil. The result is that such a history has a great deal to say to the princes and warlords of past time, but nothing to say to the ordinary folk who suffered the onslaughts of desperate soldiers.

The alternative for me, as I planned this book, was to turn to the ground war: to write a history from the standpoint of the common soldier, of villagers, and of the inhabitants of cities under the battering of merciless sieges. I was also driven to fix attention on the sight of starving armies, on famine, cannibalism, the massive plundering of food and livestock, and on churches pillaged, children and women violated, farms laid waste, houses torn apart for firewood, and men butchered. This—not the claims of rulers—was the true face of war.

Yet to dwell on the exterminating impact of war cannot be done without the unwilled raising of moral questions. These press up quietly, but insistently, to cast a shadow over the politics of elites and princes. They press up at the sight of dying armies, as troops, angry and stricken with plague or typhus, lurch through towns and villages, infecting them. And if we are there as historians, there in imagination and close enough, we wonder why rulers did not make a more determined effort to control their soldiers.

Again, behind each army we make out a horde of camp followers, crying out for food and shelter. And along comes another question: Must the villagers feed and dress them too? Soldiers march into a town, looking for billets. They avoid some houses but not others. Why? In their wide-ranging searches, they ignore certain villages, but not others. Again, why? Is it because some places had contacts at court, or managed to pay for a privilege of immunity? Or was it that the officers in charge were bribed to keep their soldiers away? Day after day, as soldiers come and go, we see villagers and townsfolk assaulted, robbed, and barked at, their faces bloodied.

In the middle of all this woe, for the historian as for the villagers, the skills of generals lose all meaning. The knowledge of "weapons systems" fades into irrelevance. Dynastic rights turn into legal abstractions. The "honor" of princes becomes palaver. "Reason of state"—the god of high politics—is drawn out and isolated, now fit to be put on trial. In short, from the moment we cut the social history of war away from the bonds of politics and diplomacy, down come all the barriers against the raising of moral questions.

Yet all at once here, strangely enough, there is a surprising reversal of intention, a return to politics. For moved and indeed liberated by the need to raise moral questions, historians are now free to cast these up against politics: free to challenge the political decisions of statesmen, to look into their tragic mistakes and moments of blind arrogance, and to pass judgment on their actions. There is nothing sacrosanct about the decisions of princes and their ministers, and there is no reason under the sun for us to assume that they were guided by political wisdom.

APPENDIX: MONEY

The gold and silver coins of preindustrial Europe cannot be converted into modern equivalents, with the aim of getting at a comparable standard of living, because the value of bullion fluctuates, and essential costs, such as for labor and bread, were then far too different from anything in our experience. A secondhand garment in silk brocade or velvet could fetch prices high enough to pay the wages of a skilled craftsman for two years. Lawyers, government clerks, university professors, and simple tradesmen had servants, in some cases teams of them. Europe was labor intensive. Unskilled and semiskilled workers (up to 35 or 40 percent of laboring populations) found it hard to pay for new shoes. And since the majority of people spent most of their earnings on food, if they saved anything at all, bad weather and a spike in grain prices easily wiped out their savings.

Europe's plethora of circulating coins, with their different gold and silver contents, forced merchants and bankers to keep their books in "moneys of account": imaginary or fictional moneys, such as the pound sterling, the *lira*, or the *livre tournois*, which existed only in account keeping. Yet trade and banking could not do without them, because they assigned practical market values to the real currencies, such as the ducat, écu, groat, taler, or florin. These coins could now be readily exchanged, the exchange rates having been fixed by the fictional moneys of the bookkeepers.

Conclusion: When encountering large sums of money in this book, readers must try to imagine values that moved alongside the cheapness of labor, the instability of prices for bread grains, the costliness (for the many) of new shoes and often of bread, and the knowledge that only a tiny minority of traders, bankers amongst them, handled gold coins every day. Petty cash ("little money") was the currency of most people: This meant coins struck from copper and from alloys of copper and silver, which always lost value in the face of the gold and silver coins of banking and big business.

Meanwhile, all the getting and spending went on in the embrace of social structures and religious ideals that promoted authority, deference, and obedience. This, too, affected prices by acting to keep down labor costs.

ACKNOWLEDGMENTS

My intellectual debt to a large number of historians is immense. The bibliography, and my notes in particular, tell the tale. If seriously done, the writing of history is always, in some respects, a collective enterprise.

No historian, I assume, ever perfects his craft, just as no novelist ever takes the art of fiction to the peak of perfection. This is as it should be, but it is also reason enough to seek the discernment and judgment of seasoned editors. In this light, I single out my publisher and editor, Peter Ginna, whose faith pulled me through a difficult time and whose keen sense of the architecture in historical argument has my grateful acknowledgment.

Led by her novelist's eye, Julia O'Faolain, the first reader of *Furies*, deserves, as ever, my affectionate gratitude. And I cannot thank my second reader enough, Dr. H. M. Serros, whose voyage through the text was made with a view to noting obscurities and infelicities of style.

Finally I must acknowledge, with grateful thanks, the work of a very wise proofreader, Mr. Michael O'Connor.

NOTES

These notes provide sources for material on the pages indicated, but give only the last name of the author and page references. Full details are set forth in the bibliography. When an entry below refers to an author listed with two or more titles, the work in question is identified by the year of publication. Examples: G. Parker (2004), Wilson (2009), Lynn (1997).

PRELUDE

For source material on the state, see my comment at the start of the notes for Chapter 10.

vii   Incident at bridge: Bourdeille, II, 132; also Wood, 305–06; Lynn (2008), 71.
viii   Standard accounts of the civil wars: e.g., Bonney (1991), 164–72.
viii   Mantuan villagers, incident: Quazza (1926), I, 526, and (1933), 184.
ix   Florence, ten thousand mercenaries: Martines (2006), 44.
x   On torture: Fiorelli; Langbein; Peters.
xiv   I owe a debt of gratitude to the following. For their work on Spanish armies: Geoffrey Parker, I. A. A. Thompson, Fernando González de León, and Ruth Mackay. On French armies: John Lynn, James Wood, David Parrott, and Guy Rowlands. On German armies: Peter Burschel, William Guthrie, Peter Wilson, Fritz Redlich, Otto Büsch, Bernhard Kroener, Ralf Pröve, and Christopher Clark. On the Northern Wars: R. L. Frost. On Gustavus Adolphus: Michael Roberts. On the Russian army: John Keep and Lindsay Hughes. On Italian armies: Maria Nadia Covini, William Caferro, Mallet/ Hale, Mallett/Shaw, and Gregory Hanlon. On English armies: Roger Manning and Mark Fissel. On the armies of the Dutch Republic: Marco van der Hoeven. On La Rochelle: Kevin Robbins. On the Emperor Charles V and war: Tracy (2002). And more generally: Frank Tallett and M. S. Anderson.

CHAPTER 1. A WAR MOSAIC

1   The young peasant: Wagner, 53.
2   Pierre La Sire: Lynn (1997), 397.
3   French army, manpower needs: Lynn (1997), 55; Rowlands, 1.
3   Peter the Great, branding: Keep, 107.
3   Prince Eugene, quote: M. S. Anderson (1988), 130.
4   Florence against Pisa: Buoninsegni, II, 790–803; Najemy, 194–97.
4–5 "The grass . . . useless people": Capponi, 273.
5   Catapulted soldier: Salviati, 248–49; message on corpse, Palmieri, 42–44.
5   Branding and mutilation: Capponi, 264–66.
6   Promise made to mercenaries: Ibid., 264.
7   "Was repugnant . . . of prey": Palmieri, 56.
7   Rumegies: facts and quotes in Dubois, 41, 102, 124, 131–32, 151, 153, 156, 162, 166, 172–73.
11 Animal skins: Léry, 135–39.
12 La Rochelle and pioneers there: Wood, 263.
13 The shoemaker: Heberle, *Zeytregister.*
13 On the Thirty Years War: Wilson (2009); G. Parker (1997); Asch (1997).
14 "Ravenous animals . . . marketplace": Heberle, 129, 119–20.
14 On Gustavus Adolphus: M. Roberts (1953–58).
14 Swedish garrisons: G. Parker in Repgen, 303.
14 Bygdea and quotations: Ibid., 404; Lindegren, 310–12.
15 Shortage of adult males: Lindegren, 317.
15 Scots sent to Germany: G. Parker in Repgen, 305.
16 "even the filthiest . . . on the ground": Palmieri, 42.
16 Lautrec's army: Zinsser, 253. Mallett/Shaw, 167, 205, say he had twenty thousand men.
17 Wallenstein's march: Mann, 290–92.
17 July 1649: Parrott, 521.
17 Violence at Moulins: Ibid.
18 On Monluc: see Monluc; Courteault; Sournia.
19 "Trees . . . the sword": Sournia, 262–71.
20 Josias Rantzau: Wilson (2009), 592.
20 Incident near Munich, 1633: Friesenegger, 31, 35.
20–21 "are ever enemies . . . they were found": Monro, 15, 252.
21 Mansfeld's soldiers: Tallett, 157.
21 "Blackened . . . splendidly dressed": Friesenegger, 37.
22 The armies of Louis XIV: Lynn (1997), 171.
22 In 1573 and 1576: Wood, 262, 36.

CHAPTER 2. SOLDIERS: PLEBEIANS AND NOBLES

24 Nobilities, good starting points: H. M. Scott, 2 vols.; Kamen (2000), Chap. 4.
24 Armies, their social composition: see the note for page xiv.

25 Charles V, quotation: Packard, 203. On Alba: Hale, 98.
25 Castillo de Bovadilla: Mackay, 154.
25 Saint-Germain's words: reported by M. S. Anderson (1988), 163.
25 Wellington's words: Coates, 67–68; Holmes (1996), 279–80.
26 Barnes and Palmer: quoted in Manning, 44.
28 The Chester saying: McGurk, 35.
28 Disease in the Derry garrisons: Ibid., 241.
28 Mutinies near Chester: Fissel, 95.
28 The Bristol report and succeeding quotes: McGurk, 33, 34, 39.
29 The English practice of impressment: Stearns (1972); and into the early eighteenth century, Brewer, 49–50.
29 Impressment in Scotland, nasty hyperbole: Manning, 50, 65.
29 Recruitment lotteries in Castile: Mackay, 133–35.
30 A "gross underestimate": Thompson (1976), 112.
30 Quotes and events in Burgos, Zamora, Salamanca, Béjar, Murcia, Albuquerque, and Portugal: Mackay, 78, 79, 154, 167, 170–71.
31 Events in Catalonia, quote, six reapers: Corteguera, 143, 147–48.
31 Catalan soldiers, quotes: Ibid., 151, 154–55.
32 Russian army, conditions, recruits, Peter I, quotes: Hughes, 70; Keep, 83, 146.
33 Sweden in Thirty Years War, conscripts, mortalities, poor boys: Frost, 205–08.
34 Italians desert Swedish ranks: G. Parker in Repgen, 307.
35 Deserted markets: Lynn (1997), 361.
35 Markets, impressment, quotes: Ibid., 361, 363; M. S. Anderson (1988), 124.
35 "Themselves forcibly," top policeman, *racoleurs*: Rowlands, 257–58.
36 On Wolfenbüttel and recruiting criminals: Burschel (1994), 94–96; Bröckling/Sikora, 74; Redlich (1964), II, 173–74; and Kapser, 73–74.
37 Hilke Wessels, quote: Burschel (1994), 105–107. Prussia, quotes: Büsch, 5.
37 Landsknechts: see Baumann.
38 Desertion in Germany: Bröckling/Sikora; Delbruck (1990), 252. Lists of deserters: Sikora in Bröckling/Sikora.
38 There are brief biographies of Thirty Years War generals in Findeisen: e.g., 443–51 (Werth), 147–58 (Tilly), 274–84 (Pappenheim), 309–16 (Gallas), and 432–36 (Banér). On the obscure Gil de Haas: Wilson (2009), 396–97.
39 The *condottieri*: Hale, 148.
39 On Caspar von Widmarckter, including his campaign diary: Gräf, 8–14, 71–72, 78, 101–50, touching the main points in my biographical sketch.
41 Bernhard of Saxe-Weimar: Findeisen, 285–93; Asch, 160–61.
41 Bernhard's contract with Louis XIII, quotes: Symcox (1974), 117–21.
42 Bernhard need for "contributions" to top up the French fee: highlighted by Guthrie, II, 97.
42 Italian quest for high officer's rank: Bilotto, 367–96, 397–419. France's aspiring "robe" nobility: Rowlands, 155–56, 169–70.
42 On Spinola's loan: G. Parker (2004), 102.
42 Fuggers: Haberer, 72–76, 240–327, 341–46.
43 The Army of Flanders: G. Parker (2004).

44   Italian mercenary forces: Mallett (1974); Caffero (1998); Covini (1998); and Mallett/Hale.

44   The Italian Wars: Oman, 105–207, Mallett/Shaw.

44   Military entrepreneurs: see Redlich (1964).

45   Quotes and the da Varano family: Law in France, 95–98.

45   Quote concerning Metz: Contamine (1984), 162.

46   Mazarin and Count of Marsin: Helfferich (2007), 480–86.

46   Captains and companies: Guthrie, I, 9.

47   In the 1590s, quote: Thompson (1976), 121.

47   Food rations: Lynn (1997), 113–23; (1993), 139–40; Smith, 39, note 10; Burschel (1994), 187–88; Creveld, 21.

47   Wages as listed: Baumann, 86–89; Thompson, 105–107; Mallett/Hale, 495–96; Keep, 103, 110. See also Hale, 109–12.

48   On bread: *Cambridge Econ. Hist. of Europe*, IV, 393; G. Parker (1985), 25. Figure of 75 percent: Cunningham/Grell, 211.

48   Sweden's armies, payment with food: Guthrie, I, 260; II, 31.

49   Oxenstierna's method of payment: Mortimer (2004), 106.

49   Mutinies: Guthrie, I, 260; M. S. Anderson (1988), 53.

49   Dutch mercenaries, quotes: "day labourer," Van der Hoeven, 49; and "continuous income," Guthrie, ii, 187. Complaints against Dutch pay, Manning, 32–33.

50   The stolen silver: Wood, 277.

50   Sforza (Milan's) mercenaries: Covini (1998), 389–90.

50   Details regarding Landsknechts: Baumann, 88–89.

51   In this jigsaw of operations: see Redlich (1964); Rowlands, 204–207, 212–13; Wood, 99; Thompson (1976), 111.

52   Fraud among army officers: Wood, 275–76; Rowlands, 259–63; Parrott, 248–50, 281–86; Hale, 113; Kroener (1992), 58–59.

52   Corruption in Milan's garrison: Ribot, in Donati/Kroener, 155–96.

CHAPTER 3. SACKING CITIES

56   Lesser sacks: Alfani, 51–53.

56   Brescia, sources: Frati, 3 vols.

56   Brescia's population: Pasero, II, 279. Frati, II, 681, puts Brescia's population at fifty thousand.

56   Background leading to the sack: Pasero, II, 251–59.

58   Four hours later: Ibid., 262–67.

59   A tumult of cries and screams: Ibid., 267–69.

59   Anselmi's account: Frati, I, 29–30.

60   Casari's account: Ibid., I, 52–60.

62   Venetian soldier and third witness, quotes: Ibid., I, 245–46, 175.

62   Booty, four thousand vehicles: Pasero, II, 269.

62   More executions: reported by chronicler, in Frati, I, 135.

63   Tartaglia's words: Ibid., I, 167–68.

64   Antwerp: the essential documentation was published by M. P. Génard (1876).

65 Iconoclasm in the Netherlands: Arnade, 90–107; in Antwerp, Wegg, 53–85, and Voet, 170–73.

66 A "grandee," quote: Israel (1998), 156.

67 Arrest of Council members: Génard, 103–105.

68 Composition of Flanders Army: Ibid., 247; G. Parker (2004).

68 "Money! Money!": Génard., 409.

68 Saturday, November 3: Ibid., 446–57.

69 The "blasphemous" flag: Ibid., 464.

69 "It was a thing miraculous": Gascoigne, 156.

70 The assault and ensuing firefight: Génard, 464–69.

71 Conduct of English troops (ignored by Gascoigne): Ibid., 466, 476–77.

71 Casualty figures: Gascoigne, 157; Génard, 468, 514–15, 522, 564; Wegg. 201; Voet, 203.

71 Gascoigne, quoted, 159.

71 Loot, value: Wegg, 201; Génard, 472–73, 475–76, 522; Vasquez de Prada, 252.

72 Tapestries and baptisms: Voet, 200, 204.

72 Marie de Soeto: Génard, 472.

73 Modern scholarship finds: Voet, 203; Israel (1998), 185.

73 Magdeburg: Wolter's old history (1845) provides a reliable narrative leading up to the sack.

　　　For English readers, the Thirty Years War is best handled by Wilson (2009); Asch; G. Parker (1997); and Guthrie, 2 vols. Mann's biography of Wallenstein is outstanding.

74 On the different political currents in Magdeburg: Wolter, 272–79; Ballerstedt, 14–21; Volkholz, 2–6, 16–17; Mann, 459–61. Lohmann and Neubauer published the accounts of the important witnesses.

75 The early morning of May 20: Guericke, 77–78; Volkholz, 19.

75 Ackermann's words: in Mortimer (2002), 67.

76 Insults exchanged at the city walls: Bandhauer, 272; Guericke, 83.

76 Guns, mortars, powder, and shortage of gunpowder: Wolter, 280–81. Volkholz denies that there was such a shortage and accuses Guericke of lying: Volkholz, 50–55.

77 Of signs and portents: This theme, highlighting Magdeburg's importance for German Protestants, has been treated by Medick in Krusenstjern/Medick, 377–407.

77 How soon Falkenberg was killed is disputed: Volkholz, 22–24.

77 Guericke's words: Guericke, 83.

78 Quote about St. Ulrich's, etc.: Guericke, 87.

78 How the fire got started has been much debated. See Guericke, 83–84. Volkholz, 48–91, sees Pappenheim as the culprit. Medick (1999), 389–90, leans to the view that it was started by Magdeburg's defenders.

78 Looters killed by fire: Bandhauer, 275–76.

79 Poor folk forced to help plunderers: Helfferich (2009), 110.

79 The Elbe "choked with the corpses of victims": M. Roberts (1953–58), II, 496.

79 Census of 1632, "rubble until 1720": Wilson (2009), 479.

80 Human remains dumped into the Elbe: Mortimer (2002), 70.

CHAPTER 4. WEAPONS AND PRINCES

82   Sovereignty: The topic has elicited a vast literature. See Martines (1968), Chaps. 4, 9–11.
82   Making of the modern state: Chittolini (1994); Tilly; Ertman; Thomson; Tuck.
82   Parliament in England: Brewer, 43.
82   New weapons: Pepper/Adams; Hall; Arnold.
84   "A morass . . . work of art": Guthrie, I, 4, 6–7.
85   Hussites: see Kaminsky.
85   Battles of Atella and Cerignola: Oman, 52–53; Mallett/Shaw, 33–34, 64–65.
86   English observer, quote: Arnold, 94.
86   Workings of wheel-lock pistol: Hall, 191.
87   Bullet velocities: Ibid., 136.
87   On the musket or "fusile": Childs, 147, 152–53.
87   New forms of fortification: Duffy, 2; Hale, 206–209, 250–51; Pepper/Adams; Pollak.
88   Quote, "fully bastioned enceinte": Pepper/Adams, 29.
88   Medieval warfare: Contamine (1984).
90   The Italian Wars, main battles: Oman, 105–243; Mallett/Shaw, passim.
90   Swiss pike and Spanish *tercio*: Arnold, 76–82; Oman, 59–62, 69–73. Deafening drums: Benedetti, 151.
91   Proportion of pike to musket: Wilson (2009), 90–91; Guthrie, I, 9–10; II, 33.
92   Siege casualties: Van der Hoeven, 13; Duffy, 88–89; Robbins, 214, 355.
92   Arms production, lead passes to Dutch: Vogel, 197–210.
93   Quote, "lots of 500" arquebuses: Pepper/Adams, 17.
93   On Christian of Brunswick's purchase: Van der Hoeven, 201.
93   Wages of skilled artisans: Zanden, 47, 129; Israel (1998), 353. My extrapolation of 8.5 percent of tax receipts is based on Gelderblom, 147.
94   Taxes, bankers, and nascent state: see Chapter 10.
96   "Engravings of upwards of 1000 different pieces": W. Shaw, 7–8.
97   On Spain, quote: Lovett, 19.
101   Charles V's words: *Memoires de Charles Quint*, 203.
101   The sum borrowed from German bankers: Lovett, 219. My projection regarding the 24,000 soldiers is based on Mallett/Hale, 495–96.
101   "Impresario of war": Tracy (2002).

CHAPTER 5. SIEGE

103   Siege, background: Cantagalli; Hook (1977); and on the siege itself, Pepper/Adams, Chap. 6. My account relies mainly on Cantagalli and Sozzini.
105   Date of Monluc's arrival in Siena: Monluc, 256; Sozzini, 265.
105   Food rations and Strozzi's misfortunes: Cantagalli, 305, 326–27; Sozzini, 270–71; Pepper/Adams, 130.
106   Military practice regarding "useless mouths": Rocca, 206–207.

106   August 1554, threatened penalties, and rich leave city: Cantagalli, 327–28, 341; Sozzini, 274–75, 283–84.

107   The trees "festooned": Pepper/Adams, 131.

107   Council of 150, quote: Cantagalli, 335.

108   Third week of September, poor folk, hospital, children, and Scipione Venturi: Ibid., 338–39, 345; Sozzini, 299–302.

109   Monluc addresses town council: Monluc, 294–99.

109   German soldiers, corpse-eating dogs: Cantagalli, 382, 386; Sozzini, 419.

109   Monluc, 335–37, slips out of Siena, mistakenly making April 22 his exit date. See Cantagalli, 400.

109   Surrender agreement, population: Cantagalli, 402–406.

109   The insider's view: Monluc, Book III.

110   The Knight of Malta was a certain Mario Donati: Sozzini, 300.

110–111   "Who lived by the sweat . . . dreadful as famine": Monluc, 317–18.

111   Duke Cosimo and Charles V: Cantagalli, 404.

112   Sancerre: Cunningham/Grell, 228–31, offers a cursory sketch of the siege.

113   On Léry: *Dictionnaire, vol. E-L, 1377–1379.*

113   Armed women: Léry, 60.

113–114   All quotes: Ibid., 65.

114   By the end of January, quotes: Ibid., 72.

114   From February 21, cannonades, quote: Ibid., 77, 81–83.

115   The disemboweled girl: Ibid., 101.

116   Donkey and horse meat, cats and dogs, quotes: Ibid., 133–34.

117   Expulsion of poor: Ibid., 135.

117   Leather, hides, parchment, "like tripe": Ibid., 135–37.

118   Excrement: Ibid., 145.

118   Cannibalism, quotes: Ibid., 146.

118   Potard and l'Emerie: Ibid., 146–48.

119–120   Cannibalism quotes: Ibid., 155, 156.

120   Surrender conditions: Ibid., 210–13.

121   Sancerre in Catholic hands: Ibid., 220–26.

122   Paris: The Wars of Religion have been well narrated by Knecht (2002) and Holt (2005). The "apocalyptic" climate is exhaustively analyzed by Crouzet.

123   "30,000 peasants . . . do the same": Corneio (1837), 246.

123   On Mendoza and the religious orders: Ibid., 251; *Brief Traité*, 274–76.

124   Henry's ragged troops were not even noticed by Sully, who was present at the siege: Sully, I, 203–04.

124   Quotes: *Brief Traité*, 273–74.

125   Quotes up to "arms of the city": Ibid., 276–77.

125–126   Quote: Ibid., 277.

126   Quote: pleading, Ibid., 274.

127   Quotes: Corneio (1837), 248–49, 262.

127   Quotes up to "fighting folk and soldiers," Corneio (1590), 36.

127   Outburst of August 9: Roelker, 191.

127   Quotes: "some mornings" and "powdered bone," Corneio (1837), 261.

128   Quotes, children eaten: Roelker, 193.

129   Surrounding countryside "eaten bare": Oman, 510–11.

129   Attempted escalade, quote: Ibid., 511.

129   Living from hand to mouth: Herlihy/Klapisch-Zuber, Chap. 4, in Florence; Burschel (1994), 70–71, on Lübeck and Hamburg; Wilson (2009), 795, on Augsburg; and G. Parker (1985), 25, on Low Countries.

130   U.S. average spent on food: *Time* (Oct. 10, 2011), 33.

130   Augsburg: My account of this siege is anchored in Bernd Roeck's *Eine Stadt* and Jakob Wagner's *Chronik*.

131   Population: Roeck (1987), 73–78.

131   Bread riots: Ibid., 105.

131   Anti-Catholic measures: Wagner, 11, 18, 21, 25.

131   Defensive works, soldiers' wages, billeting: Ibid., 19–24.

133   Felling of trees: Ibid., 22–23.

133   Of "wretched, paltry sums": Ibid., 31.

134   Massacre of four hundred people: Rebel, 9.

134   Oxenstierna's alienation of lordships: Guthrie, I, 260.

135   Financial losses: Wagner, 44; Heberle, 165. The cobbler, Heberle, bought a house near Ulm for 740 florins in 1627, but sold it in 1636 for 300 florins in the depressed circumstances of the war. Property in the city was necessarily more valuable.

135   "God-given . . . goods": Wagner, 46.

135   Seditious lines: Roeck (1989), I, 16; II, 748.

136   "merciless beatings" and "cut into pieces": Wagner, 53, 55.

137   Cannibalism, quotes: Roeck (1989), I, 18.

139   The Löwenberg surrender terms: Ibid., II, 763–67; Wagner, 59–64.

CHAPTER 6. ARMIES: AMBULANT CITIES, DYING CITIES

142   Urban populations: Nicholas, 17–20, 69; Kamen (2005), 52.

142   French troops in Florence: Martines (2006), 43–48.

143   Charles V's army: Tracy (2002), 197.

144   Spinola's army near Mainz: Eckert, 55–56.

144   On Marlborough: Holmes (2008); Konstam; and on the famous march to the Danube: Weigley, 82–85.

145–146   Mrs. C. Davies (1743), 66–67; another expedition cited by Holmes (2008), 277–78. "We miserably plundered . . . his own price," Daniel Defoe (1855), *Roxana; or, The Fortunate Mistress: and The Life and Adventures of Mother Ross*, New York.

146   Buckingham's expedition: Stearns (1978); also, from the French side, Vaux de Foletier, 95–138.

148   Lavished £10,000, and dying soldiers, quotes: Manning, 116; Fissel, 263.

149   Alan Apsley, bear-pit leavings, quotes: Stearns (1978), 122, 123.

150   On "mouths": G. Parker (2004), 79.

150   Tons of grain for bread: Fissel, 201.

151   Russian study: Perjés, 4–5.

151   Dutch provisioning train: Tallett, 256, note 106.

151   Siege of La Rochelle: details in Robbins, 210–14; Wood, 263, on provisions.

152   Ambroise Paré on Metz: Packard, 182–84.

152   Poles at Pskov: Frost, 62.

152   Alpine marching route and *munitionnaires*: G. Parker (2004), 70–90; Lynn (1997), 108–12.

153   English troops in Ireland, quotes: Gillespie, 169, 176.

154   Bread ration, calories: G. Parker (2004), 136; Smith, 39, note 10.

155   Calais retreat, quotes: C. S. L. Davies, 238–44.

155   German troops in Spain: Thompson (1976), 211.

155   Wagon and cart numbers: Delbruck (1990), 66; Tallett, 34; Creveld, 6.

156   Grandee dress, quote: González de León, 194.

157   Reflecting on ambulant cities: Perjés, 11.

158   Master craftsman's wages: Lane/Mueller, 249–52.

158   Spring fairs in Italy: Covini (1998), 369–70.

158   Value "of a black galley slave": Stradling, 241–42.

158   British army report: Smith, 45.

159   Raging Croatian soldier: Benecke (1978), 56.

159   Loads and feed for horses: Smith, 45.

159   Horses "died in large numbers": González de León, 24.

159   Torstensson's cavalry: Guthrie, II, 141.

160   "the lack of forage" and "the 30,000 men": Lynn (1997), 129; (1993), 141–42.

160   Foraging parties of thousands: Hagendorf, 296–97.

160   Huguenot campaign, quote: Wood, 241–42.

160   War horses were walked: Covini (1998), 366.

161   Generally on camp following: Lynn (2008); Engelen; Hagemann/Pröve; Kroener/Pröve; Burschel (1994); Wilson (1996).

161   "When you recruit," and Charles VIII's declaration: Lynn (1997), 338, 337.

161   Women crossing the Channel: Tallett, 132.

161   Camp followers in Flanders Army and Thirty Years War: G. Parker (2004), 252; Burschel (1994), 226–58; Wilson (2009), 401; Kroener, in Bussmann/Schilling, I, 285–90.

162   After 1660, female companions and marriage in Prussian army: Engelen, 43–55, 88, with marriage rates up to 40 percent in Berlin's regiments of the late eighteenth century.

163   On "the bishop of Albi": Tallett, 133.

163   On sutlers: Grimmelshausen (1964a); Redlich (1954), 163–64.

163   Burschel claim: Burschel (1994), 10.

164   Of 220 sutlers: Mortimer (2002), 33, 108; also Benecke (1978), 34; and G. Parker (2004), 151.

165   Jews in Thirty Years War: M. S. Anderson (1988), 69–70.

166   Letter to Ferdinand III: Benecke (1978), 71–72.

166   The colonel's words: Verdugo, 169.

167   Billeting in western Pomerania: Voss, 276.

168   Town of Vervien, billeting: Lynn (1997), 162.

168   The Russian saying: Hughes, 74.

169   French revolts: Bercé, 181–82, 192, 194.

169   Town of Sancoins, quote: Lynn (1997), 187.

170   Death rates: Tallett, 105; Hale, 119–20, 180.

170   Trapped soldiers and "vile" water: Schertlin, 25, who was in Naples.

171   August 1632, Gustavus Adolphus: Guthrie, II, 36.

171   Flanders Army, mutinies: G. Parker (2004), 253–56.

171   Charles V's army at Metz: Prinzing, 21–22; Zinsser, 159, 265.

171   Louis XIII's vanishing army: D. Parker, 11.

172   Army of sixty thousand decimated, quotes: G. Parker (2004), 177, 180.

172   Leicester's words, deserters caught: Manning, 36.

172   Italian troops decimated: Hanlon, 76–77.

173   Recruits in Derry garrisons: McGurk, 247.

173   June to September, armies of Gustavus Adolphus and Wallenstein, quotes: Wilson (2009), 506; Guthrie I, 193; Zinsser, 159.

174   Battle of Lützen: Wilson (2009), 507–11; Mann, 650–63.

174   August 1664, quote: Wilson (1998), 43.

174   Maladies of the day: see Eckert; Outram; Prinzing; Zinsser.

174   Tracking the diseases, quotes: Outram, 175.

175   Simplicius, quote: Grimmelshausen (1964), 152.

176   The study of losses: Niccoli, in Anselmi/De Benedictis, 124–28.

CHAPTER 7. PLUNDER

177   The biggest haul: Tauss, 281–88; Fučiková, 173–79; Bussmann/Schilling, III, 405–11; Trevor-Roper; Frost, 134.

178   Stockholm palaces, quotation: Turner, 12.

180   Size of Swedish army: Guthrie, I, 163.

181   The authority on war booty: Redlich (1956).

182   Maximilian, art collection, quote: Mann, 620.

182   Heidelberg's Palatine Library: Trevor-Roper, 23–26; Tauss, 281–83.

183   Augsburg's goldsmiths, objects named: Müller, 263–64.

184   Imperial army on its way to Rome: Guicciardini; Hook (2004), 116–154; Pastor, 360–89; Pieri, 577–81.

185   The assault on Rome: Pastor, 390–422; Hook (2004), 162–77.

186   Plundered sums: Hook (2004), 180; Pastor, 413.

187   The quoted historian: Hook (2004), 171. The German officer, castle of Burtenbach: Schertlin, 30.

187   Venetian public revenue: Mallet/Hale, 131; Lane, 426. Quote, "gold-embroidered garments": Pastor, 417.

187   On the numbers of victims: Schertlin, 19; Hook (2004), 178–80, says "thousands."

188   Brescia, 1512, estimated value of loot: Contamine (2000), 179.

188   Battle of Bicocca: Pieri, 542–43; Mallett/Shaw, 143–44.

189   Split in Genoese ruling class: Foglietta, 652; Varese, 306–15.

189   Description of booty: Foglietta, 654.

190 "With shame . . . wealth distribution": Ibid.
190 Customs house and bank of San Giorgio: Epstein, 314.
190 Sack of Mantua: Quazza (1926), II, 119–81; and (1933), 200–202; *Mantova*, 111–16; Malacarne, 70–77; Hanlon, 116–17; Mann, 478–81.
191 Plague deaths: Quazza (1926), II, 104–106; and (1933), 187–89; Malacarne, 68–70; Hanlon, 115.
192 Aldringen, the other generals, and Duke Vincenzo's previous sale: Hanlon, 116; Trevor-Roper, 29–36.
192 The ghetto and quote: Quazza (1933), 202.
192 Estimated value of Mantuan loot and quote: Quazza (1933), 200.
193 Quote: "three times tax revenue" and royal share of silver, Hanlon, 116.
193 On soldiers' partners and sale of booty: Malacarne, 75–76.
194 On McNeill and Goldthwaite: Caferro (2008), 190.

CHAPTER 8. HELL IN THE VILLAGES

196 Of May 1622, quote: Switzer, 66.
197 The Florentine saying: Martines (1963), 36.
197 The attack on Saint Nicolas-de-Port, quotes: Gaber, 45–46.
198 Stephan Mayer, incidents, quotes: Sreenivasan, 280–81, 282, 286, 287.
199 Colmar's immiseration: Wallace, 58–59, 173–75.
199 War came to Hesse-Kassel, quotes: Theibault (1995), 153, 157, 166.
200 Langenburg in Hohenlohe county, quotes: Robisheaux, 213.
200 Countess Anna Maria and quotes: Ibid., 216, 222.
201 For a detailed inventory of the diaries, see Krusenstjern (1997).
201 Benedictine diary, village of Erling, quotes: Friesenegger, 14.
202 April-May 1632, incidents, quotes: Ibid., 18–19.
203 July-November 1632, Croats, Imperial horsemen: Ibid., 20–22.
203 Swedes in grain chests, quote: Ibid., 26–27.
204 "War turns men into beasts": Ibid., 89.
204 Late-December scene, quote: Ibid., 36.
205 Words of the Imperial colonels: Ibid., 39, 41.
205 January 1634, and later, quotes: Ibid., 44–45.
206 Plague strike, quotes: Ibid., 53, 54.
206 Wolves and mice, quotes: Ibid., 60, 63. Compare Helfferich (2009), 322; Theibault (1995), 157.
207 On "whores and boys": Heberle, 119.
208 Bernhard of Saxe-Weimer in Weidenstetten, quotes: Ibid., 148.
209 Hohenlohe, production ratios, quote: Robisheaux, 154.
210 Quote, "cauldrons of boiling pitch": Robbins, 211.
210 Turin's burning of wounded soldiers: Symcox (2002), IV, 767.
211 The sick soldiers: Gräf (2000), 131.

CHAPTER 9. KILLING FOR GOD

212 On France's Wars of Religion: Knecht (2002); Holt (2005). On Rouen: Le Parquier; Benedict (1981).
214 Quote, "warriors of God": a turn rightly seized on by Crouzet.
214 The storming of Rouen: Le Parquier; looting, Benedict (1981), 97–102.
214 Holy war defined, quote: Birely (1988), 85–86.
215 On the Hussites: Kaminsky.
216 Ferdinand II's vow: Hanlon, 93; iconoclasm, Arnade, 90–92; and Israel (1998), 148.
216 On Philip II: G. Parker (2004), 112–13; Lovett, 119ff., 155–58.
217 Antwerp's thirty-eight thousand Protestants, quote: Israel, 219.
218 English mercenaries on Dutch side: Trim (2001), 49–50.
219 Armed friars and monks, quotes: Knecht (2000), 249.
219 Pierre de l'Estoile's words: Roelker, 190,194.
220 On the two Jesuits: Birely (2003), 82–87.
221 Württemberg, and Catholic reactions to edict: Ibid., 91–93, 110–11.
222 Gustavus Adolphus, quote: Wilson (2009), 465.
222 Swedes dismantle Roman Church: *New Cambridge Mod. Hist.,* IV, 330; Tilly, 135.
222 Muzio Vitelleschi: Birely (2003), 110–11.
224 Gustavus criticizes Magdeburg, quote: Roberts (1953–58), II, 498.
224 Magdeburg, quote, "chancellery of God": Holborn (1959), 259.

CHAPTER 10. THE STATE: EMERGING LEVIATHAN

Except for the twist on banking in this chapter, my view of the emerging European state is not new. It is about "state building," and the rudiments of this notion go back to the late nineteenth century, to Max Weber, Otto Hintze, and others. More recently, historians—e.g., Charles Tilly and Thomas Ertman—have tightened the argument by linking war and taxation more closely.
227 On the rise of bankers: Lane/Mueller (1985), 65ff.
228 Interest of 67.4 percent, charged by Genoese bankers in 1550s: Kirk, 31. On papal bankers, see Bullard, chaps. 5, 7.
228 Mary of Hungary and the 40 percent: Tracy (2002), 226.
229 The archbishop's complaint: De Maddalena/Kellenbenz, 303.
229 Charles V's debt: Tallett, 175.
229 Funding public debts: generally, Tracy (1995), I, 563–88. For Venice: Lane, 150–52. For Florence: Najemy, 139–44. Spain: Thompson (1994), 154; Lovett, 222; Gelabert, 206–09. France: Collins; Hoffman (1994a), 226–52; Bonney (1999), 123–76. The Imperial cities: Isenmann, 246. England: Brewer, 94–95, 137. The Dutch Republic: Hart (1993); De Jong, 133–52; Veenendaal, 96–139. Germany: articles by Krüger and Winnige, in Kroener/Pröve.

230   Spain, bankruptcies: Thompson (1994), 160; G. Parker (2004), 126–27; Lovett, 229.

230   Philip IV, his financial crisis, solution: Belenguer, 405–06; Boyajian, 154–59.

231   Of wholesale fraud: Boyajian, 159.

232   Fugger rights over mines: Pickl, 159–64.

233   Bardi and Peruzzi crash: Najemy, 133–34.

233   The financial fairs: Pezzolo/Tattara; Mandich, 123–51. Some students claim that debt was not rolled over at the fairs.

233   Heyday of the New Christians: Boyajian, xi.

234   War and rise of Medici: Martines (2003), 41–53; and (1988), 300–311.

236   On the rise of regular taxation, see the entries above for p. 229 regarding funding public debt; also Ertman, 70–71, 73–75, 240–47, on Spain, France, and Germany.

238   England and tax farming: Brewer, 65–66.

239   Of twenty thousand German and Swiss mercenaries: Ertman, 95; and unpaid troops, Mallett/Shaw, 279–86.

239   Debt of 100 million *livres*, then strain and bankruptcy: Wood, 283; Lynn (1997), 20–27.

239   Proprietary officeholders, numbers, 28 percent of revenue, and Spain: Ertman, 203, 119; Tallett, 186.

240   L. B. Alberti on merchant oligarchy: Martines (1963), 29.

241   French army numbers: Lynn (1997), 55.

241   Quote, "forced loans": Ertman, 136.

242   Ballooning French debt in seventeenth century: Lynn (1997), 20–27; Hoffman (1994a), 237–45; Bonney (1999), 147; Rowlands, 111.

242   Revenue and debt: Lynn (1997), 25–27; Bonney, in Bonney (1999), 141–47.

242   Quote, tsar's army: Keep, 91.

242   Quote, Swedish "war budget": M. Roberts (2002), 123.

243   Germany, payments as late as nineteenth century: Krüger, 57; Wilson (2009), 805.

243   Saxony's debt, Swedish army costs in 1649: Wilson (2009), 579, 771.

244   Dutch Union's budget, quote: Hart (1993), 218.

244   Dutch war costs, debt, taxes: Hart (1993), 71, 164; Veenendaal, 123; Manning, 32–33, on complaints against the Dutch; Tracy (2008), 181–82, on Dutch miserliness with soldiers.

246   Kings were not absolute rulers: see P. Anderson; Collins; Henshall; Mackay.

247   Germany, Brandenburg: Clark, 34–43; Ertman, 246–54; Carsten, 187.

248   Quote, the "central financial administration": Lynn (1997), 29. Corruption in French government: Rowlands, 135–49 and Parrott, 232–58.

249   Brandenburg's commissaries: Ertman, 249–50.

249   Swedish military state, quote: Frost, 122.

249   Spain, *subsidio* and "crusade" money: Lovett, 230–34; Tracy (2002), 104.

249   On Jesuits: Birely (2003), ix–x, 28–30, 61, 64.

250   Sovereignty and Roman law: see Jane Black, 19ff., 37–38, 143–44, on the idea of *plena potestas*; and on sovereignty, Luard, 100–28.

251   Quote, *Ius in armis est*: Martines (1968), 380.
251   The "balance of power" principle: Luard, 1–25; as found in Alberico Gentile, Tuck, 18; and in diplomacy, M. S. Anderson (1993).
253   Peasants and tax collector, quote: *New Cambridge Mod. Hist.*, IV, 492.
253   For early modern European reflection on the state: Tuck; Skinner; J. H. Franklin; and the essay by Arenilla.
253   Dynastic rights as "sacrosanct": Bonney (1991), 80.
255   Jean Bodin: Skinner, II, 293–96.

AFTERWORD

260   On Louis XIV and the Palatinate: Lynn, 79–87, in Grimsley/Rogers.

APPENDIX. MONEY

265   Sources: Lane/Mueller; Denzel; W. A. Shaw; Spufford; McCusker; and Braudel/Spooner.

BIBLIOGRAPHY

I have put a star in front of the English-language studies that, in my view, have made a significant contribution to the field. Example: *Geoffrey Parker, *The Army of Flanders and the Spanish Road*. Without the works thus indicated, much in the tone and accents of this book would be different.

PRIMARY SOURCES

Bandhauer, Zacharias. 1856. *Tagebuch der Zerstörung Magdeburgs 1631*, ed. P. Philipp Klimesch. In *Archiv für Kunde österreichischer Geschichts-Quellen,* xvi, 11: 239–319.

Benecke, Gerhard (ed. and trans.). 1978. *Germany in the Thirty Years War*. London.

Benedetti, Alessandro. 1967. *Diaria de bello carolino*, ed. and trans. Dorothy M. Schullian. New York.

Bourdeille, Pierre de. 1864–1882. *Oeuvres Complètes de Pierre de Bourdeille, Seigneur de Brantôme,* ed. Ludovic Lalanne. 11 vols. Paris.

Brief Traité des Misères de la Ville de Paris. In Corneio (1837), 271–85.

Buoninsegni, Piero. 1579. *Historia fiorentina*. 2 vols. Florence.

Capponi, Gino. *Dell'acquisto di Pisa*. 1733. In *Cronichette antiche di vari scrittori,* ed. Domenico Maria Manni. Florence.

Cauriana, Philippe. 1856. *Histoire du Siège de la Rochelle en 1572*. La Rochelle.

Centorio, Ascanio. 1568. *Discorsi di guerra*. Venice.

Corneio, Pierre. 1590. *Bref discours et veritable des choses plus notables, arrivées au siége mémorable de la renommée ville de Paris*. Lyon.

———. 1837. *Bref discours* (as above). In *Archives Curieuses de l'Histoire de France depuis Louis XI jusqu'a Louis XVIII*. Vol. 13. Paris.

Davies, Christian. 1743. *The Life and Adventures of Mrs. Christian Davies*. London.

Dubois, Alexandre. 1965. *Journal d'un Curé de Campagne au XVIIe Siècle*, ed. Henri Platelle. Paris.

Foglietta, Uberto. 1597. *Dell'Istoria di Genova*. Genoa.

Franklin, J. H. (ed.). 1969. *Constitutionalism and Resistance in the Sixteenth Century. Three Treatises by Hotman, Beza and Mornay*. New York.

Frati, Vasco, et al. (eds.). 1989. *Il sacco di Brescia*. 3 vols. Brescia.

Friesenegger, Maurus. 2007. *Tagebuch aus dem 30jährigen Krieg*, ed. P. Willibald Malthäser. Munich.

Gascoigne, George. 1896. *The Spoil of Antwerp*, ed. Edward Arber, in *An English Garner*. Vol. 8: 141–70. London.

Génard, M. P. (ed.). 1876. *La Furie Espagnole: Documents pour servir à l'histoire du sac d'Anvers en 1576*. In *Annales de l'Académie Royale d'Archéologie de Belgique* XXXII, 3rd ser., tome II.

Goulart, Simon. 1578. 2nd ed. *Memoires de l'Estat de France sous Charles IX*. 3 vols. Meidelbourg.

Gräf, Holger Th. (ed.). 2000. *Söldnerleben am Vorabend des Dreissigjährigen Krieges. Lebenslauf und Kriegstagebuch 1617 des hessischen Obristen Caspar von Widmarckter*. Marburg.

Grimmelshausen, H. J. C. von. 1964. *Simplicius Simplicissimus*. Trans. H. Weisenborn and L. Macdonald. London.

———. 1964a. *Courage, The Adventuress and the False Messiah*. Trans. Hans Speier. Princeton.

Gualdo Priorato, Galeazzo. 1648. *An History of the Late Warres*. Trans. Henry, Earl of Monmouth. London.

Guericke, Otto von. 1860. *Geschichte der Belagerung, Eroberung und Zerstörung Magdeburgs*, ed. Friedrich W. Hoffmann. Magdeburg.

Guicciardini, Luigi. 1867. *Il Sacco di Roma*, ed. Carlo Milanesi. Florence.

Hagendorf, Peter. 1993. *Ein Söldnerleben im Dreissigjährigen Krieg: Eine Quelle zur Sozialgeschichte*, ed. Jan Peters. Berlin.

Heberle, Hans. 1975. *Der Dreissigjährige Krieg in zeitgenössischer Darstellung: Hans Heberles 'Zeytregister' (1618–1672): Aufzeichnungen aus dem Ulmer Territorium*, ed. Gerd Zillhardt. Ulm.

Helfferich, Tryntje (ed. and trans.). 2009. *The Thirty Years War. A Documentary History*. Indianapolis.

La Noue, François de. 1957. *Discours politiques et militaires*, ed. F. E. Sutcliffe. Geneva.

Léry, Jean de. 1574. *Histoire memorable de la Ville de Sancerre*. La Rochelle.

Lohmann, K. (ed.). 1913. *Die Zerstörung Magdeburgs*. Berlin.

Memoires de Charles Quint. 1913, ed. and trans. Alfred Morel-Fatio. "Bibliothèque de l'Ecole des Hautes Etudes," Vol. 202, *Historiographie de Charles-Quint*.

Mendoza, Bernardino de. 1860–1863. *Commentaires de Bernardino de Mendoza sur les évènements de la Guerre de Pays Bas, 1567–1577*. 2 vols. Brussels.

Monluc, Blaise de. 1964. *Commentaires, 1521–1576*, ed. Paul Courteault. Paris.

Monro, Robert. 1999. *Monro. His Expedition with the Worthy Scots Regiment Called Mac-Keys*, ed. William S. Brockington, Jr. Westport and London.

Neubauer, E. (ed.). 1931. *Magdeburgs Zerstörung 1631*. Magdeburg.

Palmieri, Matteo. 1995. *La Presa di Pisa*, ed. A. M. Ferraro. Naples.

Paré, Ambroise. 1951. *The Apology and Treatise*, ed. Geoffrey Keynes. London.

Potter, David (ed. and trans.). 1997. *The French Wars of Religion. Selected Documents*. London.

Poyntz, Sydnam. 1908. *The Relation of Sydnam Poyntz. 1624–1636*, ed. A. T. S. Goodrick. Camden Third Series, XIV. London.

Rocca, Bernardino. 1582. *De' discorsi di guerra*. Venice.

Roelker, Nancy Lyman (ed. and trans.). 1958. *The Paris of Henry of Navarre as Seen by Pierre de l'Estoile. Selections from his Memoires-Journaux.* Cambridge, MA.

Salviati, Jacopo. 1784. *Cronica dall'anno 1398 al 1411.* In *Delizie degli eruditi toscani.* Vol. 18, ed. Ildefonso di San Luigi.

Schertlin, Sebastian. 1777. *Lebensbeschreibung des berühmten Ritters Sebastian Schertlins von Burtenbach.* Frankfurt and Leipzig.

Sozzini, Alessandro. 1842. *Diario delle cose avvenute in Siena dai 20 luglio 1550 al 28 giugno 1555.* In *Archivio storico italiano,* vol. 2. Florence.

Sully. 1805. *Memoirs of Maximilian de Bethune, Duke of Sully,* ed. and trans. M. de L'Ecluse. 5 vols. Edinburgh.

Turner, Sir James. 1829. *Memoirs of His Own Life and Times.* Edinburgh.

Verdugo, Francisco. 1899. *Commentario del Coronel Francisco Verdugo de la Guerra de Frisa,* ed. Henri Lonchay. Brussels.

Wagner, Jakob. 1902. *Die Chronik des Jakob Wagner über die Zeit der schwedischen Okkupation in Augsburg vom 20. April 1632 bis 28. März 1635,* ed. Wilhelm Roos. Augsburg.

SECONDARY SOURCES

Alfani, Guido. 2010. *Il Grand Tour dei Cavalieri dell'Apocalisse. L'Italia del "lungo Cinquecento" (1494–1629).* Venice.

Anderson, M. S. 1993. *The Rise of Modern Diplomacy, 1450–1919.* London and New York.

———. 1988. *War and Society in Europe of the Old Regime, 1618–1789.* London.

Anderson, Perry. 1979. *Lineages of the Absolutist State.* London.

Andersson, Christiane. "Von 'Metzen' und 'Dirnen': Frauenbilder in Kriegsdarstellungen der Frühen Neuzeit." In Hagemann and Pröve, 171–98.

Anselmi, Gian Mario, and Angela De Benedictis (eds.). 2008. *Città in Guerra. Esperienze e reflessioni nel primo '500.* Bologna.

Arenilla, L. "Le Calvinisme et le droit de résistance à l'état." In *Annales E.S.C.* 22 (1967).

Arnade, Peter. 2008. *Beggars, Iconoclasts, and Civic Patriots: The Political Culture of the Dutch Revolt*. Ithaca and London.

Arnold, Thomas F. 2006. *The Renaissance at War*. New York and London.

Asch, Ronald G. 1997. *The Thirty Years War: The Holy Roman Empire and Europe, 1618–48*. Basingstoke and New York.

Aston, Trevor (ed.). 1965. *Crisis in Europe, 1560–1660*. London.

Ballerstedt, Maren. 2006. "Belagerung und Zerstörung Magdeburgs 1629/31—Ereignisse und Hintergründe," in *Konfession*, 11–24.

Barker, Thomas M. 1975. *The Military Intellectual and Battle: Raimondo Montecuccoli and the Thirty Years War*. Albany.

Bartlett, Thomas, and K. Jeffrey. 1996. *A Military History of Ireland*. Cambridge.

Baumann, Reinhard. 1994. *Landsknechte. Ihre Geschichte und Kultur vom späten Mittelalter zum Dreissigjährigen Krieg*. Munich.

Belenguer, Ernest. 1995. *El Imperio hispanico, 1479–1665*. Barcelona.

Bell, David A. 2007. *The First Total War: Napoleon's Europe and the Birth of Modern Warfare*. London and New York.

Beller, Elmer A. 1940. *Propaganda in Germany during the Thirty Years War*. Princeton.

Benecke, G. 1974. *Society and Politics in Germany, 1500–1750*. London and Toronto.

Benedict, Philip. 1981. *Rouen during the Wars of Religion*. Cambridge.

———. 1978. "The Saint Bartholomew's Massacres in the Provinces." In *The Historical Journal* 21, 2: 205–25.

*Bercé, Yves-Marie. 1990. *History of Peasant Revolts: The Social Origins of Rebellion in Early Modern France*. Trans. Amanda Whitmore. Cambridge.

Berger, Ernst A. 1954. *Hans de Witte, Finanzmann Wallensteins*. Wiesbaden.

Bilotto, Antonella, P. del Negro, and C. Mozzarelli (eds.). 1997. *I Farnesi. Corti, guerra e nobiltà in antico regime*. Rome.

*Bireley, Robert. 2003. *The Jesuits and the Thirty Years War: Kings, Courts, and Confessors.* Cambridge.

——. 1999. *The Refashioning of Catholicism, 1450–1700.* Washington, D.C.

——. "The Thirty Years' War as Germany's Religious War." In Repgen, 85–106.

Black, Jane. 2009. *Absolutism in Renaissance Milan.* Oxford.

Black, Jeremy. 2002. *European Warfare, 1494–1660.* London and New York.

Bonney, Richard. 1991. *The European Dynastic States, 1494–1660.* Oxford.

*—— (ed.). 1999. *The Rise of the Fiscal State in Europe, c. 1200–1815.* Oxford.

——. "France, 1494–1815." In Bonney (1999), 123–76.

*Boyajian, James C. 1983. *Portuguese Bankers at the Court of Spain, 1626–1650.* New Brunswick.

Braudel, F. P., and F. Spooner. "Prices in Europe from 1450 to 1750." In *Cambridge Economic History of Europe*, vol. iv, 378–486.

Brewer, John. 1989. *The Sinews of Power: War, Money and the English State, 1688–1783.* London.

Bröckling, Ulrich, and Michael Sikora (eds.). 1998. *Armeen und ihre Deserteure.* Göttingen.

Bullard, Melissa M. 1980. *Filippo Strozzi and the Medici: Favor and Finance in Sixteenth-Century Florence and Rome.* Cambridge.

*Burschel, Peter. 1994. *Söldner im Nordwestdeutschland des 16. und 17. Jahrhunderts. Sozialgeschichtliche Studien.* Göttingen.

——. "Die Erfindung der Desertion. Strukturprobleme in deutschen Söldnerheeren des 17. Jahrhunderts." In Bröckling and Sikora, 72–85.

Büsch, Otto. 1997. *Military System and Social Life in Old Regime Prussia, 1713–1807.* Trans. J. G. Gagliardo. Atlantic Highlands, NJ.

Bussmann, Klaus, and H. Schilling (eds.). 1998. *1648: War and Peace in Europe.* 3 vols. Münster and Osnabrück.

Caferro, William P. 1998. *Mercenary Companies and the Decline of Siena*. Baltimore and London.

———. 2008. "Warfare and Economy in Renaissance Italy, 1350–1450." In *Journal of Interdisciplinary History*, XXXIX, 2: 167–209.

Cambridge Economic History of Europe, vol. iv. 1967. Eds. E. E. Rich and C. H. Wilson. Cambridge.

Canning, Joseph, Hartmut Lehmann, and Jay Winter (eds.). 2004. *Power, Violence and Mass Death in Pre-Modern and Modern Times*. Aldershot and Burlington.

Cantagalli, Roberto. 1962. *La guerra di Siena (1552–1559)*. Siena.

Carsten, F. L. 1954. *The Origins of Prussia*. Oxford.

Charles, Jean-Léon. 1965. "Le sac des villes dans les Pays Bas au XVIe siècle: Etude critique des regles de guerre." In *Revue Internationale d'Histoire Militaire* 24: 288–301.

Childs, John. 2001. *Warfare in the Seventeenth Century*. London.

Chittolini, Giorgio. "Il 'militare' tra tarde medioeveo e prima età moderna." In Donati and Kroener, 53–102.

Chittolini, Giorgio, Anthony Molho, and Pierangelo Schiera, eds. 1994. *Origini dello stato. Processi di formazione statale in Italia fra medioevo ed età moderna*. Bologna.

Clark, Christopher. 2006. *Iron Kingdom: The Rise and Downfall of Prussia, 1600–1947*. London.

Coates, Berwick. 2003. *Wellington's Charge: A Portrait of the Duke's England*. London.

Collins, James B. 1988. *Fiscal Limits of Absolutism: Direct Taxation in Early Seventeenth-Century France*. Berkeley, Los Angeles, London.

Contamine, Philippe. 1984. *War in the Middle Ages*. Trans. Michael Jones. London and New York.

——— (ed.). 2000. *War and Competition Between States*. Oxford.

———. "The Growth of State Control. Practices of War, 1300–1800: Ransom and Booty." In Contamine (2000), 163–93.

Corteguera, Luis R. 2002. *For the Common Good: Popular Politics in Barcelona, 1580–1640*. Ithaca and London.

Corvisier, André. 1979. *Armies and Societies in Europe, 1494–1789.* Trans. A. T. Siddall. Bloomington and London.

Courteault, Paul. 1909. *Blaise de Monluc: Un cadet de Gascogne au XVIe siècle.* Paris.

Covini, Maria Nadia. 1998. *L'Esercito del Duca. Organizzazione militare e istituzioni al tempo degli Sforza (1450–1480).* Rome.

———. "Political and Military Bonds in the Italian State System, Thirteenth to Sixteenth Centuries." In Contamine (2000), 9–36.

Crouzet, Denis. 1990. *Les Guerriers de Dieu.* Seyssel.

Cunningham, Andrew, and O. P. Grell. 2000. *The Four Horsemen of the Apocalypse: Religion, War, Famine and Death in Reformation Europe.* Cambridge and New York.

Davies, C. S. L. 1964. "Provisions for Armies, 1509–60: A Study in the Effectiveness of Early Tudor Government." In *Economic History Review*, 2nd series, XVII: 234–48.

De Jong, Michiel. 1997. "Dutch Public Finance during the Eighty Years War: The Case of the Province of Zeeland, 1585–1621." In Van der Hoeven, 133–52.

Delbruck, Hans. 1975–1990. *History of the Art of War.* Trans. Walter J. Renfroe. 4 vols. Lincoln.

———. 1990. *The Dawn of Modern Warfare.* [Vol. 4, above.] Lincoln.

*De Maddalena, Aldo, and Hermann Kellenbenz (eds.). 1986. *La repubblica internazionale del denaro tra XV e XVII secolo.* Bologna.

Denzel, Markus A. 2010. *Handbook of World Exchange Rates, 1590–1914.* Ashgate.

Dictionnaire des Littératures de Langue Française. 1994. Paris.

Diefendorf, Barbara B. 1991. *Beneath the Cross: Catholics and Huguenots in Sixteenth-Century Paris.* New York and Oxford.

Dixon, C. S. 2007. "Urban Order and Religious Coexistence in the German Imperial City: Augsburg and Donauwörth, 1548–1608." In *Central European History* 40: 1–33.

Donati, Claudio, and Bernhard R. Kroener (eds.). 2007. *Militari e società civile nell'Europa dell'età moderna (secoli xvi–xviii).* Bologna.

Doria, Giorgio. "Conoscenza del mercato e sistema informativo: il know-how dei mercanti-finanzieri genovesi nei secoli xvi e xvii." In De Maddalena and Kellenbenz, 57–121.

Downing, Brian M. (ed.). 1992. *The Military Revolution and Political Change: Origins of Democracy and Autocracy in Early Modern Europe.* Princeton.

Duffy, Christopher. 1979. *Siege Warfare: The Fortress in the Early Modern World, 1494–1660.* London.

★Eckert, Edward A. 1996. *The Structure of Plagues and Pestilences in Early Modern Europe. Central Europe, 1560–1640.* Basel.

Engelen, Beate. 2005. *Soldatenfrauen in Preussen. Eine Strukturanalyse der Garnisonsgesellschaft im späten 17. und in 18. Jahrhundert.* Münster.

Epstein, Steven A. 1996. *Genoa and the Genoese, 968–1528.* Chapel Hill and London.

★Ertman, Thomas. 1997. *Birth of the Leviathan: Building States and Regimes in Medieval and Early Modern Europe.* Cambridge.

Evans, Richard J. 1996. *Rituals of Retribution: Capital Punishment in Germany, 1600–1987.* Oxford.

Evans, Robert, J. W. 1979. *The Making of the Habsburg Monarchy, 1550–1700.* Oxford.

Findeisen, Jörg-Peter. 1998. *Der Dreissigjährige Krieg: Eine Epoche in Lebensbildern.* Graz, Vienna, and Cologne.

Fiorelli, Piero. 1953–1954. *La tortura giudiziaria nel diritto commune.* 2 vols. Milan.

★Fissel, Mark Charles. 2001. *English Warfare, 1511–1642.* London and New York.

France, John (ed.). 2008. *Mercenaries and Paid Men. The Mercenary Identity in the Middle Ages.* London and Boston.

★Friedrichs, Christopher R. 1979. *Urban Society in an Age of War: Nördlingen, 1580–1720.* Princeton.

Frigo, Daniela (ed.). 2000. *Politics and Diplomacy in Early Modern Italy.* Cambridge.

Fritschy, Wantje. "The Efficiency of Taxation in Holland." In Gelderblom, 55–84.

————. "'Small States' and Diplomacy: Mantua and Modena." In Frigo, 147–75.

★Frost, R. L. 2000. *The Northern Wars: War, State and Society in North-eastern Europe, 1558–1721.* London.

Fučiková, Eliška. "The Fate of Rudolf II's Collection in Light of the History of the Thirty Years War." In Bussmann and Schilling, 173–79.

Gaber, Stéphane. 1991. *La Lorraine meurtrie: les malheurs de la guerre de Trente ans.* Nancy.

Garcia, Luis Ribot. "Types of Armies: Early Modern Spain." In Contamine (2000), 37–68.

Gelabert, Juan. "Castile, 1504–1808." In Bonney (1999), 201–41.

Gelderblom, Oscar (ed.). 2009. *The Political Economy of the Dutch Republic.* Farnham and Burlington.

Gillespie, Raymond. "The Irish Economy at War, 1641–1652." In Ohlmeyer, 160–80.

Gindely, A. 1892. *The Thirty Years War.* 2 vols. New York.

Glozier, Mathew, and D. Onnekink (eds.). 2007. *War, Religion and Service: Huguenot Soldiering, 1685–1713.* Aldershot.

★González de León, Fernando. 2009. *The Road to Rocroi: Class, Culture and Command in the Spanish Army of Flanders, 1567–1659.* Leiden and Boston.

Gräf, Holger Th. "Ruolo e funzione delle testimonianze autobiografiche per la storia militare." In Donati and Kroener, 281–311.

Gray, John. 2007. *Black Mass: Apocalyptic Religion and the Death of Utopia.* London.

Grimsley, Mark, and Clifford J. Rogers (eds.). 2002. *Civilians in the Path of War.* Lincoln and London.

★Guthrie, William P. [Vol. I] 2002. *Battles of the Thirty Years War.* Westport and London.

★————. [Vol. II] 2003. *The Later Battles of the Thirty Years War: From the Battle of Wittstock to the Treaty of Westphalia.* Westport and London.

Haberer, Stephanie. 2004. *Otto Heinrich Fugger (1592–1644). Biogra-*

phische Analyse typologischer Handlungsfelder in der Epoche des Dreissigjährigen Krieges. Augsburg.

Hagemann, Karen, and Ralf Pröve (eds.). 1998. *Landsknechte, Soldatenfrauen und Nationalkrieger: Militär, Krieg und Geschlechterordnung im historischen Wandel*. Frankfurt and New York.

Haldon, John F. (ed.). 2006. *General Issues in the Study of Medieval Logistics*. Leiden.

Hale, John R. 1985. *War and Society in Renaissance Europe 1450–1620*. London.

★Hall, Bert S. 1997. *Weapons and Warfare in Renaissance Europe*. Baltimore and London.

Handbook of European History, 1400–1600. 1995. Eds. Thomas A. Brady, H. A. Oberman, and J. D. Tracy. 2 vols. Leiden, New York, and Cologne.

Hanlon, Gregory. 1998. *The Twilight of a Military Tradition: Italian Aristocrats and European Conflicts, 1560–1800*. London.

Harari, Yuval N. 2004. *Renaissance Military Memoirs. War, History, and Identity, 1450–1600*. Woodbridge and Rochester.

★Hart, Marjolein C. 't. 1993. *The Making of a Bourgeois State: War, Politics and Finance during the Dutch Revolt*. Manchester and New York.

———. "The United Provinces, 1579–1806." In Bonney (1999), 309–325.

Hathaway, Jane (ed.). 2001. *Rebellion, Repression, Reinvention: Mutiny in Comparative Perspective*. Westport and London.

Heal, Bridget. 2007. *The Cult of the Virgin Mary in Early Modern Germany: Protestant and Catholic Piety, 1500–1648*. Cambridge.

Helfferich, Tryntje. 2007. "A Levy in Liège for Mazarin's Army: Practical and Strategic Difficulties in Raising and Supporting Troops in the Thirty Years War." In *Journal of Early Modern History* 11, 6: 475–500.

Henshall, Nicholas. 1992. *The Myth of Absolutism: Change and Continuity in Early Modern European Monarchy*. London and New York.

Hoffman, Philip T., and K. Norberg (eds.). 1994. *Fiscal Crises, Liberty, and Representative Government, 1450–1789*. Stanford.

Hoffman, Philip T. (1994a). "Early Modern France, 1450–1700." In Hoffman and Norberg, 226–52.

Holborn, Hajo. 1959. *A History of Modern Germany: The Reformation.* New York.

———. 1982. *A History of Modern Germany: 1648–1840.* Princeton.

Holmes, Richard. 1996. *Wellington: The Iron Duke.* London.

———. 2008. *Marlborough: England's Fragile Genius.* London.

Holt, Mack P. (ed.). 2002. *Renaissance and Reformation France, 1500–1648.* Oxford and New York.

*———. 2005. 2nd ed. *The French Wars of Religion, 1562–1629.* Cambridge.

Hook, Judith. 2004. 2nd ed. *The Sack of Rome, 1527.* Basingstoke and New York.

———. "Fortifications and the End of the Sienese State." In *History: the Journal of the Historical Association*, 62, no. 206 (Oct. 1977): 372–87.

Housley, Norman. 2002. *Religious Warfare in Europe, 1400–1536.* Oxford.

Howard, Michael, et al (eds.). 1994. *The Laws of War.* New Haven and London.

Hroch, Miroslav. "Wirtschaftliche und gesellschaftliche Voraussetzungen des Dreissigjährigen Krieges." In Repgen, 133–49.

Hughes, Lindsay. 1998. *Russia in the Age of Peter the Great.* New Haven and London.

Ingrao, Charles W. 1994. *The Habsburg Monarchy, 1618–1815.* Cambridge.

Isenmann, Eberhard. "The Holy Roman Empire in the Middle Ages." In Bonney (1999), 243–80.

Israel, Jonathan I. 1997. *Conflicts of Empires: Spain, the Low Countries and the Struggle for World Supremacy, 1585–1713.* London.

———. 1998. *The Dutch Republic: Its Rise, Greatness, and Fall, 1477–1806.* Oxford.

Jesperson, Leon. 1985. "The Machtstaat in Seventeenth-Century Denmark." In *Scandinavian Journal of History*, 10, no. 4: 271–304.

Kaiser, Michael. "Inmitten des Kriegstheaters: Die Bevölkerung als militärischer Faktor und Kriegsteilnehmer im Dreissigjährigen Krieg." In Kroener and Pröve, 281–303.

———. 1998. "Ausreisser und Meuterer im Dreissigjährigen Krieg." In Bröckling and Sikora, 49–71.

———. 1998a. "Die Lebenswelt der Söldner und das Phänomen der Desertion im Dreissigjährigen Krieg." In *Osnabrücker Mitteilungen* 103: 105–24.

Kamen, Henry. 2000. *Early Modern European Society*. London and New York.

———. 2005. *Golden Age Spain*. Basingstoke and New York.

Kaminsky, Howard. 1967. *A History of the Hussite Revolution*. Berkeley and Los Angeles.

Kapser, Cordula. 1997. *Die bayerische Kriegsorganisation in der zweiten Hälfte des Dreissigjährigen Krieges, 1635–1648/49*. Münster.

Keegan, John, and Richard Holmes. 1985. *Soldiers: A History of Men in Battle*. London.

Keep, John L. H. 1985. *Soldiers of the Tsar: Army and Society in Russia, 1462–1874*. Oxford.

Kellenbenz, Hermann, and P. Prodi (eds.). 1994. *Fiskus, Kirche und Staat im konfessionellen Zeitalter*. Berlin.

Kellenbenz, Hermann. "Lo stato, la societá, e il denaro." In De Maddalana and Kellenbenz, 333–83.

Kiernan, V. G. "Foreign Mercenaries and Absolute Monarchy." In Aston, 117–40.

Kingra, M. S. 1993. "The *Trace Italienne* and the Military Revolution during the Eighty Years War 1567–1648," *Journal of Military History*, 57: 431–46.

Kirk, Thomas Allison. 2005. *Genoa and the Sea: Policy and Power in an Early Modern Maritime Republic, 1559–1684*. Baltimore and London.

★Knecht, Robert J. 2000. *The French Civil Wars, 1562–1598*. Harlow.

★———. 2002. *The French Religious Wars, 1562–1598*. Oxford.

Konfession, Krieg und Katastrophe. Magdeburgs Geschick im Dreissigjährigen Krieg. 2006. Magdeburg.

Konstam, Angus. 2010. *Marlborough: Leadership—Strategy—Conflict.* Oxford.

★Kroener, Bernhard R., and Ralf Pröve (eds.). 1996. *Krieg und Frieden. Militär und Gesellschaft in der Frühen Neuzeit.* Paderborn and Munich.

Kroener, Bernhard R. "'Kriegsgurgeln, Freireuter und Morode-brüder.' Der Soldat des Dreissigjährigen Krieges." In Wette, 51–67.

———. "'. . . und ist der jammer nit zu beschreiben': Geschlech-terbeziehungen und Uberlebensstrategien in der Lagergesell-schaft des Dreissigjährigen Krieges." In Hagemann and Pröve, 279–96.

Krüger, Kersten. "Kriegsfinanzen und Reichsrecht im 16. und 17. Jahrhundert." In Kroener and Pröve, 47–57.

Krusenstjern, Benigna von. 1997. *Selbstzeugnisse der Zeit des Dreis-sigjährigen Krieges: Beschreibendes Verzeichnis.* Berlin.

———, and H. Medick (eds.). 1999. *Zwischen Alltag un Katastrophe. Der Dreissigjährige Krieg aus der Nähe.* Göttingen.

Lane, Frederic C. 1973. *Venice: A Maritime Republic.* Baltimore and London.

★Lane, Frederic C., and R. C. Mueller. 1985. *Money and Banking in Medieval and Renaissance Venice.* Vol. 1. Baltimore and London.

Langbein, John H. 2006. *Torture and the Law of Proof.* Chicago and London.

Law, John. "The Da Varano Lords of Camerino as *Condottiere* Princes." In France, 89–103.

Le Parquier, Emile. 1907. *La Siège de Rouen en 1562.* Rouen.

Lindegren, Jan. 1985. "The Swedish 'Military State', 1560–1720." In *Scandinavian Journal of History*, 10, no. 4: 305–336.

Lloyd, Howell A. 1973. *The Rouen Campaign, 1590–1592: Politics, Warfare and the Early Modern State.* Oxford.

Lockhart, Paul Douglas. 1996. *Denmark in the Thirty Years War, 1618–1648. King Christian IV and the Decline of the Oldenburg State.* London.

★Lovett, A. W. 1986. *Early Habsburg Spain, 1517–1598.* Oxford and New York.

Luard, Evan. 1992. *The Balance of Power: The System of International Relations, 1648–1815.* London.

Lynn, John A. (ed.). 1990. *Tools of War: Instruments, Ideas, and Institutions of Warfare, 1445–1871.* Urbana and Chicago.

———. 1993. *Feeding Mars: Logistics in Western Europe from the Middle Ages to the Present.* Boulder, San Francisco, Oxford.

*———. 1997. *Giant of the Grand Siècle: The French Army, 1610–1715.* Cambridge.

———. "A Brutal Necessity? The Devastation of the Palatinate, 1688–1689." In Grimsley and Rogers, 79–111.

———. 2008. *Women, Armies, and Warfare in Early Modern Europe.* Cambridge.

*Mackay, Ruth. 1999. *The Limits of Royal Authority: Resistance and Obedience in Seventeenth-Century Castile.* Cambridge.

Mackillop, A. and S. Murdoch (eds.). 2003. *Military Governors and Imperial Frontiers c. 1600–1800.* Leiden.

Malacarne, Giancarlo. 2008. *I Gonzaga di Mantova.* Vol. 5. *Morte di una dinastia.* Modena.

Mallett, Michael. 1974. *Mercenaries and their Masters: Warfare in Renaissance Italy.* London.

*Mallett, M. E., and J. R. Hale. 1984. *The Military Organization of a Renaissance State: Venice c. 1400 to 1617.* Cambridge and New York.

Mallett, Michael, and Christine Shaw. 2012. *The Italian Wars, 1494—1559: War, State and Society in Early Modern Europe.* Harlow, London, New York.

Mandich, Giulio. "Fiere cambiarie concorrenti (genovesi, fiorentine, veneziane) nel 1622–1652." In De Maddalena and Kellenbenz, 123–51.

*Mann, Golo. 1976. *Wallenstein: His Life.* Trans. Charles Kessler. London.

*Manning, Roger B. 2006. *An Apprenticeship in Arms: The Origins of the British Army, 1585–1702.* Oxford.

Mantova: La Storia. 1963. Ed. Leonardo Mazzoldi, R. Giusti, and others. Vol. 3. Mantua.

Marcos Martín, Alberto. 2000. *España en los siglos xvi, xvii, y xviii: Economia y Sociedad.* Barcelona.

Marnef, Guido. 1996. *Antwerp in the Age of the Reformation: Underground Protestantism in a Commercial Metropolis, 1550–1577.* Trans. J. C. Grayson. Baltimore and London.

Martin, P. 2002. *Une guerre de Trente Ans en Lorraine 1632–1661.* Metz.

Martines, Lauro. 1963. *The Social World of the Florentine Humanists.* Princeton.

———. 1968. *Lawyers and Statecraft in Renaissance Florence.* Princeton.

———. 1988. "Force Loans; Political and Social Strain in Quattrocento Florence." In *Journal of Modern History,* 60: 300–11.

———. 2003. *April Blood: Florence and the Plot Against the Medici.* London and New York.

———. 2006. *Scourge and Fire: Savonarola and Renaissance Florence.* London and New York.

McCusker, John J. 1978. *Money and Exchange in Europe and America, 1600–1775: A Handbook.* London and Basingstoke.

*McGurk, John. 1997. *The Elizabethan Conquest of Ireland: The 1590s Crisis.* Manchester and New York.

Medick, Hans. "Historisches Ereignis und zeitgenössische Erfahrung: Die Eroberung und Zerstörung Magdeburgs 1631." In Krusenstjern and Medick, 377–407.

———. 2001. "Historical Event and Contemporary Experience: The Capture and Destruction of Magdeburg," *History Workshop Journal,* 52: 23–48.

Melton, Edgar. "The Junkers of Brandenburg-Prussia, 1600–1806." In H. M. Scott, II, 118–70.

Mentzer, Raymond, and A. Spicer (eds.). 2002. *Society and Culture in the Huguenot World, 1559–1685.* Cambridge.

Meumann, Marcus. "Soldaten familien und uneheliche Kinder. Ein soziales Problem im Gefolge der stehenden Heere." In Kroener and Pröve, 219–36.

Monod, Paul Kleber. 1999. *The Power of Kings: Monarchy and Religion in Europe, 1589–1715.* New Haven and London.

*Mortimer, Geoff. 2002. *Eyewitness Accounts of the Thirty Years War, 1618–48*. Basingstoke and New York.

———— (ed.). 2004. *Early Modern Military History, 1450–1815*. Basingstoke and New York.

Müller, Hannelore. "The Art of the Augsburg Goldsmiths in Times of War." In Bussmann and Schilling, 263–69.

Murdoch, Steve (ed.). 2001. *Scotland and the Thirty Years War*. Leiden.

Muto, Giovanni. " 'Decretos' e 'medios generales': la gestione delle crisi finanziarie nell' Italia spagnola." In De Maddalena and Kellenbenz, 275–332.

————. "Apparati militari e fabbisogno finanziario nell' Europa moderna: il caso della Spagna 'de los Austrias.' " In Donati and Kroener, 23–52.

Najemy, John M. 2006. *A History of Florence: 1200–1575*. Malden, MA, and Oxford.

New Cambridge Modern History. 1957–1961, eds. G. R. Potter, G. R. Elton, others. Vols. 1–5. Cambridge.

Niccoli, Ottavia. "I morti, la morte, le guerre d'Italia." In Anselmi and De Benedictis, 119–33.

Nicholas, David. 2003. *Urban Europe, 1100–1700*. Basingstoke and New York.

Ohlmeyer, Jane (ed.). 1995. *Ireland from Independence to Occupation, 1641–1660*. Cambridge.

Oman, Sir Charles. 1991 reprint. *A History of the Art of War in the Sixteenth Century*. London and Novato, CA.

Osborne, Toby. 2002. *Dynasty and Diplomacy in the Court of Savoy*. Cambridge.

Otte, Enrique. "Il ruolo dei Genovesi nella Spagna del XV e XVI secolo." In De Maddalena and Kellenbenz, 17–56.

*Outram, Quentin. 2001. "The Socio-Economic Relations of Warfare and the Military Mortality Crises of the Thirty Years' War." In *Medical History*, 45: 151–84.

Packard, Francis R. 1922. *Life and Times of Ambroise Paré (1510–1590)*. London.

Parker, David. 1980. *La Rochelle and the French Monarchy: Conflict and Order in Seventeenth-Century France*. London.

★Parker, Geoffrey. 1985. Rev. ed. *The Dutch Revolt*. London and New York.

★———— (ed.). 1997. Rev. ed. *The Thirty Years War*. London and New York.

★————. 2004. Rev. ed. *The Army of Flanders and the Spanish Road, 1567–1659*. Cambridge and New York.

————. "The Soldiers of the Thirty Years War." In Repgen, 303–15.

————. "Early Modern Europe." In Howard, 40–58.

★Parrott, David. 2001. *Richelieu's Army: War, Government and Society in France, 1624–1642*. Cambridge.

Pasero, Carlo. "Il dominio veneto fino all incendio della Loggia (1426–1575)." In *Storia di Brescia*, II: 3–396.

Pastor, Ludwig. 1950. *History of the Popes*. Vol. IX. London and St. Louis.

Pearse, Meic. 2006. *The Age of Reason: From the Wars of Religion to the French Revolution*. Oxford and Grand Rapids.

★Pepper, Simon, and Nicholas Adams. 1986. *Firearms and Fortifications: Military Architecture and Siege Warfare in Sixteenth-Century Siena*. Chicago and London.

★Perjés, Géza. 1970. "Army Provisioning, Logistics and Strategy in the Second Half of the 17th Century." In *Acta Historica Academiae Scientiarum Hungaricae*, 16: 1–51.

Peters, Edward. 1985. *Torture*. New York and Oxford.

Pezzolo, Luciano, and G. Tattara. 2006. "Una fiera senza luogo. Was Bisenzone an offshore capital market in sixteenth-century Italy?" In *Working Papers*, Dept. of Economics, University of Venice (Ca' Foscari), No 25/WP. ISSN 1827-336X.

Pickl, Othmar. "Gli Asburgo austriaci e la concorrenza delle grandi banche dal XIV secolo alla fine del XVII." In De Maddalena and Kellenbenz, 153–75.

Pieri, Piero. 1952. *Il Rinascimento e la crisi militare italiana*. Turin.

Polišenský, J. V. 1978. *War and Society in Europe, 1618–1648*. Cambridge.

Pollak, Martha. 2010. *Cities at War in Early Modern Europe*. Cambridge.

Porter, Stephen. 1994. *Destruction in the English Civil Wars*. Stroud and Dover.

Potter, David. 1996. "The International Mercenary Market in the Sixteenth Century: Anglo-French Competition in Germany, 1543–1550." In *English Historical Review*, CXI, 440: 24–58.

Prak, Maarten. 2005. *The Dutch Republic in the Seventeenth Century*. Trans. Diane Webb. Cambridge.

Prinzing, Friedrich. 1916. *Epidemics Resulting from Wars*, ed. H. Westergaard. Oxford.

Pröve, Ralf. "Der Soldat in der 'guten Bürgerstube': Das frühneuzeitliche Einquartierungssystem und die sozioökonomischen Folgen." In Kroener and Pröve, 191–217.

Quazza, Romolo. 1926. *La Guerra per la successione di Mantova e del Monferrato (1628–1631)*. 2 vols. Mantua.

———. 1933. *Mantova attraverso i secoli*. Mantua.

Racaut, Luc. 2002. *Hatred in Print: Catholic Propaganda and Protestant Identity during the French Wars of Religion*. Aldershot.

Rebel, Hermann. 1983. *Peasant Classes: The Bureaucratization of Property and Family Relations under Early Habsburg Absolutism*. Princeton.

Redlich, Fritz. 1954. "Der Marketender." In *Vierteljahrschrift für Sozial- und Wirtschaftsgeschichte*, 41: 227–52.

———. 1956. "De praeda militari: Looting and Booty, 1500–1815." In *Vierteljahrschrift für Sozial- und Wirtschaftsgeschichte*, 39. Wiesbaden.

★———. 1964. *The German Military Enterpriser and His Work Force*. 2 vols. Wiesbaden.

Repgen, Konrad (ed.). 1988. *Krieg und Politik, 1618–1648. Europäische Probleme und Perspektiven*. Munich.

Ribot, Luis. "Soldati spagnoli in Italia. Il castello di Milano alla fine del XVI secolo." In Donati and Kroener, 133–96.

Riccardi, Luca. "An Outline of Vatican Diplomacy in the Early Modern Age." In Frigo, 95–108.

★Robbins, Kevin C. 1997. *City on the Ocean Sea: La Rochelle, 1530–1650. Urban Society, Religion, and Politics on the French Atlantic Frontier.* Leiden, New York, Cologne.

Roberts, Michael. 1953–1958. *Gustavus Adolphus. A History of Sweden, 1611–1632.* 2 vols. London, New York, Toronto.

———. 1973. *Gustavus Adolphus and the Rise of Sweden.* London.

———. 1979. *The Swedish Imperial Experience, 1560–1718.* Cambridge.

———. 2002. *Gustavus Adolphus.* Harlow. [New ed. of the 1973 book.]

Roberts, Penny. 1996. *A City in Conflict: Troyes during the French Wars of Religion.* Manchester and New York.

★Robisheaux, Thomas. 1989. *Rural Society and the Search for Order in Early Modern Germany.* Cambridge.

Roeck, Bernd. 1987. *Bäcker, Brot und Getreide in Augsburg: Zur Geschichte des Bäckerhandwerks und zur Versorgungspolitik der Reichsstadt im Zeitalter des Dreissigjäharigen Krieges.* Sigmaringen.

———. 1989. *Eine Stadt in Krieg und Frieden: Studien zur Geschichte der Reichsstadt Augsburg zwischen Kalenderstreit und Parität.* 2 vols. Göttingen.

Rogers, Clifford J. "By Fire and Sword: Bellum Hostile and 'Civilians' in the Hundred Years War." In Grimsley and Rogers, 33–78.

★Rowlands, Guy. 2002. *The Dynastic State and the Army under Louis XIV. Royal Service and Private Interest, 1661–1701.* Cambridge.

Ruff, Julius R. 2001. *Violence in Early Modern Europe.* Cambridge.

Salm, Hubert. 1990. *Armeefinanzierung im Dreissigjährigen Krieg. Der Niederrheinisch-Westfälische Reichskreis 1635–1650.* Münster.

Scott, H. M. (ed.). 2007. New ed. *The European Nobilities in the Seventeenth and Eighteenth Centuries.* 2 vols. Basingstoke and New York.

Scott, Tom (ed.). 1998. *The Peasantries of Europe from the Fourteenth to the Eighteenth Centuries.* London and New York.

Shaw, Christine (ed.). 2006. *Italy and the European Powers: The Impact of War, 1500–1530.* Leiden and Boston.

Shaw, William A. 1896. *The History of Currency, 1252–1894.* London.

Sikora, Michael. "Des 18. Jahrhundert: Die Zeit der Diserteure." In Bröckling and Sikora, 86–111.

Skinner, Quentin. 1978. *The Foundations of Modern Political Thought.* 2 vols. Cambridge and New York.

*Smith, Dianne L. 1993. "Muscovite Logistics, 1462–1598." In *Slavonic and East European Review,* 71, no. 1: 35–65.

Sournia, Jean-Charles. 1981. *Blaise de Monluc: Soldat et écrivain (1500–1577).* Paris.

Spufford, Peter. 1986. *Handbook of Medieval Exchange.* London.

*Sreenivasan, Govind P. 2004. *The Peasants of Ottobeuren, 1487–1726: A Rural Society in Early Modern Europe.* Cambridge.

Stearns, Stephen J. 1972. "Conscription and English Society in the 1620s." In *The Journal of British Studies,* 11, no. 2: 1–23.

———. 1978. "A Problem of Logistics in the Early 17th Century: The Siege of Ré." In *Military Affairs,* 42: 121–26.

Stevens, Carol B. 2007. *Russia's Wars of Emergence.* Harlow.

Storia di Brescia. 1961, ed. Giovanni Treccani degli Alfieri. 5 vols. Brescia.

Storia di Milano. 1957. Fondazione Treccani degli Alfieri. Vol. 8. Milan.

Storia di Torino. 1998–2002, ed. Giuseppe Ricuperati. Vols. III–IV. Turin.

*Stradling, R. A. 1994. *Spain's Struggle for Europe, 1598–1668.* London.

Swann, Julian, and Barry Coward (eds.). 2004. *Conspiracies and Conspiracy Theory in Early Modern Europe.* Aldershot.

Switzer, H. L. "The Eighty Years War." In Van der Hoeven, 33–55.

Symcox, Geoffrey (ed.). 1974. *War, Diplomacy, and Imperialism, 1618–1763.* London and New York.

———. 2002. "La trasformazione dello stato." In *Storia di Torino*, IV, 719–867.

★Tallett, Frank. 1992. *War and Society in Early Modern Europe, 1495–1715.* London and New York.

Tauss, Susanne. " 'Robber Is the Most Noble of Occupations': The Looting of Art during the Thirty Years War." In Bussmann and Schilling, 281–88.

Theibault, John C. 1993. "The Rhetoric of Death and Destruction in the Thirty Years War." In *Journal of Social History*, 27: 271–90.

★———. 1995. *German Villages in Crisis. Rural Life in Hesse-Kassel and the Thirty Years' War, 1580–1720.* Atlantic Highlands, New Jersey.

★Thompson, I. A. A. 1976. *War and Government in Habsburg Spain, 1560–1620.* London.

———. 1994. "Castile: Polity, Fiscality, and Fiscal Crisis." In Hoffman and Norberg, 140–80.

Thomson, Janice E. 1994. *Mercenaries, Pirates, and Sovereigns: State-Building and Extraterritorial Violence in Early Modern Europe.* Princeton.

★Tilly, Charles. 1992. *Coercion, Capital, and European States, AD 990–1992.* Cambridge, MA, and Oxford.

Tlusty, B. Ann. 2001. *Bacchus and Civic Order. The Culture of Drink in Early Modern Germany.* Charlottesville and London.

★Tracy, James D. 2002. *Emperor Charles V, Impresario of War: Campaign Strategy, International Finance, and Domestic Politics.* Cambridge.

———. 2008. *The Founding of the Dutch Republic: War, Finance, and Politics in Holland, 1572–1588.* Oxford.

———. "Taxation and State Debt." 1995. In *Handbook*, I, 563–88.

★Trevor-Roper, Hugh. 1970. *The Plunder of the Arts in the Seventeenth Century.* London.

Trim, David J. B. "Ideology, Greed, and Social Discontent in Early

Modern Europe: Mercenaries and Mutinies in the Rebellious Netherlands, 1568–1609." In Hathaway.

———. "Huguenot Soldiering c. 1560–1685: The Origins of a Tradition." In Glozier and Onnekink, 9–30.

Tuck, Richard. 1999. *The Rights of War and Peace: Political Thought and the International Order from Grotius to Kant.* Oxford.

Turnball, Stephen. 2006. *The Art of Renaissance Warfare: From the Fall of Constantinople to the Thirty Years War.* London and St. Paul.

Ulbricht, Otto. "The Experience of Violence during the Thirty Years War: A Look at the Civilian Victims." In Canning, Lehmann, and Winter, 97–127.

Upton, A. F. "The Swedish Nobility, 1600–1772." In H. M. Scott, II, 13–42.

★Van der Hoeven, Marco (ed.). 1997. *Exercise of Arms: Warfare in the Netherlands, 1568–1648.* Leiden, New York, Cologne.

Van Horn Melton, James. "The Nobility in the Bohemian and Austrian Lands, 1620–1780." In H. M. Scott, II, 171–208.

Varese, Carlo. 1835–1838. *Storia della repubblica di Genova.* Vol. 4. Genoa.

Vásquez de Prada, Valentin. "Gli uomini d'affari e i loro rapporti con la corona spagnola nelle Fiandre (1567–1597)." In De Maddalena and Kellenbenz, 243–273.

Vaux de Foletier, François de. 1978. *La Siège de La Rochelle.* La Rochelle.

Veenendaal, Augustus J. "Fiscal Crises and Constitutional Freedom in the Netherlands, 1450–1795." In Hoffman and Norberg, 96–139.

Voet, Leon. 1973. *Antwerp: The Golden Age. The Rise and Glory of the Metropolis in the Sixteenth Century.* Antwerp.

Vogel, Hans. "Arms Production and Exports in the Dutch Republic, 1600–1650." In Van der Hoeven, 197–210.

Volkholz, Robert. 1892. *Die Zerstörung Magdeburgs (1631) im Lichte der neuesten Forschung.* Magdeburg.

Voss, Wulf Eckhart. "For the Prevention of Even Greater Suffering: The Curse and Blessing of Law in War." In Bussmann and Schilling, 275–83.

Vries, Jan de. "The Political Economy of Bread in the Dutch Republic." In Gelderblom, 85–114.

Wallace, Peter G. 1995. *Communities and Conflict in Early Modern Colmar: 1575–1730.* Atlantic Highlands, New Jersey.

Weigley, Russell F. 1993. *The Age of Battles: The Quest for Decisive Warfare from Breitenfeld to Waterloo.* London.

Wette, Wolfram (ed.). 1992. *Der Krieg des kleinen Mannes. Eine Militärgeschichte von unten.* Munich and Zurich.

White, Lorraine. 2001. "Spain's Early Modern Soldiers: Origins, Motivation and Loyalty." In *War and Society,* 19, no. 2: 19–46.

★Wilson, Peter H. 2009. *Europe's Tragedy. A History of the Thirty Years War.* London and New York.

———. "New Approaches under the Old Regime." In Mortimer (2004), 135–54.

———. 1996. "German Women and War, 1500–1800." In *War in History,* III, no. 2: 127–60.

———. 1998. *German Armies, War and German Politics, 1648–1806.* London.

Winnige, Norbert. "Von der Kontribution zur Aksize: Militärfinanzierung als Movens staatlicher Steuerpolitik." In Kroener and Pröve, 59–83.

Witt, Peter-Christian (ed.). 1987. *Wealth and Taxation in Central Europe.* Leamington Spa, Hamburg, New York.

Wohlfeil, Rainer. "Esercito e società nella prima età moderna (secoli xvi e xvii)." In Donati and Kroener, 197–209.

Wolter, F. A. 1845. *Geschichte der Stadt Magdeburg.* Magdeburg.

★Wood, James B. 1996. *The King's Army: Warfare, Soldiers, and Society during the Wars of Religion in France, 1562–1576.* Cambridge and New York.

Worthington, David. 2004. *Scots in Habsburg Service, 1618–1648.* Leiden.

Zanden, J. L. van. 1993. *The Rise and Decline of Holland's Economy: Merchant Capitalism and the Labour Market.* Manchester and New York.

Zinsser, Hans. 1985. *Rats, Lice and History.* London.

Zwierlein, Cornel. "Fame, violenza e religione politicizzata: gli assedi nelle guerre confessionali (Parigi, 1590)." In Donati and Kroener, 497–545.

INDEX